Advance Pr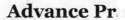

"...A great achiever

"Standby for Broadcast is a conter ..... 22, a book darkly funny...hauntingly lyrical."

~**Wayne Johnson**, Author of The Snake Game, Deluge, and The Devil You Know.

"A forthcoming and brave testament to our capacity to transcend the grip of trauma"

"The author's remembrance brims with both heartache and insight, the latter often painfully excavated from the former. [Kari] Rhyan's predicament is one not often represented in popular discourse – The PTSD suffered but those who see the effects of combat without partaking in combat itself. Bracingly candid...deeply affecting."

~**Kirkus Reviews**

"A poignant literary effort"

"In contrast, dark comic moments help lighten the load. Consider pill-popping, hard drinking Rhyan having an orange-haired therapist named Johnnie Walker, or the thought of dismembered holiday gingerbread treats likened to the revolving door carnage that enters the ER."

~**BlueInk Review**

"Eerily reminiscent of M.A.S.H."

"I was absolutely consumed by this book. It was amazingly written and, as a serving member of the armed forces, touched some very sensitive topics."

~**Online Book Club**

Advance Praise

"Fast paced and dark as hell."

~**Matt Borczon**, Author of A Clock of Human Bones, Battle Lines, and Ghost Train

---

"Childhood demons and combat wounds cause one Navy nurse to examine her life"

"Rhyan writes with high emotion...dramatically constructed and terrifyingly realistic, Standby for Broadcast is a cry for greater outreach to those who serve in auxiliary roles in times of warfare, who are forced to deal with the horrific effects without the sympathy reserved for combatants.... a moving memoir."

~**Chanticleer Book Reviews**

"Rhyan doesn't demand sympathy from her readers, but earns it"

"Rhyan presents herself in a way that's sympathetic but not perfect. We see her as a child being stomped on by her mother, her mother's boyfriends, her aunt, and her older cousin, then we see her as a nurse turning off her emotions while she tries to keep a triple amputee alive."

~**Jess Costello for IndieReader**

Advance Praise

"Five Stars"

Rhyan's memoir begins the day her shrink, Johnnie Walker, informs her there will be no more drugs for her and that she (Dr. Walker) is sending her to a civilian hospital. The narrative alludes to a potentially violent incident that occurred at home the previous night. The description of the worry and stress clearly show how difficult it is for Rhyan to maintain her composure and calm.

Although much of the story takes place while Rhyan is a patient in the hospital, her program of healing and recovery demands that she explore her complex issues. As she does the required writing of her timeline and in her combat journal, her story shines a light on her resistance, including the hidden family issues.

Standby for Broadcast is a story filled with the angst and insight that can only be provided by someone who has been present to the travesty and camaraderie of a war zone. Kari Rhyan tells her story in a way that draws in and enlightens the reader without overwhelming. She has a unique capacity to share her stories in a manner that opens a door on a world many people never experience. Standby for Broadcast is an absorbing story for anyone interested in the complexity of living in and through a war zone as well as surviving the return from it.

~Portland Book Review

Copyright

Standby for Broadcast

A Memoir by

Kari Rhyan

Acknowledgements

The author would like to thank the following for their support:

Wayne Johnson (Editor)

Karen Subach (Editor)

Ivana Mijalkovic (Illustrator)

Bill Raymond (Collaborator)

Special thank you to Matt Borczon, Wolfgang Carstens, and Epic

Rites Press/Tree Killer Ink for keeping it courageous

eBook Conversion by Bill Raymond, Optical Authoring

https://opticalauthoring.com

On Anonymity and Process

This is a true story about trauma. As such, I've obscured the identities of real individuals and locations. Physical descriptions have been altered and pseudonyms used for persons and places (The Willows Hospital, for example, does not exist). Characters herein are amalgams of persons (Rodney, for instance, is a composite of one British nurse and five Navy corpsmen--all of whom taught me similar lessons). Dialogue, therefore, has been reconstructed throughout to realize a feeling or a truth. Timelines have also been compressed for the benefit of storytelling. Lastly, other than the public figures who visited Camp Bastion, the subjects of various news stories, and my immediate family members, the only whole character in the following pages is the one I knew least and sought to reach most.

-Kari Rhyan

For my family

BOOK I

CHEERS

I wanted to live the life of a prince
because I thought saints were born
saints...
I looked in the dirt
and found wisdom is learnt
through a costly process
of success and failure.
- Atlas Sound, "Quick Canal"

Chapter 1

I'm deteriorating at an alarming rate.

Spreadsheets and pie charts, no matter the relevance or illustrative panache, do not excite the paranoid neurotic holding my sensible, good nature for ransom. Abercrombee N. Phantom, my alter ego and former inner nihilist, skims the hospital budget cast by the tabletop projector, but from a perspective *so* distorted her eyes list over its bold-red bottom-line (then land with a thud).

"Pfft!" says the Phantom.

The Commanding Officer shoots the upstart a dirty look, but his canon falls flat; though partially obscured by hair wisps the size of shrews, the Phantom's face still possesses all the subtle charms of a slapped-ass abutting a roll brush. Meanwhile, our Comptroller waits out the Mexican standoff from the business end of our long mahogany table, thumb cocked atop a wireless mouse. *Medicated and motivated*, I think. Caffeine plus Fear equals Efficiency and, on occasion, one hell of a Hail Mary.

Not this time.

Fifty-six coughs and two Diet Cokes later, our Money Man tees-up a ten-year action plan (an oxymoron if there ever was one) to slow a spiral that begins now and "doesn't look good."

I should be consulting my mental tickler of staff I can easily fire or furlough. That'd be the sensible thing to do. I am, nevertheless, more consumed by containing the Phantom, who can't be bothered by a looming hospital closure nor the unscrupulous steps it will take to avoid it. Truth be told, she has only devoted herself to four things over the last nine days. In short and in no particular order, the Phantom: drop-kicked a couple corrupt peers right in their careers; looked like a walking bag of ass in a shit-show of brass and bootlickers; bought a .357 revolver; AND (*why deny it?*) amassed an impressive cache of hollow points. She's stockpiling the cavity rippers in her credenza because, according to *her* deluded calculations, the end must be nigh.

The Comptroller clears his throat (number fifty-seven). It's louder, closer. He thinks I'm sleeping. I slowly raise my head and toss away my shrews so he can better see my eyes. A flash of concern cuts across his, but quickly recedes after I mouth "Thank you." The Comptroller *slash* Money Man *slash* Troll (my favorite) is one of the good guys. He wants to make a difference. He said as much when we first met a year ago, and just before I laughed in his face. He'd make me his mentor right there on the spot.

Strange kid.

I glance at my phone: one hour in *and halfway to freedom!* The projector bakes my panic as I try to keep time. Counting-off coughs, Cokes, and bullets (just) dampens my urge to scream. The Phantom, or, rather, We, or (actually) I...*I* wedge the steel toes of my black boots under the legs of the high-backed leather chair that's been mine, and mine alone, for the last year. I'm swiveling back and forth, back and forth.... I'm a maniac in *Blueberries,* or Navy blue camouflage flecked in gold and silver, now riddled with *Irish Pennants*--the untidy threads that come with so much washing and living and swiveling.

The Phantom tells me I'm a fool of a full-commander.

Though a few inches taller than an average woman, I find my

backrest--high by design--a little too high. But, like most precocious children who've worn out their welcome, I'm comfortable. Quite comfortable, though I fidget and (last I checked) have pupils the size of crazy--or dilated just enough to yield pale gray rings growing dimmer by the day.

I have no pearls of wisdom or condolences to offer the other directors, half of whom are still staring at the missive with their traps open or frenetically clicking their ballpoints (telegraphing an SOS to a department head or a drinking buddy or mommy, one could guess). One worm is texting his concubine *slash* secretary on a government-issued Blackberry.

"I hate these people."

Did I say that out loud?

The Petty Officer seated across from me half-stifles the giggle that skids through her nose and bounces out on the projector she faithfully mans. In the meantime, I go back to the business of hatching plans.

◆ ◆ ◆

The meeting ran over, and I'm late (*goddammit!*). I've got an appointment with a shrink. It's a session I can't miss, else the paddy wagon pull up to my office door and take me away. They can log their concerns on the dry erase, for all I care. Open door policies are fucking passé.

I push my 39th birthday present back up to the bridge of my nose as I climb the stairs to the Seventh Deck. Bifocals--weighted in seasons--shouldn't feel heavy, but everything does today. This pair is six months new and already kaput. I need a new exam. This concerns me more than the meeting's takeaways, which I've already data-dumped into my "Who the Fuck Gives a Shit Folder," and where it rests (shoulder-to-shoulder) with my Navy's Core Values: Honor, Courage, and Commitment.

I hurry down the hall toward Johnnie Walker's office. She's trying to help me stop this. I blow through her doorway and to the far left side of her dark green sixty-grit sofa and am suddenly blinded by her thousand-watt hairdo: It's orange today, like a clown's.

"I'm gonna transfer you to a civilian hospital," says Johnnie. *She's really serious this time.*

"California or D.C.?" I ask.

"The Willows. It's in Tampa."

"Florida isn't really my thing."

"That's ok, Commander. You won't be sightseeing."

"Uh-huh...and when am I leaving?"

"Soon," she says.

"I'll need bennies."

"Can't give you Xanax. Not anymore."

"Why?"

"Because you're an alcoholic."

"I don't even drink that much," I tell her.

"That's NOT the point."

"What *is* the point?"

"Benzodiazepines and Opioids are no better than wine for someone like you. You know all this."

"Someone like me?"

"You're numb," she replies, "and withdrawn. You look like shit."

"*Nice.*"

"I'm sorry, ma'am, but you do."

I do, I think. And I'm angry, impulsive, forgetful, and manipulative. If this wasn't bad enough, my outlook on the future is on the extreme left side of my one-page questionnaire designed to give shrinks a heads up on Trouble.

(I know all of this too.)

Johnnie Walker says I'm having a breakdown, and my dissociative behavior is getting worse.

"I don't deny it," I mutter.

"How did you sleep last night?"

"Not very well," I say.

"How so?"

"I lost my temper."

"While you were sleeping?"

"Yes and no." A voice crack on the "no," and a clue I'll cry before the hour is over, so I'm careful to keep the appointment short. Two's always a crowd when I blubber, and any self-respecting desk jockey would be smart to follow my example, though I take my stoicism to *a whole 'nutha level*. It's a craft, really: a calling card for suitors, a hurdle for interlopers, and a bailiwick for these pretentious boardroom buttholes disguising themselves as my shipmates. So, the voice crack pisses me off, naturally, along with everything else that's been happening without my goddamn say so.

I'd been a happy-go-lucky officer once upon a time, taking orders and absorbing criticism with a resting heart rate of sixty. My gusto, forged in the very white trash trenches I'd eventually escape from, had been spit-shined to reflection on blue carpets--carpets I'd initially be called upon for being "a punk ensign." But I'd straighten up fast. Once sorted, I'd control my capillaries like fjords, halting the onslaught of blushes and flushes. *Show them no fear*, I'd tell myself. So I waltzed through my day at sixty beats per minute (no more no less) and, if it ticked-up, I slowed it down. My biorhythm had a time signature: 6/8, or *snappy cool*.

"What are you thinking about?" Johnnie asks.

"Nothing," I say.

Nothing flows through me now. Everyone keeps dumping grievances and bullshit on me, though, just like they always have because "Rhyan fixes shit." That's what I do, or what I did, before resigning as the Director for Mental Health only ten minutes ago. A couple years back I was sent in to fix the ailing directorate with its flubbed time cards and hostile work environment, courtesy of a couple underhanded head-butting shrinks. After I cleaned house, the Commanding Officer kept me on. "You're a shoe-in for captain," he said. "Just keep doing what you're doing."

Yay. Got anything else?

Yes. There was more--*much* more. In addition to garnishing, firing, and banishing, there were plenty of other things on my To Do List: double-dealing, secret-keeping, power-grabbing, and ass-kissing--all sorts of bureaucratic bullshit moves that proved none of us executives had ever truly graduated from grade school. But those days are gone. *I ain't keepin' nothin' in!* My Id is a goddamn lunatic nun--absent of habit--singing from a mountaintop she's sure to be pushed off. Chaos is the name of my game. I must find it or create it, situation depending. So says the nun *and* the gun I purchased for the Phantom's itchy trigger finger: *I'm* King of the Mountain now, bastards.

Johnnie jots something down. *Crazier than bird shit on bat wings in kangaroo pouches,* I suspect. She stares at me for a beat through the bottom of her lenses (she's also myopic--in vision AND aim).

"Your Safe Phrase...what's it again?"

"Abercrombee N. Phantom," I say.

"I don't get it," she says and flips my record over to write something in the margin of my progress notes. This is likely to marginalize any influence I have left.

"But it's funny, right? This Phantom whatnot?"

"Yeah," I say. "It cracks me up."

I'm too tired to delve into the minutiae of how my Safe Phrase, once funny as hell, has deftly recast itself from savior to executioner. I say zilch. I chalk it up to self-sabotage (I'm an ace). I keep answering Johnnie's questions and promise myself to find a different phrase to snap me out of these blind rages, which, unfortunately, are becoming more frequent and intense.

"And your Spouse said the Safe Phrase?"

"No," I say. "There wasn't enough time."

"Everyone okay?"

"Yes," I say. "Physically, yes."

Johnnie looks sad. I look away.

"You *need* this," she says.

I try to reset myself so I can meet her eyes, but end up staring over her shoulder and outside the window at a brick wall. It's a stone's throw away and *much* more interesting than all this shit.

"Come on, Kari...talk to me," she says.

I'm Kari now, I think to myself. I'm Kari whether I like it or not. The mask is still on, though not the one belonging to the Phantom schmo who makes an appearance every time her triggers are tripped. I mean the *Kari Mask*, the ego--a healthy cover if worn for the right reasons (like placating a shrink, for example, but these days I can't even do that). These days, I spend most of my time protecting me from me, whether it's neutralizing one of the Phantom's knee-jerk reactions, feeding my ego with empty achievements, *or* getting a handle on this *Other Gal*, whom I haven't nailed-down, let alone met. She's the one my shrink wants to talk to, and I wish *she* would get on with it already and sing like a canary.

But Johnnie has had it. She's washing me out like a bad dye job. "I've seen it too many times," she says. "You know our numbers...Kari?"

"They're dismal," I say.

She's referring to our base suicide rates. Marines mostly. It's a pattern. Many had multiple traffic violations, drug and alcohol problems, or domestic violence issues before doing themselves in. But I'm not suicidal, or even homicidal. I'm lumped-in with a special group of hard-charging catatonics (at best) and miscreants (at worst). Two members, local Gunnery Sergeants nicknamed The Smash Brothers, returned home from Afghanistan around the same time I did. Both had a history of impulsive behavior--the least of which was yanking aggressive male drivers out of their car seats and bitch-slapping them at red lights. The Brothers met in our clinic, bonded over slapping, war, and sundries, and became fast friends. Hope, however small, sprang anew. The Brothers are doing just fine, last I heard. Cheers to happy endings!

I should've been able to reach out to someone, what with a hospital full of caregivers. But that's bollocks; I'm a sad reminder to those who've deployed, and I'm misunderstood by those who haven't: a caregiver who can't take care of herself or anyone else. I approached another officer (once) at a barbeque, figuring, if it worked for The Brothers, then it could work for me. Smitty had been our radiologist in Afghanistan--a frag and bleed hunter and a good one, at that. I'd thought, *Smitty will relate.* A strappy guy with a nickname to match (forfeiting his given, Bernard) just HAD to relate. And, like me, he'd seen a shit-ton of blood and guts.

So I told Smitty I wasn't doing well, and that my nightmares were really getting on top of me. He took a swig from his lager and scuttled away before I could finish. He was well across the yard by the time he took his lips off the nip where he quickly rejoined a conversation about CrossFit.

Oh, that I could CrossFit this shit away....

"When do you think I'll blow?" I ask.

"Between now and two years," says Johnnie. "That's been my experience with..."

"Someone like me," I finish.

"Yes," she says.

"I'm not that bad."

"Kari, you are *ill.* Keep repeating it to yourself."

"Okay," I say.

"And no more narcotics," she adds, "you need a clear head for the next six weeks. You need to *feel.*"

That's the point, goddammit.

I leave Johnnie and lumber down the hall to my corner office: I walk with my feet perpetually pointed outward at ten and two o'clock (similar to a gutted toad on display). Still, it's a mellow stride. My Kid inherited the same walk. A few steps later, I get a mental lock on the next junior medical officer I'm to dupe for my candy. We have scads of doe-eyed residents who'd just *love* to please an asshole like me (warts and all).

I enter my office where the walls are blighted with accolades, awards, and degrees--none of which mean anything to me now. Nor do the cast of physicians, nurses, and corpsmen I used to manage. All of them knew the score: I dropped the contract of a doctor, described by one of my underlings as a gelatinous little man, who called our Marine base (filled to the gills with traumatized drill instructors) a "veritable game preserve" for his nascent Traumatic Brain Injury practice. Many of the drill instructors had deployed as many as five times in the last ten years. Now they're here, on Parris Island, whipping recruits into shape and being poached by medical providers on the side. Some have cracked (threatening, pushing, and punching- -the usual suspects). Some Marines have just snapped (pick a *'cide*, any *'cide*).

I move past the static and sit behind a large desk that cuts the room in half. I inherited the behemoth from yet another banished employee. Suffice it to say I've ditched the Shackleton Model of Leadership. Stranded in an ice field, the 20th Century Explorer kept all whiners in his tent and under his thumb to spare the rest of his men the agony. But this isn't the South Pole. No, sir! It's South Carolina. We send all our ne'er-do-wells far away and over the floes (aka the base across town).

And what of the mid-century oak, ma'am?

No way, you Chauncey fucking dickhead! Su escritorio es mi escritorio. *Now fuck off!*

I pick up my pen and use it to dial my Spouse. We've got a lot to discuss, but I'm sobbing by the time I get to the final digit and have to hang-up. First, I'll beat back the Phantom. Second, I'll catch my breath. Third, I'll figure out a way to downplay the crisis--something I used to do incredibly well (I lived for it, in fact).

Still, last night was hard enough. We sleep with Arnold, our Schnoodle: part Poodle, part Schnauzer, and slightly loathed by my Spouse for his overwhelming lack of manliness. Arnold awoke in a tangle at 12:21, having wedged his small paw between a wrist and a bracelet. It slid until the chain was clear up his leg, and well past the joint. Torqued-down like a mother, the dog screamed bloody murder and settled into a slow sickening bellow of unremitting pain. The Phantom took hold immediately. (It always starts behind the eyes--a red flash. My heart pounds until everything inside of me hurts. Then I explode.) After freeing Arnold with tin snips, the Phantom picked up our Blu Ray player and threw it across the room where it smashed against our hope chest. Only this time, for the finale, the Phantom screamed "FUUUUCK!" for five...interminable...seconds.

Thud. The all-too-familiar weight of insanity was back, but quickly supplanted this time by such a gut-wrenching shame I nearly fell to my knees; I saw my beloved's brown eyes poised in cross-examination, asking *who* (the fuck) *are you?*

I should've dropped right there, cutting my knees open on the small bits of plastic and metal strewn across the hardwood we had shellacked together. Or I could have just answered the question: "I'm the drunken, pill-popping boss and patient of a shrink named Johnnie Walker. I'm a six-figure Cry Baby. More, I'm a shitty Wife and Mother. I need help, my love, and I'm so fucking sorry." Instead, I went back to bed. It's ironic, I must admit, as is the stigma that'll strike the death knell on my military career the second I step on that plane.

Damn. How on God's green earth did I become...this?

I was a decent human being back in the day--a *Gilligan* of sorts. I wasn't a goldbricker, a nag, or incompetent (I'm batting .667 this season, thanks to the bennies and Two-Buck Chuck). Many of my high-level peers, however, reminded me of my 5th Grade teacher, Ms. Madill, who never stood up or stepped out from behind her desk. She controlled us with a rigid schedule and a chubby little finger that pointed out directions. Still, I don't remember her for the inertia as much as I do for the two-word response she gave a boy who asked the most complicated question I've never tried to answer.

"What's war, Ms. Madill?"

"A mistake, Michael. Now go sharpen my pencil."

I've been in the Navy for eighteen years, have studied everything from Sun Tzu to Chris Hedges, and have yet to find a better answer (though Hedges came close with *War Is a Force That Gives Us Meaning*).

I'm so tired.

I used to be a bunch of other great things as well: reliable, pragmatic, compassionate, and optimistic. My leadership agreed. I promoted out of the Emergency Room mid-career and was placed at a desk with an end-to-end calendar pad that tore away the months like a postictal esthetician; my new admin duties, quite simply, made me hate the written word. Considering I had always been a better writer than a talker, this was bad news. I used to read and journal for pleasure, but in the Navy I deployed words to dupe and stall others year after year. (I once composed a proposal that would save my command several hundred thousand dollars. Never mind the eight nurses whose contracts were terminated. Never mind they were given thirty days notice, though I knew for six months. Never mind I received a Navy Commendation Medal for all of it.) But there would be no turning back. I had permanently exchanged my scrubs and stethoscope for a black cable-knit sweater, a clipboard, and a motivational nature portrait. Peers in similar predicaments had hung-up patience-preaching glaciers (*No job is too big*, I'd thought) or rolling greens with golf balls begging to be driven (*Focus, Kari!*).

I spin around to face the framed tsunami on my six. It's imploring me to ride the wave of change or I'll find myself beneath it (*Change or die!*). I nicked the portrait a few years ago from a shared office in San Diego where I racked, stacked, and scrambled each night to prepare a one-page Snapshot of our Admiral's ship, or Medical Center, as it were. It sounded easy but it wasn't. The Admiral, over-privileged by default, hadn't the patience for a pickle in his Happy Meal. So his number two, a bugged-eyed Bearcat with a fearsome resting bitch face, jumped on anyone she pleased.

Number Two tailored each attack to our weakness, so she'd ask *me* redundant questions. This served two purposes: One, to bait my circumlocution which would eventually be used to, two, embarrass the living shit out of me. The ass chewing happened on the first day. My Snapshot started off grainy: I mince words when nervous. Having no sense of sport, the Bearcat stopped me in my tracks while the Admiral silently watched from the head of the table. He had no pen or paper--his interest, or lack thereof, was implied.

If only they'd given me a chance to settle in and find my flow that first day, it would have been different. I was good under pressure. As a teen, I worked on assembly lines next to ass-groping crank addicts at a local car plant, and still managed to produce and produce. Now a nurse, I'd toughened up even more by way of bedpans and crash carts. But getting a harness on admin panic was a completely different animal (claws and all).

"Whoa! Wait a minute," the Bearcat interrupted.

"I'm sorry, ma'am. Did I miss something?"

"Rhyan? What *exactly* did you do all night?"

"I worked, ma'am."

"Are you sure?"

"Yes, ma'am," I said. "I rounded the wards...staffing ratios look good...no deaths. Yes, ma'am. It was a quiet night."

My answer was met with silence (different from quiet).

"Did I miss something?" I asked.

Silence.

"A temperature?" I asked, shuffling my notes.

"Temperatures don't excite me," she finally replied.

"Yes ma'am."

"So, are you ready to give a proper report?"

"Yes, m...ma'am." A stammer (voice cracks be damned, but stammering is the pits).

After batting me around for another minute, she *dotted-the-i* on her first impression.

"Good naval officers don't act like you."

I guess good naval officers weren't Yes Men, either. Unlike my fanged faultfinder, I devoted myself to pleasing people. In fact, if I took every person I routinely catered to and lined them up single file, the procession would be a mile long. And, at the very end, behind my ultra-creepy, overly chatty, Craigslist-tricking, former colleague (known affectionately as Slime Ball) would be me. The Bearcat knew I cared about our patients and knew I wanted to please her. But she also knew I was scared shitless, so she shot and dressed me just for kicks. I'd make it my mission to please my Bearcat and Admiral from that day forward.

After The Gruesome Twosome left the room, the Director for Nursing Services, who'd been seated to my right the entire time, turned to me and said it'd been a good mentorship moment. *Fucking stuffed*, I thought. *A mentorship moment?!* After a week on the job, I'd eventually learn to *Embrace the BOHICA* (Bend Over, Here It Comes Again). What else could I do? Quit? *Yeah right.* I was ass out. I took control of my fjords, which is to say I stuffed back my anger and fear, and perfected the dopey Gilligan grin I had used as a kid. Eventually, I became a groomed godhead, watching other officers and sailors fry for colloquial missteps (dip shits) or under-preparedness (dirt bags) OR just being goddamn nervous (weak). Most meetings I never said a word. I didn't want to get walloped. As one Navy chief put it in Kuwait when a corpsman had asked for help with a patient: "I don't wipe ass anymore." So, like the Chief and Director, I don't help underlings. They'd have to toughen up on their own. Still, it sucked (a word too common, too lowlife, yet there were no other words). It *sucked* to stand by and do nothing.

It didn't matter by that time; I'd consciously rooted myself within an insidious cadre of automatons--those who had divested themselves of kindness two or three ranks ago, when all I *really* wanted was to fit in, and, corny as it sounds (and much like the Troll), to be part of something I was proud of.

I am ashamed.

Yet as frightening as Bearcats and BOHICAs could be, these weren't the bad parts. In the midst of my job transition, and well before my fall from grace, I was selected to deploy to Helmand Province to work the ER within a British trauma bottleneck called Bastion Hospital. Not a bad thing, in and of itself; I'd be part of something worthwhile and return to bedside nursing, a place where I was human and the mission was clear. It was to be my third deployment, but my first to Afghanistan and the first as a mom. Of course, I balked at the thought of leaving my two year old behind. Who wouldn't? But I reckoned it would be best to go before the Kid's long-term memory kicked-in. So, I went and, eight months later, came back callous and would go on to become hostile.

Hostile indeed.

Deployments change people, sure. But I was on the fast track to the next rank when I came back and had to reassume my duties *tout de suite*; there were deadlines to meet and inspections to pass. My changes were gradual at first, imperceptible even. Then I fell off a precipice--some flimsy scaffolding of my own design that I've yet been able (or willing) to re-ascend.

So I'll leave the confines of my corner office, the one on the First Deck with the best view of our flag, half-mast this mackerel-sky-Monday for another dead politician. But first, I need twenty-four more breaths so I can punch all eleven numbers to inform my Spouse, my Northern Wind, who'll (once again) steady my sails, that I'm going to Tampa. I'll punch in the numbers then telegraph a message to the Phantom.

It's okay to heal.

We don't have a choice, I tell her. We can't ride a desk or work an ER ever again. My gusto is fucking gone and won't return for anything less than a catastrophic hemorrhage of my very own.

*Never in a million years...*Post-Traumatic Stress Disorder and its grubby little co-conspirator, addiction, had just taken my career and were making inroads towards my family and, quite possibly, my life.

Chapter 2

I'm haze gray and underway when I arrive in Tampa, early in the afternoon and fresh from a few hundred miles of scotch. My genial airport driver goes mute after I tell him my destination. Thirty minutes later, we pull up to The Willows where he quickly liberates my luggage from his trunk. I slip a twenty-dollar tip into his hand before he beelines it back to the driver's seat; when the Phantom is dormant, all I want is to be liked and accepted.

I sling my pack over my shoulder, take my suitcase, and meander through The Willows' front entrance. There's a pot for Joe, thank Jesus, but the machine has no creamer, cups, or coffee. Just a sign on the front with a smiley face saying, "Sorry." *Goddammit.*

The Willows appears well-manicured at first blush and sprawls across seven palm-fronded acres (according to the brochure I'm reading) and, aside from the heavily-secured entry, cameras, and extrapyramidal effects, seems collegiate. A man with blonde hair and magenta scrubs scoops me up and escorts me through two gates, and down a trail towards a designated military unit in the middle of campus.

We cross over a small wooden bridge that links two esplanades separated by a narrow bog. A blue-haired teen and another magenta are having a conversation about "ownership" on a wooden bench. Further on, Magenta and I come upon a disheveled woman burping a swaddled baby over her shoulder with another magenta beside her.

The fuh?

Upon closer inspection, I see the baby is but a doll and the woman is soothing it between drags with gentle shhh's whistling through an absent incisor. Professional intuition tells me the woman must've suffered a stillbirth.

I remain on the heels of Magenta and am about to look away when, just as I pass, the woman casually flicks ash on the doll's head. I come to a halt and see the doll's head has a black fontanel (soon to be a goddamn blowhole) where the woman puts out her Winston. *Yep. I'm home.*

I arrive at a locked psych unit where twenty service members convalesce. They've been plucked from parent commands like feral dogs in need of obedience school.

I'm taken to a small room off the entry for vital signs and am told to blow into a breathalyzer.

It registers 0.0. *How?*

It occurs to me the last beverage I actually *remember* having was just prior to takeoff. *Oh, yeah...Alcohol plus Poly-pharm equals Blotto!* I even drink in my dreams.

After introductions, two techs begin a strip search, and anxiety grips me. A short old Hispanic lady (Cuban, I think, on account of the curves) steps into the room, sees my panic, and pulls me aside.

"Hello, Kari. I'm Riza."

"Hi," I say.

"I'm going to be your therapist for the next six weeks."

"Sounds good."

The strip search resumes, only slower this time. Riza keeps yammering. She tells me we're each born with a resiliency bucket, and that mine happens to be overflowing onto my sandcastle. *What the shit is that?!* I wave off her metaphor and say my problem is the simple consequence of too many drinks, but she prattles on. "We're going to punch holes in your bucket...Kari?...Kari?"

"What?"

"It's okay to cry."

Riza says the last word in a hush. It's the sort of inflection used to calm a kid with an *owie*. On cue, I surprisingly give in to the moment and picture myself an apoplectic toddler, boiling mad at the pail washing all her hard work away. Thankfully, the thousand-yard stare I perfected eons ago holds true. Lots of military folks have it, but I call mine "The Foat." Named after the Myotonic Fainting Goat that goes rigid and blank should its comfort zone be violated by, say, another goat (or a stiff breeze), the Foat doesn't fail. Yet the tears trickle down my face. I feel defeated, in need of Johnnie's brick wall again (for a whole host of reasons).

After the search, I sit in the patient lounge and wipe the anguish away with my shirtsleeve while the staff rifle though my backpack for contraband. I hear my containers full of pills rattling around behind the nurses' station until, finally, the noise stops. *Bagged and tagged and far away,* I observe.

The rest of the patients are at lunch, save a young man slunk in a beige recliner eating a frozen prepackaged peanut butter and jelly sandwich. He's wearing white Oakley's with mirrored violet lenses. *Frogskins*--all the rage with the kids back home. Froggy seems fixated on the tube where a busty brunette in black denim hot pants works under the hood of a pick-up truck. After she sorts out the engine, the scene switches to three guitar-playing Ken dolls with shaggy hairdos and frosted tips.

Froggy stares and eats, eats and stares. *Kids today...* His black hair envelopes a gray streak that begins at his right temple and ends at the back of his head--less like a skunk stripe and more like a ram's horn. My eyes gravitate to the tattoo branded in big black swoops across the inside of his right arm: *0311.* A Marine Corps Rifleman. I saw similar tattoos come through Bastion's double doors. He wasn't one of mine, though. No, sir! His body is intact, and there are no visible scars. He's unscathed. We're all unscathed. It's why we're here.

"Don't mind Riza," Froggy tells me. "She only wants to save the world."

"Okay...thanks."

He stops eating and staring, and introduces himself. "I'm Brian," he says, offering his hand over the empty recliner between us. Brian's voice is soft and his smile easy. Behind the sunglasses, I imagine his eyes a light brown like my Spouse's. Soft voices and easy smiles best belong on darker complexions, but it's the confidence I love most. I myself run on short supply. Originally from Delaware, I'm nine parts

Potato Farmer and one part Native American. This means I'm pale, yet ruddy, and perpetually overburdened by garbage-dumping douchebags. And who the hell are you people anyway? DuPonts?

The culprits are my kin, actually. As with the Bearcat, they slurped-up their young like *Balut* (fertilized duck embryo still-in-shell). I'd often joke I was raised by wolves but, honestly, White Fang would've been a better parent (as would've a duck). All my life I secretly wanted to be part of a different clan, and so it appears I am now. Brian gives me the skinny on Riza, a Vietnam War widow rumored by patients to have been battling the drink for the better part of forty years. I file the intel away for future use; it's the perfect social history to exploit in order to avoid talking about my own crapola. "What was your husband's name? Where did he serve? How did you two meet? Gimme some pills?"

The approach doesn't work on just anybody. It requires tact, along with some other crucial ingredients. For one, I'm a real sweetie when I want to be. Not saccharine like the nice neighbor lady down the street who made you brownies. I'm sweet like a cagey kitten with a docked tail that's in desperate need of a butt scratch and a bite to eat. I can get close to most people with very little effort (notorious boundary crosser that I've been). Even if I were to explain my many tendencies to Brian, he would *still* perceive me a Gilligan, which is to say harmless. If I'm put on the defense for any reason, however, displacement and stoicism are my homies. They're a potent combination. Let's say, for example (and for real), a shrink wants to get to the root of why I dream about limbless vampires floating around in mucky blood every night. He'd have to tolerate my inquiries first, if not, solely. This is the way Kari protects her weird, anxiety-ridden Id, or the Phantom, the Flying Nun *slash* Fire Starter--still minus the habit, but *soaked* in petrol.

The fact that I'm a nurse by trade only complements the ruse. I've been known to cite the DSM-V, the Holy Bible of mental health diagnoses, to distract psychiatrists with clinical questions. It isn't long before I'm asking about schooling, investments, or their family photos haphazardly turned just so. People just *love* to talk about themselves--shrinks especially. It only takes a second to pick my trajectory and--*Whoosh*--I'm off, moving at breakneck speed away from the dirtiest word I know: Me. And, if they still want to prod, then all bets are off because, if shutting down doesn't work, the Phantom explodes.

I also have this thing: If I receive a compliment, I'll twist it around or deflect the attention to its originator. Once my spidey senses hone-in on another's insecurities, I'll either assuage or exploit. I perfected this skill to sleazy proportion in the Navy, fooling some of the most sophisticated thinkers around. *Kari really has her shit together.* Right....

I suspect I've been a fraud since birth; my great-uncle Arthur dubbed me "Little Bullshitter." Granted all this, I'm most comfortable when invisible.

The last advantage I have, or had, was status. After the Phantom overtook Little Bullshitter, I managed staff like a horse-trader, ignored multi-million dollar budgets, and doled out corrective actions as necessary, sometimes unnecessarily AND (sometimes) to the *very same* people charged with my care. It was a conflict of interest which, depending on who you asked, benefited me in a big way; I dodged the tough questions in therapy for months without hassle, but was simultaneously squelching a scream that had been begging to be delivered for the last three to thirty-five years (give or take).

Riza wants to conduct my admission interview.

"You ready, Kari?"

"When can I sleep?" I ask.

"Tonight," she says.

"Good luck," says Brian.

Riza leads me to an empty group therapy space where three wooden chairs unceremoniously face each other in the center of the room. She's brought along a demure social work student with long hair and thick glasses. The lamb is hugging her notebook to her chest and anxiously smiling at me from behind her four eyes. Riza isn't smiling. She's far too busy sizing me up through my shrews. I imagine red flags signaling back and forth behind her eyes--a semaphore from ship to ship, and a testament to the fathoms she must descend because, unlike our Navy's Fleet, I am *sunk*. After a fistful of shrinks tried and failed, now it's become Riza's job to get me to surface.

It's a pity none of my advantages will work on Riza. (Not a goddamn one.) There's simply nothing at stake for her. I'm not her boss, her peer, her family member, or her friend. I know her type, and they're a pain in my ass. The experience of having honed my defenses for the last four decades only serves to confirm the obvious: Riza is hewn from burl, resplendent in her natural imperfections and strength. In other words, she's twenty years older than me and she isn't about to take any of my regressive adolescent tactics.

The alcohol is long gone and the haze lifted. I'm sober, goddammit. Worse, I'm coherent and crawling out of my fucking skin without Xanax.

The Phantom is coming.

There's nothing to count. No Cokes. No coughs. Not even the plastic clock over the blackboard is ticking. The second hand, much like my handle, is in flux. I could count my heartbeat, but now it's too fast and, every time I try, it only speeds up.

In desperation, I don a figurative Eisenhower, a Navy jacket made famous by Ike that's fashioned to snuff out an officer's fear. It's a simple correlative: Fear goes down and Confidence rises. Or does it? I puff out my chest and look at the two from behind my figurative Oak as if they were my subordinates coming in for a bitch session. The Phantom is hovering, but I'm determined to toe a professional line.

Then Riza totally mortifies me. "What brought you here?"

It's a simple question, I think. I must've asked ER patients the same thing hundreds of times from behind a triage window. But, being on the receiving end, I find it curt.

I search myself and come up with nothing.

I target the student. It'd be easy to get her talking, but Riza senses the shift. "Kari?...Kari?"

"Huh?" I ask.

"Please answer the question, Kari."

Uncle, I think. Mercy I want. "Whatever," I say and take a deep breath, then the Phantom kicks-off (calmly, at first):

"I guess I drink too much. Red wine. Scotch when I want it to go away. It doesn't. I get angry. I drink some more. I can't sleep. I take pills. Xanax. Percocet. Ultram. Docs give me anything I want. Klonopin. Vicodin. Ambien. Anything....

"I live on base. The river view is nice. Eighteen year olds march past my house. My Kid cries. I can't play games. I yell at her. I stare at the walls. My Spouse says I'm miles away....

"I'm losing my friends. They can't handle it. Why should they? I'm fucking crazy! I don't want to hurt myself. I don't want to hurt anybody, but sometimes--believe me--I want to hurt something. I bought a gun. I'm not going postal. I need it to protect my family. The world is so ugly....

"I quit yesterday. The Skipper didn't want me to, but screw this. It's all bullshit. Everything I've worked so hard for. It's all a lie, and it's all gone. I have flashbacks. People in front of me, they have no arms. You guys have arms right now, but sometimes you won't. I'm a nurse. I'm supposed to see these things. It's true. No one put a gun to my head. No one put a gun in my hand. They locked up our FUCKING NINES the day we touched down...."

Breathe....

"I volunteered for the Navy. All part of the job, right? RIGHT?! Those things. Every day. I want them to see it ONCE! A British General saw. He cried while I cleaned. Poor bastard. *My* Admirals? FUCK 'EM! They're out of touch and out to lunch. They fly their fat asses in on the 30th and out on the 1st. Three days of smiles equals two months of combat pay. Capitalizing. Visiting the dining facilities. The admin spaces. Passing out coins. Collecting a few. Visiting the fucking TOC Roaches. Planning FUCKING MURDER! Doing their part. For the machine. Shaking hands. A grip and a grin. Acting like the royalty they aren't."

COME ON! the Phantom screams. IT'S *TIME TO BLOW!*

"THEY ARE NOTHING! They tell me *I know how you feel, Rhyan.* NO, YOU DON'T! *I've seen what you've seen, Kari.* NO, YOU HAVEN'T! *Thank you for your service, commander.* AND FUCK YOU TOO, SIR! MA'AM!"

Breathe...

I can't.

Breathe...

"I can't!"

Tell them!

"Any proof, SIR?! How 'bout you, MA'AM?! A black, red, and green? Do I see it on your barreled FUCKING chest?! A Purple Heart?! A COMBAT ACTION?! Yeah, OKAY BASTARDS! You get ribbons for drinking soda and eating pie. YOU no longer get to TELL ME what to do! NOT ANYMORE! I'll drag ALL you SCUMBAGS over! Come over to BASTION, you FUCKERS, you TURDS, you goddamn DINOSAURS with your precious DATA that says nothing but *NADA!*

"Come over to Bastion where Britain's floors are soaked in YOUR mess! I'll SMASH your face in it and, GUESS WHAT?! I'll smash it again! And AGAIN! AND AGAIN! Is that OKAY? Well, I don't GIVE a SHIT! This is MINE and it's FUCKING YOURS, ADMIRAL, SIR! YOU RING-KNOCKING SON OF A BITCH!

"FUUUUUUCK!"

The bastard clock behind Riza tells me the floor has been mine for thirty minutes, though I only recall bits of what the Phantom vomited up. Not surprising. The *Global Assessment of Functioning* (GAF) score I spied on my admitting paperwork was a 25. Considering the normal value for a mentally sound individual ranges from 80 to 100, I landed somewhere between Joan of Arc and a White

Rabbit:

You're NOT late for anything, the Phantom tells me. *And you're NOT going anywhere. The battle is HERE! You wanna get tied? Well, go right ahead. So you won't mind, then, if I get MY licks in first before YOU go up in flames! RIGHT?!*

Riza looks up from her notes. Her eyes are red and watery. Tired or sad, I cannot say. From my periphery I see the student gawking at me like I'm a furry speck in her plate of agar. I don't like to be studied, so I turn and look at her squarely. She quickly addresses her shoes, and her discomfort eases mine, though not nearly enough.

My Eisenhower, more hair shirt than power suit, is scratching at my fibers--a penance for my sins of evasion. I want to go back to Johnnie's sofa, a plush comfort compared to this. *Breathe,* says Other Gal.

Other Gal, my long-lost Canary in the coalmine, also tells me to *Stay.*

Riza takes a deep breath. "You're good at hiding behind your words," she says. Her heavy accent leaves an honest residue I try to ignore. "Your next six weeks will be busy."

"Is that so?"

"Your program will be divided into four parts. First, you'll go to Alcoholics Anonymous meetings every day."

I look out the window, detesting the cliché. Half my family members are AA Alums.

"Second, you must write down your entire Combat Timeline and read it out loud in The War Room." I feel all the blood rush from my face and pool in my guts. "It's okay," Riza says. "*The War Room* is just like this room...."

The Foat kicks-in, and I stare over her shoulder at a blackboard. There's a quotation written in perfect cursive in the upper left-hand corner. *The War Room: A place that means more than stories being told, where the strongest people in the world share their battles within themselves.*

"Kari?"

"What?"

"I copied that for you," says Riza.

The tears want out, but I refuse to lose it in front of a Student.

"*The War Room* is a safe place," says Riza.

Yeah, I think, *like Abercrombee N. Phantom is a Safe Phrase.*

"Only service members with combat trauma are allowed in," she says. "Well, and one therapist. We rotate. You'll see me in there from time to time." Riza flips through her notes. "This uh...Johnnie Walker?" she chuckles. "That's a first."

"What?" I ask.

"It's nothing," she says.

"You think it's funny," I tell her, "that an alcoholic has a psychiatrist named Johnnie Walker."

"Could be," she grins.

"I'm not an alcoholic."

"How much do you drink, Kari?"

"A few glasses a night."

Riza makes a note and returns to *The War Room.* "I know you think you can't do it. It's scary. But *The War Room* is only the beginning. Each time you talk about your traumas, terrifying memories will become less intrusive and, eventually, they'll file themselves away."

"You're right," I tell Riza. "I can't do it."

"Then you're cheating yourself."

I Foat.

"How many times have you deployed?" asks Riza.

"Three."

"You'll have to write about the others, too," Riza says.

"This doesn't seem right," I say, trying to work an angle.

"What doesn't seem right?"

"That I'm even allowed in."

"Into *The War Room?* Of course you are. Why wouldn't you be?"

"My stuff isn't combat-related," I say.

"But you were in a combat zone."

"The Navy says it's not combat-related," I insist. (It's true; hospital types fail to qualify for Combat-Related Special Compensation if medically retired for PTSD acquired on the job. Gore comes with the territory for someone like me.) "Look it up," I tell her.

"Kari, I'm not splitting hairs here. You've seen horrible things, and the other soldiers need to hear your story almost as much as you need to tell it. They need to hear how much you tried."

Can she shut up?

"You're rare, Kari."

Nope.

"It's always bittersweet," says Riza, "to have a nurse or a doctor as a patient. Bitter, of course, because we see how it's tearing you apart. But the other patients learn *so much* from you. Most of them see officers as the bad guys."

"They should," I say.

"You're a breath of fresh air, whether you know it or not."

I Foat.

"But DON'T treat the other patients. That's our job, okay?"

Duh, I think. "Any corpsman here?"

"No, but we get our share." Riza wipes the corner of her eyes and looks down at her notes.

"You have a history of family trauma," she says.

"So?"

"So, we have to address that, too," Riza says.

My Eisenhower finds its starch. "Like hell, we do. I'm here because of Bastion. Not that shit."

"I disagree," she says.

"It was ages ago!"

"It's part of the program AND part of the problem," she says.

It's also a nice segue to the third goddamn thing I have to do: compose an Autobiography. I'll have to read the trash in front of other *baluts* doing time in *The Resilience Room*--a different room in a different unit.

"But I don't know them!" I plead.

Riza says talking to strangers can be easier than talking to those we know, or even love.

I'm pissed. I want to snatch the notes out of her hands and chuck them into the hallway. But, before I can do that, Riza hits me where it's so dark and scary a brown recluse would sooner free its prey and race it for the hills than stay. The fourth thing: "You have to write a letter to the person who hurt you," she says. Our eyes lock, "Then you have to read it to me."

"Uh-uh," I say, "no fucking way!"

"It's only to me. It'll be *private*, Kari."

"It doesn't *sound* very FUCKING private, *Riza!*"

"We're cleaning out everything," she says. "No more concealing. Cleaning. It's what you must do to complete the program. You've suffered *two* traumatic events. A hundred, if counted individually. All were intentional AND malicious, and those are the hardest types to bounce back from."

I Foat.

"It's no wonder," she says.

"What?" I ask.

"It's no wonder you've lost faith."

Her crucifix glints in the afternoon sun pouring through the windows. I start preparing for a sermon that never comes.

"You've lost faith in *us*, Kari. In *everyone*. You've lost it in peers, leaders, family..."

"Wrong," I interrupt. "I love my family."

"I'm not taking about immediate relatives."

I Foat.

"You've lost faith in humanity," she says.

I Foat.

"You've also stopped fooling people." Riza motions to my lap and

I look down with the student in feeble solidarity. My thumb knuckles are bloody. I must've picked at them mercilessly the entire time.

"It's bothering you," she says. "I can tell."

I look up at her, then at the Student (who rejoined us somewhere between war and family), put each knuckle in my mouth and deliberately tear off the loose skin with my teeth, making them bleed all the more: the Phantom may *pop smoke*, but she never disappears.

The student looks constipated, but Cuba is unfazed.

"First group starts in ten minutes," says Riza. "I'll see you then."

"Yay."

Chapter 3

"Shut the fuck up, Riza!"

Yikes.

"Damn!" he rages. "Why you gotta be such an ASSHOLE all the time?!"

I laugh my head off from across the room. Since the Phantom swooped in several months ago, I crack-up whenever people lose their shit in public places. Call it a sympathetic response. Cuba ignores my howling and re-addresses Zeke.

"You aren't trying," says Riza.

"Oh *real*-ly?! I'm not *try*-ing?!" Zeke glares at Riza with arms tightly folded over swollen fists showcasing a few split knuckles in various stages of healing. Zeke isn't a picker, like I am. He's a puncher, and a stocky Southerner who wouldn't be caught dead without his Wintergreen Copenhagen or bold-faced irreverence. My first foray into group healing tells me Zeke's outbursts are common-- especially if the subject matter revolves around "a bunch of hokey bullshit." Take meditation class, for example. We have it on Tuesdays.

Riza turns in her chair to face Zeke and says to him in that accent- -the honest one, which nobody can deny. "You make me really sad."

"Boo-hoo," says our jolly good fellow, "I don't give a shit!"

"I don't believe that," says Riza.

"Then YOU'RE in denial!" shouts Zeke.

"You *care*," she insists. "It's why you're angry with me."

"Whatever," he says.

"AND *I* care, Zeke. Please take our work here seriously."

"It doesn't matter," he says, "I don't need this. I already know how to find peace."

Some nod their heads in agreement. We knew where to find it, all right. War, a peace in its own, was replaced with booze, pills, road rage, and fist fights. I'm passive by nature, preferring the first two, but don't put anything past the Phantom instigator. First, it's a revolver. Next thing you know, it'd be arrest, for whatever reason (brandishing, maiming, etc...). Case-in-point: The Phantom hates the Juggalo, a carcass-wielding gang of ass clowns bent on toppling the local establishment by flinging dead raccoons at 7-Eleven cashiers. *SCREW those dudes AND their screwworms*! Even anarchy requires an element of style. With the right provocation (and the wrong Slurpee) it'd be open season on those dorks.

Riza's brow furrows and she says, more to the ground than to anyone in particular, "Oh Zeke...*Please* don't throw away your second chance."

Or is this his third? Zeke has been here over three months, save a few days post-tantrum on the F Unit, or "The Eff U," a place brimming with window-lickers and blowholes. He doesn't want to meditate, but he doesn't want to go back to The Eff U again, either. I agree with Riza. He cares. He'll try again. Maybe not today, but he'll try.

Don't treat them, Kari.

Riza looks around to see if any of us are watching the cautionary tale unfolding before our very eyes. Mine strain to pay attention, but I scan the room once more before closing my eyes to transcend amongst misanthropes: Brian, the Marine I'd met earlier, sits motionless to my left and is still wearing sunglasses; a girl two seats to my right noshes on what's left of her paper coffee cup; a blonde guy with holes for eyes stares at Cup Girl and me from across the room; and a sweet-looking red-headed kid slouches in the corner, bouncing his knees to, what could only be, the palsied rhythms of his own troubled mind. Meanwhile, I'm picking at my whatnot and bleeding from my wherever, and a lanky guy next to Riza is sleeping.

◆ ◆ ◆

After meditation, the patients reconvene in the lounge for Daily Goals. Noah is refreshed from his early evening nap, and sneaks up behind Brian to do his best Corey Hart impression.

"I-wear-my-suuun-glasses-at-goals!"

"You come up behind me like that again," says Brian, "and I'll shove'em up your ass."

"Oooo...tough guy!"

Brian slowly turns away from Noah and spits into an empty coke can. Dipping is forbidden indoors, though the only people who really give a shit are the therapists who went home for the evening. Still, Brian tries to respect the graveyard crew who let him slide. Zeke, however, puts it on blast during banker's hours by purposefully dipping Long Cut in group therapy just to gross-out Riza with the grounds that collect in his teeth. Not even Brian checks him for it because "it's good morale."

"Hi, I'm Noah!" Neither picker nor puncher, Noah is a performer (and the little bastard's always on when he's not asleep).

"Hi, Noah," says everyone, save Brian, who trails off with a "Hi, asshole."

"My goal today was to take a shit, but I haven't yet."

"There's always tomorrow," says everyone.

Constipation is a genuine concern at The Willows. Opiods, God bless 'em, did a number on our plumbing before we arrived. Now that we're here, the hospital isn't exactly what you'd call a Club Med. There's a small gym on the unit but, from the look of it, most prefer to bide their evenings with DVDs and carbs. Hence, most are overweight and ALL are on a stool softener. It's one of the many reasons Zeke calls us "broke dicks."

Not one to be outdone, I've put on thirty pounds since Afghanistan secondary to the shoddy metabolism I nurtured while at Camp Bastion, eating a quarter of what I usually did back in the States. The self-starvation was a little on account of Bastion's British Scoff House cuisine (Yorkshire pudding, black pudding, gammon, curry, hunger strike, repeat...). But food was food in Afghanistan and we knew how precious it was. Over there, if you had "three hots and a cot," you were doing pretty well. So I kept trying to eat the stuff, but treated myself once a week when I wasn't on call, taking the twenty-minute hike to the cafeteria at Camp Leatherneck, a U.S. Marine base that conjoined with Camp Bastion. Leatherneck was the stouter base of the two, and had all the soda and pie a visiting dignitary could eat. Camp Bastion, by contrast, was more austere in tea and kit *slash* food and equipment, but had a trauma hospital of exceptional reputation that dumped twenty percent of Great Britain's total world blood supply into The Sangin Valley, an IED hotbed that contained the gravest injuries (and greatest saves) modern medicine has ever known--*more* than enough to make a Bearcat bawl. Amazing, considering U.S. casualties didn't absorb the Queen's stores; America pumped-in her own Bastion blood supply, but stock still dwindled, leaving hospital staff to donate blood between shifts.

Bastion, or, more specifically, The Sangin Valley, was hell on earth. Anyone who says otherwise hasn't been there, and to them I say "Fuck you." Walk two hundred and four paces from your cot to your hell a hundred times over and we'll talk. If you can do that, then do it again, but this time ditch the fucking vanilla latté and pick up a Tea One (brown water, milk, and a cube, goddammit), and we'll talk again. Then do it constipated with shrews in your face.

So, needless to say, I wasn't very hungry in Afghanistan. After the deployment, I shrugged off yoga and proceeded to stuff my face for two years straight with the calorie conversion rate of a male elephant seal in-between mating seasons. I even developed an anal fissure (nice), which has required a couple surgeries. This explains my predilection for, and copious supply of, opiates.

Hi, I'm chubby and constipated. I'm also new here, so I won't have a goal until tomorrow, when I'll tell you I want to lose ten pounds in a day or present in *The War Room* without shitting my pants. Constipation be damned, but I like goals I can never reach. It makes self-deprecation that much easier.

"Hi, my name is Brian."

"Hi Brian," says everyone.

"My goal today was to read in *The War Room*," he says, "and I did."

Zeke says good job. Sylvia says good job. Noah is far away; Noah hasn't presented yet, so he disappears behind his eyes and takes a long drink of red Mountain Dew. Not a full-on Foat, but close. Hopefully The Dew makes a turd (dream big, says I).

"Hi, I'm Zeke."

"Hi Zeke," says everyone.

"My goal today was to kill Riza, but I didn't do it."

"Ezekiel!" shouts an old black lady barely visible above the medication counter. *Man, I wish I had her set of pipes.* Whenever I lay down the law at home, my Kid hides for fun, or barters for *even more* fun. Maybe Miss Dorothea can help me "grow a pair." She, for all intents and purposes, is my new Magenta Mama. It certainly seems so as Zeke, angry bastard that he is, quiets down *pronto*. She's been a nurse for decades and is a devout southern Baptist whose life mission is to get her patients to take Daily Goals seriously.

"Now listen up, everybody! Be sure to get yourselves to AA tonight. And, don't forget, service is at eight o'clock. Hope to see a few of your friendly faces at worship tonight. Are you going, Miss Kari?"

On cue, all heads turn to see what the new girl will say. "Will there be a blood sacrifice?" I ask.

Mama frowns.

"Good one!" says Noah.

"Miss Dorothea be like, 'Ya'll motherfuckas need Jesus!'" says Zeke.

And with that, Miss Dorothea shakes her head and goes about her regular duty of taking our ungrateful vital signs.

◆ ◆ ◆

I go to my room and drop the shades. I don't want dinner. I need to sleep, but my mind races as I try to comfort myself with an old bedtime routine. Not the kind my Kid and I share; thinking about that stuff would only make me more anxious than I already am. I'm raw enough. I'm walling off my loved ones like I did after Afghanistan. I'm not ready to lose my head, but, when I do, I hope a fellow inmate does me the good service to laugh. With no booze, pills, or *pistola*, I'm gonna need *something*.

There's always tomorrow....

"No, Kari. There ain't any monsters."

My mother pulls the covers up to my neck and moves across the room to turn off the light. Sheryl can't afford a two-bedroom, not even in a rent-assisted complex where the water bugs constantly crunch underfoot in the dark. She sits next to me on my twin bed, directly across from her own. Her movements are slow and careful. Although sidestepping a few toys and a couple six-legged tenants, I know her measured pace is more for my benefit; I need time to gather courage for the next question.

"What about vampires?"

"Nope," she says with her face just above mine.

The last question takes the longest.

"And you're never gonna die. *Right?*"

"Never ever," she whispers.

◆ ◆ ◆

I wake at 3 AM. Needless to say I slept through AA. *Miss Dorothea is going to kill me*! Yet the graveyard nurses in the lounge are indifferent to my presence; insomnia is the one constant within our patient population. I see my skittish roommate, Cup Girl, or Sylvia the Masticator, curled-up in one of the recliners. I know she'll sleep under the bright fluorescents of the lounge until she's able to get a better read on me. She's tight with Brian and Zeke, though. The Honey Badgers (as the staff have renamed them) are all Marine Sergeants who've parlayed the shittier aspects of this inpatient stint to better suit their three-way Tease-a-Thon.

Yesterday, Zeke was eavesdropping when I asked Sylvia if she was going to AA that evening.

"Hell yeah, she is!" said Zeke.

"Well you're supposed to go too," said Sylvia, "and I haven't seen your ass there in a week."

"Don't get salty with me because you're an alcoholic."

"Your mom's an alcoholic!"

"Dirty wino!"

"Oh, come on, Zee, I'm not that bad!"

"Really Syl? Your fuckin' lips look like they blew a purple Smurf last night!"

"BAM!" said Brian.

They didn't really (the lips), but wine was one of the things that landed Sylvia at The Willows. Zeke saw her the day she admitted (from a beige recliner, perhaps), so he'd know. Either way, I definitely related to the way they downplayed their pain; I spent my elementary school years as one of five white kids (ten, if you counted the teachers) at an all-black school. It was the early 80's and we were kids. Shade wasn't thrown so much as it was flung:

"Your Mama!"

"Your Pops!"

"Your Granny on tops!"

"Your Whole Generation!" (Irony would be taught in middle school.)

I was never called a honky, just as Sylvia would never truly be called a drunk who couldn't hack it. But smurfs, mamas, and vermillion borders are always in play. Besides, it's good morale to belong.

I don't *belong* anywhere. Even if I weren't losing my mind, I can't mix with my peers anymore. They tunnel like gerbils through the bowels of someone else's notion of excellence (I'd rather be in Bastion). I wear too much brass to make fun of said gerbils in the presence of junior sailors (I'd rather be in Bastion). And I'm too numb to engage with my Spouse and Kid, who are--for lack of a better description--incredibly unfortunate. I *could* talk turkey with the nurses behind the counter, trading blowhole and butthole stories, but, to them, I'm just another patient with bats in her belfry. So, for the next six-weeks, I simply belong to The Willows.

I don't want to wake Sylvia with the television, so I go back to my room to retrieve my iPod and the marbled composition book Riza gave me earlier. I place the book on the table. It's where I'm supposed to write my Autobiography, Combat Timeline, and other conscriptions of torture. I put my figurative headphones on because the last thing I want is to be alone with my thoughts; practiced in the fine art of dissociation, my imagination is still strong. I have to imagine the music, since The Willows confiscated all my personal electronics. I stare at the composition book for "a few more tracks."

At last I have one of the nurses flip a coin to determine which I'll start first. The Autobiography wins.

My name is Kari. I was born in Wilmington, Delaware during the spring of 1973. My mother Sheryl worked as a secretary in an old TV repair shop owned by my great-uncle Arthur. I remember being in the shop a lot as a preschooler and knew, even then, Uncle Arthur loved his niece. He must have because he kept Sheryl on even though she was mean to his customers.

One of my first childhood memories was that of a phone conversation I overheard in the shop. I was playing with rubber stamps and invoices while Sheryl argued with a potentially litigious customer with a broken Zenith.

"Oh, that's bullshit! We fixed the thing last week and what you're talking about now is something new. Oh, yeah? Well go ahead and fuckin' sue me. I don't have a pot to piss in, so good luck getting JACK SHIT!"

Click.

Uncle Arthur ran out of his office with a half an Italian sub in his face. "NO! NO! NO! You can't talk like that!*"*

"Oh, come on!" Sheryl said. "That asshole's been trying to get something extra out of us every time, and every time I tell him to go fuck himself. He'll call us when he's ready to pay for a repair. Trust me. I KNOW people!"

He threatened to fire her (again) and she protested (again), saying he wouldn't be able to find another secretary "who'd do this shit for a pittance." Then she called the shop a shithole and complained about the tits and puss all over the place; Uncle Arthur's three sons worked as repairmen and had a predilection for Playboy, in that the centerfolds covered every square inch of wall space and, sometimes, the surface of every desk.

Sheryl motioned to the "twat shot" left casually beside her typewriter and, as predicted, Uncle Arthur caved.

"Take it easy on the customers. Okay, Sher?"

"You're the boss," she said and got back to work--only this time with a sunny disposition. That's the thing about Sheryl: She could be ugly one minute and warm the next. She made excuses for her outbursts, chalking them up to fits of "whimsy." One such incident occurred when she threw a heavy cream-filled doughnut (my favorite) from clear across the room at my head. It landed in my cereal bowl, instead, drenching my face and shirt with Cheerios. I'd been "eating too fuckin' slow."

Like me, Arthur and the sons tolerated Sheryl's whimsy because she was always the life of the party when she wasn't pissed off. She was efficient, too; all was ship-shape with Sheryl calling the shots. Uncle Arthur may've been the boss, but Sheryl was the Skipper. Or maybe that's just how I saw it because Sheryl was my world.

Despite his shop's lowbrow aesthetic, Uncle Arthur was a gentleman who never swore and treated all women, whom he attracted in throngs, with respect. His sons, on the other hand, used their good looks to shake down as many women as possible, leaving Sheryl to field her cousins' calls from jilted women whose spurned indignation spanned three counties. I assume Uncle Arthur didn't like his sons' behavior, but all three were kick-ass tube men, so the photos stayed up. It didn't really bother Sheryl, a weather-beaten woman in her late 30's whose mantra, a stiff dick has no conscience, absolved her cousins' conduct as far as she was concerned, and would only use the smut for leverage whenever she didn't get her *way. The sons weren't so bad: each had a different color Labrador I could play with whenever they stopped by between jobs. I liked the chocolate Lab best. So, I associated my second cousins more with dogs than pussy. Clearly, Uncle Arthur needed Sheryl, and she, a belligerent single mother, needed him. He paid a salary of $200 per week with medical insurance, the latter of which came in handy. I'd always be sunburned in the summer and, quite often, sun poisoned. The citizens of the greater tri-state* area (comprising Delaware, New Jersey, and Pennsylvania) were *manic summer tanners, and my mother was no exception. Sheryl would go down the shore and bask from nine to five whenever possible. I was, literally, toast if she didn't score me a spot at PWP Camp.* Parents without Partners *was, back then, a place where gutter-class singles could unload their children in order to fully explore their own contraction-potential for melanoma, hepatic encephalopathy, crabs, etc...*

PWP would at least douse us kids with bug spray and slather on the SPF before telling us to scram. But, with Sheryl, my skin would be blistering in the water. By the end of the afternoon, she'd be on the sand, golden brown, attracting beer bellies with strong shoulders. I'd be rocking the zinc on the second sunny day. If there be a third, jeans, a flannel shirt, and a hat. More sunny days would score me a doctor's visit, a couple lances, creams, and Opiods.

The medical insurance was, indeed, a godsend, but the salary was barely enough to keep us warm in winter, and, although our apartment wasn't much (we'd graduated to a two-bedroom by that time), *it never lacked for visitors, cold or not. There'd always be a mishmash of people stopping in: Drunk boyfriends, stoned family squatters, and one psychiatrist.*

Dr. Sutton came highly recommended by Godmother Shandy (Sheryl's twin), who'd been seeing him for years as her couples' therapist. Aunt Shandy thought Dr. Sutton was the best thing since Freud. Not that she, an 8th grade dropout, even knew who Freud was. Nor was she cognizant of the phallic stage she perpetually inhabited; Shandy had sex with Dr. Sutton regularly on Sheryl's living room couch while I was in class across the street at Logan Elementary. Sheryl had given Shandy a copy of my house key and, while hers hung on a packed ring in anonymity from her hard-hitting husband, mine was a lure neatly snapped onto my belt loop. It said:

"This is a latchkey kid who comes home, roller skates in the kitchen, pisses off the old ladies downstairs, takes her Flintstone Vitamins (five to seven of them because they taste better than Pixie Sticks or Pez), makes Kraft Macaroni and Cheese, and sits in front of the TV until her mother returns from work, so, if you do manage to snatch her before she gets to the front door, it'll probably be a good three hours before anyone notices (good luck)."

But Friday was different. Other than the usual aromas of long-departed malpractice would be the unmistakable fragrance of Jean Natte Powder wafting out from our upstairs apartment. Millicent Agatha Dwyer, my grandmother, used the same powder puff between her legs for over ten years according to family legend (and later proven when I began cleaning her apartment in my teens; the puff, kept in the bottom drawer of her dresser, rested on top of a long, deep tin of Natty J).

Millie was a cold comfort. A severe manic-depressive who barely managed on Lithium, she exhibited a number of side effects that combined to make her a pariah. In addition to having a marginal grip on reality and being ninety percent deaf, she (and we) suffered from Bruxism (rabid teeth grinding) with crepitus so loud it achieved a decibel equivalent to that of a cowbell (POP, RAKE, POP, PLUNK). She constantly shuffled her feet while seated and wore carpet holes in front of her favorite chairs. The holes, my wolf's bane, told me which chairs to avoid when visiting family; Millie would hike up her floral muumuus and sit down bare-assed in any home she visited. Last, but not least, she'd been born with NO boundaries or filters whatsoever:

"*I caught your grandfather diddling the German maid again!*"
POP, PLUNK, POP....

I was in the middle of watching an episode of my favorite afterschool show, Gilligan's Island, *and wondering how my best friend's gigantic Afro had become tiny cornrows overnight. I was still a greenhorn, ethnically speaking--be it style, shade, or otherwise. So, I watched* What's Happening!! *after Gilligan to brush up; LeShawn had looked like a completely different person at school, and it was still freaking me out. I always turned to TV to field life's questions. I wasn't so much a kid as I was one of Sheryl's plants; she fed and watered me, sure. But life? Coping? I'd figure that stuff out on my own.*

"*His Army buddy was in there, too, doll!*" POP, RAKE, POP, POP....

I'm not sure why Millie thought a 2ⁿᵈ grader would appreciate a thirty-year old anecdote about an adulterous love triangle involving a dead sadist, his best friend, and a "whore kraut," until it suddenly dawned on me that she was fucking crazy. Yet I loved her very much, like I loved Uncle Arthur. The hugs and kisses I got back then were mostly from them, along with the candy I devoured, the cassettes I listened to, and the Stride Rites *I demolished (and, later, the Classic Suede* Nike *I'd come to worship). Millie and Arthur represented my Camelot--evidence that grace could still exist with nudie pictures on the walls and a cheating husband (et al.) in the bedroom.*

I don't remember my mother's hugs. I'm not sure if that's because she never gave me any, or the other stuff was so bad, or I just plain forgot. Years later, when Sheryl and I talked about those times, the conversation would always devolve into the same canned rhetoric: "Don't you remember any of the good stuff, Kari?!" That's when I'd usually bring up our bedtime routine. They were the only instances I ever saw my mother let her guard down. I told her those moments had been peaceful and loving until she eventually ruined that, too. She told me she answered "all the monster shit" so I'd "go the fuck to sleep already."

So I don't remember her hugs, though I remember running her errands. I went to the 7-Eleven every Saturday morning to get two-packs of Merit Lights, a carton of milk, the Sunday paper, and (if there was change) a pack of baseball cards. Baseball was bigger than football back then and I'd already had designs on cashing-in on their appreciation by the time I turned eighteen to buy Sheryl the house she always wanted: I'm a natural born optimist who always planned and prepared--in this case--to cover the cost of Sheryl's dream house.

I approached the register with my goods, but Keisha, who'd been selling cigarettes to me for the last six months, put a stop to that one woeful Sunday, thanks to the new laws prohibiting tobacco sales to minors. She pointed to the sign above the counter. It had big red words she knew I could read. I was a good reader--the best in 2nd grade. My teacher, Mrs. Overstreet, advised my mother to skip me from the 2nd to 4th grade, but Sheryl said I was "too backwards and immature," so I stayed behind.

"But the cigarettes are for Sheryl," I told Keisha.

"Come on, Kari. You know I can't. Your mama can come down and buy them herself. Now go on."

I put the milk in my rear basket, the baseball cards in my pocket, and tied the newspaper to the banana seat of my pink Huffy; the last time I came home with half-a-paper hadn't been pleasant. After the yelling and breaking of things, Sheryl wouldn't let me back in the house until I retraced my trail and retrieved every single scrap on the highway, where a section or two must have fallen out. Sheryl's boyfriends read the sports page in the afternoons when they woke, and it was important, goddammit!

But, now, this was to be worse. Sheryl didn't have a habit. She had a compulsion. She clung to her cigarettes and the smell clung to me. I took a deep breath after cinching up my purchases and hit play on the boom box tied to my handlebars, singing AC/DC's "Dirty

Deeds," while pedaling the mile-ride home. I was trying to look like a bad-ass, but was stuck "Like a Rock" in Segar-ville with the rest of the white trash: scrawny, jean-jacketed with a black and white checkered Black Sabbath painter's cap covering my tangled brown hair (no rat tail, thank Jesus), a flannel shirt, big rose-tinted eyeglasses, and Lee Jeans. I felt like a number, that's for sure: one in a long line of hill people with no role model in sight. My pseudo parents were an amalgam of 70's and 80's rock stars: Uncle Arthur kept me well supplied with music (Bon Scott and Ozzy Osbourne were my dads in times of need. Likewise, Debbie Harry and Pat Benatar served as my mothers). I played air guitar alongside them to resounding applause every night in my room because they always drowned-out the whimsy that would invariably be occurring in the next room. I wasn't permitted to listen to rap because Aunt Shandy would've called me a nigger-lover. The only black people Shandy tolerated were those from Motown days gone by because "those niggers could sing!" Still, I loved hanging with Leshawn and his cousins, who started breakdancing in front of our elementary school in the fall of 1980. Leshawn always vouched for me, though I looked like a tool. The only cool thing I could get away with wearing were the suede Nikes Millie bought for me. God forbid I wear an Adidas tracksuit. Sheryl echoed her big sister's cultural attitudes, unfortunately, as did her boyfriends. I remember winning some coin with an essay I wrote at school. I used the money to buy her boyfriend, Phil, a pair of Clamshell Adidas. The response from him? "I'm not wearing those nigger shoes!" Then he tossed them to the side.

Sheryl and Phil were waiting for me as I approached the apartment. I prayed they had half-a-pack left. I climbed the stairs and went straight to the kitchen where Sheryl was waiting. Phil had gone back to sleep, which was bad because my mother tended to make nice in the immediate presence of a new man she'd just banged.

"Sorry, Mom. Keisha told me I can't buy cigarettes for you anymore."

"What?!"

"Well...I...I mean I..."

"Spit it out!"

"I told her she could, but she..."

"But WHAT!?"

"I can't buy them, Mom! She'll get arrested and..."

"FUCK THAT! Go back, RIGHT NOW, and tell that NIGGER the cigarettes are for ME!"

"That's a bad word, Mom. Don't say that."

"You sound like your CHEATIN' ASSHOLE FATHER when you talk to me like that. STOP CUTTIN' ME UP!" ("Stop cutting me up," analogous to "Stop criticizing me," was said anytime I expressed a personal opinion.)

"I'm not cutting you up, Mom. Just please don't be mad at Keisha. She's really nice."

Then Sheryl picked up the carton of milk and threw it straight down on the linoleum floor and screamed "FUUUUCK!"

I stop writing. I don't want to think about her--my mother, my Skipper. I stare at the last page and see I've left a third of it blank. That spurs me on more than the revelation of becoming the person I loathe. Filling white space is but one of a long line of obsessions that fool me into thinking I have any control over this goddamn life.

Sheryl's instructions became, at once, clear: "This is how to handle stress, you little shit: throw things, yell, scream if you have to, cuss at will, name call, accuse everyone AND ANYONE but yourself, yell some more, deflect, deny, project, and displace all over place. But not you, Kari! NOT YOU! YOU stay silent! Take my shit. Take EVERYONE's shit! Hold it in and DON'T YOU FUCKING CRY!"

She didn't say that, of course. Sheryl wasn't that eloquent and wouldn't have copped to a single thing. Instead, her "FUUUCK" hung in the air and told me what to do: Dissociate. I simply went somewhere else.

Sheryl, broken and sad, had been raised by a war-mongering psycho and a sweet basket case. You'd think she'd want to protect me. You'd think she'd never want me to experience what she'd experienced. But no. And I could never leave Sheryl because, if I did, she would kill herself. She said so every season, it seemed, and it fucking terrified me. I was hers to abuse and a toy she'd neglect, so I stopped having opinions. I did as she said and loved her the way she wanted.

I take a breather. *It's all too much.* Blind loyalty and fear: the parasites of our family tree, much like the red chiggers that clung to the Spanish Moss on the Cackalacky oak trees, just outside my windows on base housing, and outside my office and pretty much everywhere.

I'd been perfect for the Navy; a warm transfer--a carcass barely there--being passed from a witch to a bug-eyed Bearcat. Easy pickins' me. A *Balut!* An *amuse-bouche!*

Fuck'em, says the Phantom.

I take my pen and resume.

Grandma Millie had spent the night and watched the milk spectacle from the living room recliner. "Oh, Sheryl! That's terrible. Don't yell like that. Come on, doll...she's just a LITTLE GIRL!" POP, POP, POP.... Millie didn't like yelling. Her heart couldn't take it. Paced to manage a third degree block, Millie's heart had a solid GPS. She'd been punched and kicked for years by Sheryl's father, but she still hadn't become desensitized enough to tolerate Sheryl the Terrible's *similar mistreatment of me. Sheryl was just like her father, though, holding her heart in her fist and threatening to stomp away with it at a moment's notice, so Millie's cries fell on (equally) deaf ears. This was Sheryl, after all--a woman who referred to Brazilian nuts as "nigger toes."*

"I DON'T FUCKIN' CARE, MOM! That nigger KNEW they were for ME! What's a seven-year-old kid want with cigarettes ANY

way?!"

And, just like that, Sheryl stomped out to get her ciggy-pops. I didn't understand her hatred. Even though I'd come home with broken glasses from repeated fights with Lakisha, Leshawn's older sister, I never hated her or called her names. I'd made that mistake once when Sheryl dropped me off at Head Start for the first time. "Don't leave me with those niggers and spics, Mommy!" My four-year-old self ran down the hall toward my mother, begging her not to go. The profanities flew as the teacher was right on my heels. My mother was long gone, though, ironically embarrassed by my behavior. Unlike Shandy, who's a bonafide racist pig and would've laughed her ass off, Sheryl is all talk. I'd turnaround to see the look in the teacher's eyes, and immediately felt awful (just as I had with my Spouse the day I chucked the Blu Ray). And Lakisha, who'd overheard my slurs while walking down the hall toward her first class, would never forget it.

All I wanted was to be liked and accepted around the neighborhood, and, eventually, I was. Still, Sheryl had told me while putting Scotch Tape on my glasses that I'd better learn to "fight those niggers," though the extent of her follow-on instruction was: "If they nigger-pile you, just grab hold of a little one's hair. The shit comes out like cotton candy!"

As I stood there watching the milk seep under the refrigerator, I thought about Andy--my father. Andy, a draft-dodger, who allegedly told Sheryl to sniff gas and run around the garage until she aborted. Andy, who's smiling and doting in my baby pictures, contrasted by Sheryl, who had a smile that was positively asystolic. Andy, who took me to see the first Rocky, wore Andy Capp hats, and would always shout "There they go!" at the horse track. Poor Andy, the gambling man. He must've bet on an attractive young woman, later realizing, not so much that the carpet didn't match the drapes, but rather her heart didn't match her beauty.

Sheryl used to be pretty. Maybe she still was. I couldn't tell. I

*loved her like no other and knew I'd be lost without her. My
happiness was contingent upon hers. I followed her cues to the nth.
It was a cross I willingly bore because to acknowledge the obvious
was too goddamn painful: My mother didn't love me, or couldn't
love me.*

*It was clear Andy hadn't wanted Sheryl, but I like to think he
would've taken me if he could've. But Sheryl hung onto people like
she hung onto knick-knacks--only she valued her bell and spoon
collections more. She kept Andy away from me, save for once, when
I was eight and he showed-up unexpectedly at Uncle Arthur's
funeral. I knew then, like I know now, that he abandoned me to save
himself.*

And I didn't (and still don't) *blame him one bit.*

It's six in the morning when I finish, so I head back to the room
for a ninety-minute snooze. My head is pounding, but a small sense
of accomplishment relaxes me just enough to take me to dreamland,
and fast.

In a flash, I'm awake again. A nurse says Riza is waiting for me
down the hall in one of the quiet rooms. I put on my slippers and
shuffle down the hallway with a vague recollection of a nightmare
about deer, of all things. When I see them, which is often in our neck
of the woods, they serve as gentle reminders to pause, take stock,
breathe, that life is not so bad.

I enter the room and see Riza seated in the far corner. She is
absent her usual pen and notebook. She seems more serene, but I
know it's just a front for all the questions she'll ask.

"You're late this morning," she says.

"I started journaling in the middle of the night," I tell her, "and I
got on a roll."

"You had a nightmare?"

I talk about the Deer Dream, the only one I *can* remember, and
because it's fresh. There were two deer. A doe was standing in the
corner of my Kid's bedroom. The Kid and I were sleeping in a twin

bed on the opposite side of the room. As per usual, my daughter was sleeping the sleep of the profoundly innocent. I was wide-awake in the dream, faking sleep because I was scared shitless: The doe had a huge head with slanting yellow eyes, and its body was half the size it should have been to support a dome so ghastly. Everything was silent and still, save a tremolo that pulsed as if a Theremin were just behind the doe, deep in the shadowy corner, which, by then, was a goddamn chasm. And I dared not move else I startle the doe or wake my Kid, who would surely scream because this thing was worse than scary.

When I began to shake, I was transported through the darkness and into a small forest at the bottom of a valley. My Kid was nowhere in sight and I was surrounded by trees with falling leaves. Maples. I was a little girl. I knew it because I was wearing the same black and white checkered *Black Sabbath* painter's cap I wore when I was seven.

I was at recess with a bunch of other kids aimlessly walking around in the leaves. My eyes shifted from the kids up to a slope. A huge buck was at the top of the tree line. He was a fantastic eighteen-pointer. Unlike the doe, he was proportionate and majestic. Then, as quick as anything, he charged toward us. I tried to dart left, then right. Nothing. I could only lie down and close my eyes as I heard his breath and his gallop, a tympani of terror the likes of which I'd never known in sleep (and I've had some doozies).

All the kids were on the ground, but he was going to trample *me*. Then I felt the wind, and the wind alone, as it took the last bit of my breath. Just when I thought I was dead, I looked up in time to see the buck's broad backside disappear over the slope from whence he'd come. The leaves were trailing behind until the wind, too, was gone.

We children rose to our feet. When my bearings returned, I looked down to see a lone parchment wrapped with a red ribbon. The ribbon was the shade of old blood. The black ink inside, more scrawled than printed, read:

In this world there is no Kari Rhyan.

"What do you think it means?" Riza asks.

"I have no idea."

Chapter 4

"Hello, my name is Kari."

"Hi, Kari," mumbles the group (dead heads, every last one.)

It's early, I think, but mornings are *my* time to shine. I'd been a rooster-baby since birth and, seven days in this goddamn cuckoo's nest, I straight-up know the score AND the drill. I'm the cock-of-the-walk, man, and ready to *Crack On!* (British slang for *Just Do It*, only more get-the-lead-out-of-your-ass.) Plus, this goal--already fixed to nail-down--is but another Snapshot. Whether I'm briefing a Bearcat or a few cranky inmates falling asleep in their Fruit Loops, it's all the same to me. "My goal today is to start my Combat Timeline," I say (with a voice crack). *Goddammit....*

Noah interrupts. "Which therapist you got?" The unit has three. If it were up to us, we'd exchange our crummy scab-pickers for one of the other two. The grass is always greener, even in the clink, where denial reigns supreme like a chalupa on an anthill. Still, none would ever exchange their therapist for the one Zeke and I share.

"Riza," I tell him.

"Oooo, that Riza is one...piece...of *ace*."

"Sick," I say, though his Chris Farley is way better than his Corey Hart, I must admit.

And it's a nice gesture; Noah started me off with a guffaw--one to go along with my false sense of security because he knows scribbling down the horror will burn up what little scaffolding we Crazies have left.

Am I to be rebuilt? I think.

Yes. AFTER Riza drains you!

(Kiss my ass, Phantom.)

But Julien, still in pajamas with his back to the group, is a real piece. He's a busted-down, three-year Army private, and quite the catch if you're into rapists and vodka (the latter being the reason he's here amidst victims; the place to which he was originally assigned, a unit strictly for addicts--minus the clear and present trauma--was full). Julien is a dirt bag. A scoundrel. A black hole. Sylvia says he's selling the drama to garner sympathy from judge and jury for his upcoming court martial. Strategic, too: His lawyers need ample time to mount a shitty defense because, make no mistake, folks--he's guilty as sin.

I met Julien yesterday while working on a puzzle. The lounge is rife with jigsaws (hot air balloons, baby animals, and Kinkades--*lots* of Kinkades). I looked at a big stack on the table under the flat screen with yet another video of tan women and acoustic guitars. Sylvia said the "Starbucky" puzzle at the bottom was a real bitch that everyone avoided. So, I snatched-up the Van Gogh and took it to the empty worktable because, like Vinny, I was keen on cutting myself off. It turns out Sylvia was right. Massive and monochromatic, Starbucky was all mine, save for Miss Dorothea's occasional intrusion; she's using the puzzle as a ploy to get at the Canary. *Fat chance.* You get Kari until you begrudge her a benny, then you get the Phantom and a bird and I don't mean Canary. *God, I miss Xanax.*

Still, the solitude was impressive for the first couple hours. My worktable nearly kissed the medication counter--good for working my magic on the Med Molls. Like me, most patients pander for pills and, unlike me, for cell numbers from young nurses who'd sooner cauterize their own genitalia than give away narcotics or phone numbers to a bunch of muggles like us. The inmates were fools for trying. Much like I was a fool for thinking I could scoot through my day without talking to anyone.

Julien slid up to me while I was working the edge pieces of my swirly blue sky and blue buildings and blue goddamn foreground. "What up? Your name's Kari, right?"

I nodded, but my eyes stayed on Starbucky. I'd appraised Julien earlier that day (if a shiver counts). I'd been talking to Tommy, the sweet redheaded kid with nervous knees. He'd asked me to teach him Sudoku. Julien walked past the tutorial and into the alcove to smoke.

Tommy stopped talking and only resumed after the door closed behind Julien.

"What's that about?" I asked.

"He's not right," said Tommy. The hairs on the back of my neck went up. Kinda like they had in Julien's immediate presence.

"So, whatcha in for?" Julien had asked me.

"This and that...you know," I said, doing my best impersonation of an imprisoned confidence man.

"I got you," Julien replied with downcast eyes.

My gut told me not to ask, but I'm a nurse: it's reflexive for me to show interest or, with someone like Julien, feign interest. He's a human being, after all, so I took the bait.

"Alcohol?" I asked. He had a look, or an aura--something similar to Shandy Fletcher's. It was the color of grizzle.

"Yeah...and I got a hearing next week," he muttered. "So, uh...I gotta look like I'm tryin'. Ya know how it is."

"Right," I said, searching for a better response. I'd hoped it was a Smash Brothers scenario: Property damage, inciting a riot, coon tossing.... Heck, even grave robbing would've been better than what he'd tell me.

"What'd they get you for?"

"Rapin'," he said. Anyone who calls rape "rapin'" is already guilty in my book. Rapin', as casual as workin', talkin', fuckin', or shittin'. After my gasp, he tried to reassure me.

"Oh, I'm gonna win, no problem. Stupid bitch. That shit was consenshul, believe me."

"Consensual," I corrected.

"Yeah!" he pointed. "Consenshul."

He looked and smelled like a smiling, sweaty ass crack, and was moving closer to me. Just as the Phantom was going to take him by the neck and shove fifty shades of duck egg blue down his gob, I was rescued.

"Hey there, Julien!" Noah popped-up from behind and, unlike

the deference he showed Brian, gave Julien two *hard* pats on the back.

"You shit yet?" Julien asked snidely.

"Nah. *Eins schizer, mein kampf!*" Noah exclaimed (with a fist pump two inches from Juliens face).

"What the fuck does that mean?"

"One shit, my struggle," I interrupted.

Julien turned back toward me, I assumed, to woo me a little more, but Noah interrupted again. "Hey Jules!"

"What now?"

"You see the new girl?" Noah asked, motioning toward a neighboring ward. Julien said he hadn't, so Noah walked him down the hall to the window that separated the two units. "Only gonna take a second but, trust me, she's fire!"

I didn't see the transaction, but I sure-as-shit heard it. Noah started off loud, and only got louder. *Embarrass, then frighten*, I thought. I didn't care for the method (too Bearcat), but wasn't one to spoil an awesome delivery--especially if the target was a rotten pedophile.

The girl was thirteen.

"So, here's the thing, Jules...between you, me, and everyone else on the unit, YOU'RE A FUCKING FAKE!" Miss Dorothea ran down the hallway with two techs, but not before Noah shouted. "STAY AWAY FROM THE LADIES, DUDE, OR I'll RUB YOU OUT LIKE A CUNT FUR BLANKET!"

I guess Noah had a Phantom of his own. An ignoramus but a gentleman, Noah had been the youngest sibling in a houseful of older sisters back in Montana, and felt it his duty, now, to look after Sylvia and me. Word on the street had it a nurse dropped the dime on Julien (two to one odds, Miss Dorothea) after the charge nurse was unable to block Julien's transfer in. The info eventually leaked out to one of the patients (even odds on Noah, the town crier), but it hadn't quite trickled down to me.

Julien emerged a minute later, head down, and walked back to the medication line, reassuming the position he never should've left. This time, though, he stood behind Tommy, who promptly left the line and, with it, the comfort of his scheduled Klonopin dose.

He's not right....

Not long after, Miss Dorothea followed Noah as he traipsed up the hallway and into the lounge, pushing a cart with a television on top. He smiled as he passed Julien.

"Hey, I've got that tonight!" Julien protested.

"Fuck you, Diaper Sniper! Victory is ten parts possession!"

Good one.

Miss Dorothea shook her head as Noah smiled and pushed the cart into his room.

As I was coming up through normal rank and file, I'd supervised many sailors just like Noah--corpsmen mostly--and was always secretly thankful whenever they'd land underneath my umbrella of influence. Noah's antics were similar to those of an older corpsman I'd worked with in Bastion: Rodney Nowak couldn't shut his mouth to save his life. He, too, had Attention Deficit Hyperactivity Disorder, a condition that has all the potential of being a modern day marvel if nurtured properly.

Rodney was only a couple years younger than me, but twice as fast. If assigned as a trauma runner, he could get two shock packs from Blood Bank to blood moll (often times, me) in less than two minutes. That being said, it was the Brits' lead Rodney and I were following. The Brits had the combat medicine gig down pat. We were saving patients who had had no hope of surviving a mere six months prior. Innovation came fast, but Rodney was faster still, which was why the Brits called him "lovely" (oh, how he hated that!). In fact, Rodney and I nearly set a Bastion record, delivering 118 units of blood products into one casualty, replacing his total blood volume five times over while the surgeons preserved what they could and sliced off the rest. The Brits dubbed the massive transfusions "The Bastion Stew," and the resuscitations themselves "The Bastion Way." They were things of beauty, so to speak.

Though I had to Foat my way up to speed when I first got to Bastion, The Stew and The Way were a walk in the park for Rodney. He'd cut his teeth on the Green side, or Marine side, when he turned thirty-one, right after his caduceus was sewn into the shoulder of the summer whites he'd rarely wear: he'd been on a personal mission ever since his older sister died in The Towers. His sister, fifteen years his senior, was more of a mother figure to Rodney. He was devastated. After that, it was digital camouflage or nothing for Rodney. He was a Fleet Marine Force corpsman, but, like me, still seemed a pacifist by nature. Yet he was a crazy son-of-a-bitch who kept a kill card in his wallet to remind him of how close he, himself, came to death two years earlier.

So the ma'am and sir bullshit was chucked after our first day in Bastion. Not to mention we'd cut off two danglers *slash* limbs in the ER--live and direct--from The Sangin Valley, a deathtrap that kicked off the day we arrived. Many injuries were those of U.S. Marines. Rodney had taken off their danglers with his own set of trauma scissors that fateful day, when he started notching the snips on the handle. And God forbid anyone borrow them.

Rodney, out there or not, was a good corpsman. That's why it pained me a great deal when he medically retired from the Navy and, even more so, when I'd learned of his current hospitalization (across the world) in Texas. I imagine him pinging all over his goddamn unit like Noah, who's uncharacteristically quiet at the moment.

Noah is pulling time on Starbucky with me while the nursing staff observes.

"Thank you for the other day," I say.

"No thanks needed," he says.

The nurses observe and chart. *Patient socializing appropriately. Patient still withdrawn. Patient wants crab wonton from P.F. Chang's.* Who can say? It's all part of the drill. I've been given a good once-over twice this week by the charge nurse and, both times, could tell she was gauging whether or not to "ready the leathers." Karma is having her way with me, I think, for enjoying the rush I'd get every time I joined in on a patient takedown (drunks and tweekers, mostly). We'd use cloth bindings instead of leather but, still, there was something *really* soothing about subduing a lunatic.

Now *I'm* the lunatic, stalling on my Combat Timeline, playing with Starbucky, and willing to bet my last Dulcolax the charge nurse has the straps stashed under the counter between a red pen and a yellow highlighter. It's all tools of the trade--those and bite blocks.

Eff her.

I leave Noah with Starbucky and mope over to our schedule that's taped to the lounge wall next to the laundry room, and just off the gym no one uses.

"Art Therapy," I mumble. "Pfft!"

Sylvia overhears as she's folding her load on top of the dryer. "You never know, ma'am. Painting might help."

"Like that painting of a polka-dotted pony helped you?" asks Zeke, breezing past.

"Jesus, stalker! What's your problem?!" says Sylvia.

"Just asking," he replies.

"Well, it wasn't a pony."

"Then what the hell was it?!"

"MY INNER FUCKING DEMON!"

"Killjoy," says Noah.

I laugh my head off as per usual. Miss Dorothea tells us to pipe down. She reminds us that we have ten minutes until art.

"Wanna P-Funk?" Zeke asks Sylvia, who snatches the Parliament from his fingers, then follows him out to the smoke deck.

Soon after, the charge nurse herds us over to a small room with fifteen desks configured in the shape of a U. The art therapist is a tall, gangly hippie with long blonde hair and bright blue eyes. She'd just come from The Eff U, and I get the feeling she's a little on edge. It's hazardous duty for an art therapist. I reckon any occupation that wrangles the subconscious out from hiding to be inherently risky. She must've seen a fair share of meltdowns and probably had a few of her own.

I sit between Sylvia and a kid named Stefano. Admitted for marijuana abuse and childhood trauma, Stefano had been in the Army all of three months and was considered a *Pogue*--a soldier who serves in the rear and never sees combat, or *Person Other than Grunt*. We all like Stefano because he never pretends to be anything other than what he is: A teenage thug. The judge told him to choose between the Army and jail and he chose the Army. Still, he's a better soldier than Julien, who's on hiatus right now with his lawyer, poking holes in a child's story, no doubt.

The art therapist tells Stefano she likes his name.

"Thank you," he says, "but I don't care for it much."

"Why? It's unique," she says.

"My mom watches *The Guiding Light,* and she went ahead and named me after her favorite character. Now HOW in the FUCK am I supposed to be a thug when I'm named after a crusty old white dude?!"

"You're doing a pretty good job," I say.

"I know," he says, beaming.

"You're stupid," says Sylvia.

The art therapist smiles stiffly and turns doll-eyed toward the center of the room. There, she unwraps a giant loaf of clay and uses a long, closely guarded, cutting wire to slice away twelve blocks. Each block is roughly one foot square, and we're permitted to use more if artistic expression calls for it. I look away from the cutting wire and Foat over to Zeke. He has Copenhagen in his slot, and he looks thrilled with arms folded. I'm a novice like everyone else. Such skills do not translate to our military trades and, besides that, we're little more than cavemen, now, trapped in survival mode at the bottom of Maslow's Pyramid. We don't know how to self-express unless we're yelling, punching, sobbing, or Foating. The art therapist reassures us that sculpting is intrinsic to human nature because people have been doing it since the beginning of time and blah-blah-blah.

We aren't allowed to use sculpting tools. Plastic knives take the place of scissors. Tongue depressors substitute for sharp metal plaster spatulas. And dull pencils (most definitely) replace shank-like calipers. We're instructed to stare at our clay for a moment and sculpt the first thing that comes to mind, allowing our hands to move over the clay, because the goals are self-awareness and anxiety reduction and blah-blah-blipity-blah.

The art therapist walks over to a paint-splattered boom box that's set on a broken, lopsided stool in the corner of the room. Spa music soon fills the air and Zeke's jaw tightens.

"I'm NOT listening to this patchouli BULLSHIT!"

Patchouli pleads with Zeke's chi. "Try it, Zeke. It's relaxing."

"No way! Give me the other half of that joint stashed in your purse, THEN we'll talk."

"Okay," she sighs, "play whatever you want."

"YES!"

"Nothing with foul language, please."

"Yeah, yeah, yeah...."

"Lil' Mama," Noah demands. "'Lip Gloss' is my jam. Do it!"

"No, no, no," says Sylvia.

Noah sings, "Mac mac Loreal yep 'cause I'm worth it!" He's been wearing sunglasses all day. Wrap around knock-offs. *Prepping for The War Room, I see.* Noah must be channeling Brian, who's conspicuously absent at the moment.

Zeke pulls up his sleeves and rifles through a plastic tub of donated CDs. I spy nine skulls rung around his left arm. I'd cared for enough Marines to know those are Zeke's kills. Finally, he makes his choice. It's thrash. The singer screams, "Let the bodies hit the floor! Let the bodies hit the floor!"

Kids today....

I bolt to imagination land, grab my ear buds and an iPod, and hit *shuffle*, then *repeat*, and play--'til the second coming--a haunting dirge wrapped in a cadence that marches out in aching two-by-two's. "Eisler On the Go" seems like just the thing. I sing along with Billy Bragg, "I don't know what I'll do, I don't know what I'll do...."

Goddammit, I don't. But I stare at my block of clay, and do. Using a plastic knife, I carve out an isosceles triangle, then take a corner and smash it up against another. Isosceles becomes an L. *That's more like it,* the Canary says. *Time to nail the sole, Kari. Without the sole, we got nothing.*

I take a pencil and etch out the base, then serrate the bottom. This guy needs plenty of traction. *Yes, he does,* the Canary chirps. *Amen!* She's wide-awake for this shit. Up until now, the Canary's public appearances were isolated to dreams and Riza's scab-picking sessions.

Keep going. She wants me to keep going, so I keep going.

It's shit, the Phantom observes. *Make a snowball, instead. Go on. Chuck it at Patchouli's head! THAT'S what you can do!*

Steady, whispers the Canary.

I use the pencil to firm up the treads, and will use it once again to make the laces. They need to be spot on. No room for sloppy. Sloppy is for the busted. Cinched tight to the end is the only way to fly as it carries to the cuff in a perfect knot tucked-in at the top.

"I don't know what I'll do," I sing louder, "I don't know what I'll do." Patchouli comes over and taps me on the shoulder. I pull out an imaginary ear bud.

"The proportions are dead on," she says.

"I know."

"What's that on the edge?" she asks.

"Eagle, Globe, and Anchor," I reply and quickly replace the ear bud.

Ok, the Canary says. *Finish it.*

No.

You gotta, she says.

"No!"

The Phantom screams, *Throw the fucking chair then! It'll be a one-way ticket to The Eff U for you!*

Shhh...finish.

I take a tongue depressor and hack at the top. It doesn't matter where it starts or where it stops, so long as it doesn't cross the plain, the cuff, or the knot.

Stefano passes a note. *Snakes?* it reads. I look up and he's staring at me, as is Sylvia. Stefano is passing a clay ball back and forth between his hands and waits for his answer. Sylvia is making a picture frame. Zeke is making a bottom half of a denture container, or cup, with one hand over his face. Noah's gone. Sweet Tommy, still red-headed, and still anxious as hell, is making a vase for his sister. I can see his knees under the table going a million miles an hour.

"No, not snakes," I say.

Now you've done it, says the Phantom.

The Canary agrees. *You've done it, Kari. Bravo.*

Sylvia nudges me. I pull out a bud.

"You ok, ma'am?"

I say yes, but the tears stream. I wipe them away with both hands and fold the salt into the clay. I need the moisture anyway; Stefano drank the cup of water that was supposed to keep my goddamn clay moist. "I don't know what I'll FUCKING do," I sing.

I pick up the pencil one last time. *This one's for me.* I crack off its tip and gouge out the snakes.

The Phantom is on a hiatus. No. The Phantom is *helping. Now bend it,* she says.

"But it'll break," I say.

Sylvia nudges, but I ignore her.

No, it won't, says the Phantom

No, it won't, says the Canary.

I bend it and it doesn't break. *Oh, God.*

Patchouli waves a hand in front of my face, and I put Eisler on pause. The room is quiet. Zeke still has his hand over his face. Noah is nowhere. Everyone else stares at what I've made. Brian walks through the door and stops short. I can imagine the horror of it as it passes through violet hues. "That!" Brian points. "*That's* what I see in nightmares."

It's a Marine's boot, amputated from owner, with flesh and bone exploding from the top like a gory puffed-pastry. The tibia is bent at a sickening right angle. The fibula is but a spire. The skin billows over the cuff. The muscle is fragged, pocked, and shredded. It's twelve inches high and ten miles wide, and I can't get around it or through it or beyond it. My chest hurts so fucking bad. I need my Spouse! I need my Brits!

Patchouli breaks the silence. "Does anyone else want to make a comment about Kari?" She means to say "Kari's piece," but Freudian slips are "a real motherfucker" as Noah would say if he were here. Before Patchouli can correct herself, Sylvia interjects. "Yes, she's very talented."

Yes, you are, the Canary affirms.

Eh, I think, *it could do with a bit of paint.*

◆ ◆ ◆

Riza snatches me up after art therapy. Good news must travel fast, but she doesn't want to talk about the boot. She'd rather talk about the AA meetings I haven't been going to.

I'd gone once, actually, but some Bible thumping-Red Robin-gorging psychosomatic Harley dude hijacked the eighty-six minute meeting. Oh, that I could've eighty-sixed *him!* His shit dogma was shockingly similar to Shandy's Molson-guzzling eldest son's, Rich Fletcher's, bullshit. Rich was a part of a motorcycle gang with sleeveless jean-jacket cuts, one whose club badge (a lower lip tattoo that, when turned inside out, read *fuck you*) had been branded on Rich once he had few felonious atrocities under his overburdened belt. He and his old lady *slash* punching bag often crashed at our

Water Bug Palace between leases.

"You have to go, Kari."

"Huh?"

"You have to go to AA," Riza repeats.

"I can't."

"Why?"

"Because I was raised by a bunch of drunk druggie assholes who swore by it," I tell her. Alcoholics Anonymous did wonders for my mother, who, not too long ago, was tits-deep in a case of socially secured Coors Light. It was equally effective for her friends and boyfriends, all of whom attended, preached, and fell out. Fairy Godmother Shandy is a *dry* drunk, so bully for fucking her! She speaks of AA in holy whispers. Thus, her wizened palate must make her King of the Shit Heads.

Riza stares at me.

"What else do you wanna hear?" I ask.

"No, that's fine," she says, then pauses briefly and looks me dead in the eye. "But you'll have to come to terms with your humble beginnings before you leave here."

What the fuck does THAT mean? I wonder. *Oh, yeah. The Autobiography. How could I forget?*

"There is an alternative, though," Riza says, pulling out a book from her tote bag. *Now* that *makes sense*; the difference between a social worker and a shrink is all in the tote. I'd originally thought Riza a psychologist or a psychiatrist when we first met, but most psychologists only carry conjecture, and psychiatrists, medication. The tote has a washed-out slogan on it that I can't read, but I can make out a word: *Hope*. A light bulb sits by the slogan with a dove hovering over. *Moth to flame?*

"Take this," says Riza. She hands me a book with a chained butterfly on the cover: *Rational Recovery*.

"This is more your speed," she says. "Read a little every day."

"Do I still have to go to AA?" I ask. (This from a woman

nicknamed "The Goat" in college. Different from the Foat, I had fallen face-first on a sidewalk during a drunken jog back to campus one evening. Later, I would receive twelve stitches on my chin from an intern who purposefully cut each stitch a hair too long.)

"No, Kari," confirms the exasperated Cuban. "You don't have to go to AA anymore."

"*Noice!*"

Chapter 5

Thirteen days done, and no phone call from my command. They had shipped me off during National Nurses Week and Mental Health Awareness Month, which is to say the second week in May. The banners around Naval Hospital Beaufort said as much when I walked out nearly two weeks ago. Worm, bless his heart, was the only one who managed a comment: "Well, I hope we don't have to go through *this* again," he said a little too loudly as I passed a poster about suicide prevention. Worm was bummed because he had to pick up my slack.

Thank God for my Spouse and Kid, with whom I speak daily. I desperately want to get better for them, though my Spouse always says, "No, Kari, get better for YOU!"

In the meantime, Sheryl, my whimsical Skipper, occupies the middle bedroom between my Spouse and the Kid. Sheryl passed along some of her sage advice before I set sail for Tampa. The pep talk, still ringing in my ears, is the best since Cotton Candy. "WHOO-HOO, Kari! It's party time now! You can act as CRRAAAZY as you want! It sounds like a FUCKIN' vacation, if you ASK ME!"

Sheryl, who'd had a stint in rehab herself, *would* think that. And who the hell asked her any-goddamn-way? Me, that's who. Now that I really think about it, I always needed her approval--even to go to The Willows.

"Well," I replied, "I don't plan on imploding anytime soon."

"Wow!" Sheryl said. "You should be a fuckin' professor."

"Why's that?"

"You use all them fancy-ass words all the time."

Great, a Gilligan with a few fancy-ass words adds up to little more than a Nutty Professor. I'm a hack with a few shitty coping mechanisms, mincing words until aggressors have the good sense (or sympathy) to leave me be. Sheryl, chigger-infested, possesses neither good sense nor sympathy. So what's a Gilligan like me to do?

Invite my Skipper to stay with me, hereafter and until the end of time.

Skipper Sheryl has been residing with me off-and-on since her second divorce. I relocated her only once to give my first marriage a fighting chance. Sheryl--UV worshiper she was--jumped at the chance to move to Florida. So, I funded the move, bought her a condo, and handed her a boatload of cash--all while praying her pursuits kept her on the straight and narrow. Fat chance: Sheryl manipulated a poor young co-ed into becoming her personal slave. So it's no wonder how Sheryl, despite her mania and colorful colloquialisms, managed college life. The co-ed, however, would finally rebuke Sheryl's abuses in their senior year. The girl (who looks a heck-of-a lot like Riza's Student sidekick) had been the recipient of a classic Sheryl stomp--in front of the Student Union, no less. Only this time the campus wasn't about to tolerate any of Sheryl's shit, let alone her FUUUCK. Professors rallied to remove Sheryl from the Psychology Program. But, try as they might've, the Chancellor took pity; Sheryl was three months from graduating with a bachelors degree, so the Chancellor--Sheryl's Higher Power *Du Jour*--bought her side of the story, which was that the co-ed kept harassing her. I've never seen a mouse harass anything, but anything's believable on Sheryl's island. And so, with a psychology degree in hand, Sheryl was released to prey upon the innocent and vulnerable--something she's been doing already for quite some time.

I began holding my Skipper accountable after she obtained full-time employment with a health agency. "How about a few hundred bucks for rent?" I'd ask her, but she cranked-up her antics instead and began picking fights with the neighborhood Filipinos (calling them nips and such; I'd find out via hate calls from my homeowner's association). Meanwhile, I continued to press her for cash.

"I don't have a pot to piss in!" Sheryl shouted, though she lived rent free with a car I'd given her. (Most of the money, I'd later find out, was spent on mail-order diet meals, McDonalds, and massages.)

Then, one rainy afternoon, the Director for Nursing Services pulls me into her office. "Good news. You made Commander."

"Great," I said.

"And you're on the short-list for Afghanistan."

My heart sank.

"Lieutenant Commander Rhyan? Are you okay?"

"My Kid just finished breastfeeding," I mumbled. "My marriage just fell apart...my ex is gone."

"I see."

"What are my odds of going?"

"One hundred percent within the next year."

What about Commander Tucker or Lieutenant Commander Lowell? Nary a deployment between them, Tucker and Lowell were mid-level managers like me and were tight with the chain of command, so I knew they'd never be fingered.

"You DID fill out the family contingency packet, did you not?" the Director asked, interrupting my panic.

"Yes, ma'am. My mother is my contingency."

"Then you're lucky. A grandmother is the best alternative. Wouldn't you agree?"

"Sure." What was I supposed to tell her? That it felt like a kick to the uterus? It wouldn't have mattered; once they have their minds made up, there's little else to say. Yes Man that I am, I'd been on the short end of preferential treatment since I commissioned. I knew the score and the drill and wouldn't cause a ruckus. The Navy took care of me. It clothed and fed me. Who was I to argue? Just prior to 9/11, another senior nurse corps officer would tell me: "With all the travel, money, and health benefits, you'd be crazy to get out."

Seeing as I'm now one hallucination away from The Eff U, I beg to differ. There's a saying in the Marine Corps--*Every Marine a Rifleman*. The Navy is different. Not all Navy nurses work traumas. They could with a little training; I gave blood most days. In fact, the Brits sent their military midwives and civilian National Health Service nurses to Afghanistan--many of whom worked traumas during mass casualties. Anything is possible on my island. Too bad my island only exists in Bastion--a place where everyone was treated equally and pulled his weight without complaint.

I'd been strategic in my career, or so I thought, and rogered-up for two deployments at random before planning my family. For the first, I was called away from the base of Kilimanjaro, having just completed the climb, when I received a phone call from my Department Head to go "some place hot." I booked it back and caught a flight bound for the Philippines. That was the first. Would Afghanistan be my last? Hell if I knew. What I'm trying to say is I'm a fucking team player, and always have been.

So, as my contingency plan required, I begged Sheryl back into my home. This suited Sheryl just fine because her brand of affection involved crawling up my ass. The Kid and I were screwed. I couldn't trust anyone else to take care of the Kid. "Your husband's an asshole," Sheryl had told me, "and I don't know why you married him in the first place." *Because he was funny and harmless.* "And your sister's a fuck-up." Cassie, pound-for-pound, is a better nurse and human being than I could ever be. But I believed Sheryl instead. Besides, my happiness had always hinged on hers since birth. I was a mess: A Parent without a Partner who'd sooner die than burn her kid on a beach, but duty called. I told my Director I preferred to go immediately--well before my Kid's long-term memory kicked-in. *Nature's mercy,* I'd reckon, then I short-sold the Florida condo I used to stash Sheryl in, and that was that.

I phoned the Skipper to tell her the good news.

"Is Bastion in a dangerous place?" Sheryl asked.

"Not really," I guessed. "It's busy, though."

"Blood and guts?"

"That's what I'm hearing."

Sheryl considered all the information. "Well, I know my kid, and this one might fuck you up for good. Can't you say no?!"

"It'll be fine," I assured her, "tons of Americans and Brits there."

"Brits? Why the fuck you working with those bloody curs?!"

"Huh? They're part of our coalition, last I checked. And don't call them that. I'm nervous enough already." (Rumor had it the Brits banished Americans who couldn't perform.)

"Well, that's what my father called 'em, so that's what they are." Prior to joining the Army, my mother's father, the small sadistic Devil who abused my grandmother Millie, was a FOB, or *Fresh Off the Boat,* from Northern Ireland. He'd go on to fight in Germany and Korea. While on furlough, he'd take his little girls to church in their Sunday best. Afterwards, he'd take the twins to the barracks to verbally abuse random privates for the rest of the afternoon while his daughters looked on. *Watch and learn.*

My Grandfather would be fifty years old and retired when he jockeyed for a spot in Vietnam to "fuck up some slant eyes." He was offered a training position, instead, to which he promptly wrote back and told God and everyone to go fuck themselves. His warring Id made my Phantom look slapstick, and the whole family revered him for the whimsy.

Flash-forward to now where Sheryl refuses to fill out employment applications. She'd wanted *me* to fill them out as I'd done for her in Florida--a good thirty of them that garnered only one hiring response, but I can't help her in South Carolina because I'm so fucked up I can't see past my cavity rippers. So, yesterday, I phoned Sheryl and, after much hemming and hawing, told her she didn't have to work. It was either that or shoot her in the fucking head.

Sheryl is also destroying what little reputation I have left at this very moment. Once again, her antics are on the rise: My Spouse said Sheryl began verbally abusing our hospital's appointment clerks the day I left for The Willows. I'd put her under my military health insurance six months before and, as a result of her packs-per-day and ensuing lung disease, she requires more hospital visits. Sheryl quit smoking twenty years earlier. Rotten on the outside, and inside apparently, my mother is still loved. I'm still Sheryl's little girl. The good life, strictly reserved for TV families, wasn't meant for me. Real life is supposed to *hurt*. My primary duty was-is-and-always will be keeping Sheryl's head above water. My Spouse even pinch-hits for me by doting on my mother while I'm away. "But love doesn't act like that," my Spouse said of Sheryl.

It doesn't matter. *I deserve this.*

All this leaves me to wonder how I'm going to handle Sheryl if I can't overcome Bastion. My emotions have given way to the Foat, and the Foat is barely hanging on by a hair. *I might murder my mother one day,* but I'm not telling Riza; she's incredulous with the revelations about Sheryl. I dished the dirt to her after we discussed *Rational Recovery*. The Cuban's response is now playing dueling banjo with my mother's shitty advice. "You're going home to THAT?!" she asked. Riza's question was rhetorical. If not, I made it so because I didn't say anything more. I was doomed to Sheryl's circles and cycles.

Yes, my home-based parent is a loudmouthed jerk, but my parent command has remained silent on all fronts. Can you blame them? They'll work on their death spiral, and I'll work on Starbucky. It's par, says I, because (fancy-ass words or not) I'm no better than Sheryl: In addition to my ever-growing hostilities, and just prior to meeting my second Spouse, it'd been public knowledge that I'd been a lewd and lascivious caitiff. One who'd use her manipulative flying nun-tendencies and clumsy wiles to fuck over and/or offend ass-loads of suitors and a shit-ton of friends. If Sheryl was my Circus Bear, then I worked the tightrope, where the thrills were alive with the sound of impending insanity. I'd slowly come to find there's yet another stage between Foating and murdering, and that's fucking. I was trying like hell to feel anything again. And my poor dalliances either ran away or smothered me with no in-between. The ones who clung, however, were eventually discarded; I went for those who ran away--the ones I'd never win over. There was a curious similarity among the latter group of women: they hated their mothers. Oddly enough, I didn't hate mine at the time and was rather maternal, myself, prior to going off the deep end. Those who ran away were content to work out their mommy issues until finding out I was more damaged than they were.

Then there was a third type of woman--the bi-curious straight girl. They wanted to get me in the sack with their boyfriends or husbands. Though I'd never, they were an amusing distraction. *Hello, ladies! Please save me from my Skipper.*

Thank God for my Spouse. She's the fourth type: stable and sublime (and she loves her mama). Pity for her she arrived just before I went totally bonkers but, then again, she tells me she loves me no matter how far I fall. "We all have flaws, Kari. It's not that I love you in spite of them. I love you because of them." In these trying times, everyone needs reasons to live. My Spouse and Kid are mine. I'll gladly purge my memory for them (or take a half-pike into shark-infested waters, which is kinda what all this feels like). Still, I don't think my Spouse ever bargained for the Phantom.

Rodney, my Bastion corpsman, told me there's a perfectly logical explanation for our rage during one of our many phone conversations. He calls it *Crank Vet Syndrome*, whereby we believe our pain is worse, or more important, than everyone else's. Rodney calls me once a week to tell me all kinds of awesome things. Ever since Bastion, he has insisted on keeping in touch. At first it was monthly. Then his contact ratcheted up just before his second hospitalization. Rodney talks about his shit all the time now. He talks about it so much he doesn't listen to anybody else's. Rodney is a clan leader with no clan. Meanwhile, I don't talk about my shit at all. If I talk about it, then I'd have to address it, and *eff that*. Rodney doesn't address anything. He just bitches and collects traffic tickets and plots revenge. Crank Vet lives in me too--a fact further illustrated when Riza told me after I'd said "fuck this and fuck you" during one of our scab-picking sessions: "Just because you have PTSD, Kari, it doesn't give you the right to act like an asshole." I guess the Phantom and Rodney haven't gotten the memo yet.

Speaking of lewd and lascivious, I'd received a public post via Facebook, a site we're told not to surf (oops), notifying me that the Worm (of Worm and Concubine) was promoted to Commander. So I sent an email, from Caitiff to Worm, congratulating him. He said thank you and told me to hurry back because there is so much work to do and blah-blah-blah. He showed no concern for my wellbeing, and this is no surprise. I didn't write to him for sympathy. So why torture myself with such correspondence? I'm preoccupied with my own insignificance. Self-loathing isn't so much a gas as it is a miasma. My military career is over. It's a fact, and it makes sense; I wouldn't want me in charge of anything either. Troll says my subordinates miss me. Troll says he misses me, too. But Troll is doe-eyed like the rest. I don't have the heart to tell them it's all a lie--that when you get to the higher ranks, and you find out senior leadership doesn't give a shit, it's like finding out you never had a mama. I'll take Worm's indifference, though, because I need to punish myself; my neighbor, a Marine pilot, told me when he found out I'd quit my position as the Director for Mental Health, "Well, how are my guys supposed to get better, *commander*?!" Don't ask me, man. My command doesn't give a shit if I get better or not.

Brian's command calls him often, lucky kid. He works at the School of Infantry on Camp Pendleton (not-so-lucky kid, considering his trouble and strife). He receives visitors, too. One threw me for quite the loop last night, but I digress. There I was, officially installed at the Willows with my Skipper and Bastion issues, pandering for pills from the med molls, when one of them buzzes in a kid on a Segway. He's wearing shorts and has two metal prosthetics from the thighs down. I look at his face, my vision flashes red, and I pinch my eyes shut. As I hear him ride by, I turn to look again. This time at his shoes. *Nike Blazers. High-tops. Red. Suede. Swoon....*

"Nice shoes," I say.

He slows, turns his vehicle to face me, stops, and says thank you before proceeding to Brian, who's waiting for him at a big table, one that can accommodate his friend's equipment.

Red Blazer was one of mine. I bet my thumbs on it. I'd seen his face before, but didn't know his name. I didn't know any of their names; after my first day in Bastion, I'd only know them by number, and number alone, because the identifier would have to match the one found on their blood packs.

Red Blazer and Brian joke. Brian removes his sunglasses for the first time: Light brown. Golden. Just like my Spouse's. Then I go to my room and have a panic attack. I pull the covers over my head and hyperventilate until I'm so exhausted I fall asleep. It's the only way I can manage a nap nowadays, so bully for me! It is a minor attack on the freak out scale, I know, but I would rather have popped a bennie and been done with it.

Now Riza says I'm to go to *The War Room* today. It's my first time observing, and Noah's turn to present.

"Hi, I'm Noah."

"Hi," says everyone.

"My goal today is to read in *The War Room*."

A voice crack on the "room," so the Honey Badgers say, "You've got this shit," and "You can do it," and "We'll be right there the whole time." I Foat and widen my lids to hold back the tears.

We dish our Daily Goals until it's a wrap. I have one hundred and twenty-two minutes until I'm due in *The War Room*. If Noah has the sack to present, then I should have it to finally start my Combat Timeline. I pull out the marbled composition book from my nightstand and head over to Starbucky. I clear a spot on the tabletop and flip the book, working back to front and upside down, to put my Autobiography and Timeline on a crash course toward center.

My name is Kari. I was commissioned by the Navy at age twenty-one in the spring of 1995. I've deployed three times: the first to the Philippines, where I was part of a medical offensive that would win over hearts and minds by handing out Motrin and scabies medication to poor Muslim families living on dirt floors. The

Motrin worked third-world miracles for children with tertiary tuberculosis, and for fifty-year-old elders with goiters the size of Fiats. As I watched our pharmacy pass out treats by the baggie, I was approached by our medical officer-in-charge.

"Doesn't it feel good to do some good?" Lieutenant Commander Maddick was surveying the scene with his hands on his hips, but his exuberance was cut short as our general surgeon, Lieutenant Commander Blake, laughed. Maddick was mad. Blake too: we had two fully functional operating rooms with more than enough medication and talent to give fifty civilians a fighting chance (and fifty more after we got another shipment of supplies), but there the rooms waited, empty and untouched, unless we were logging inventory.

The supplies were for Special Operations casualties that'd seldom materialize. (I had a good SEAL friend named Mark, whom I met when he and his teammates crashed my twenty-sixth birthday. They later jumped off my roof into the pool with my cake. Though Mark and I would have a fling, he was one in a long line of male friends I'd experiment with to try to "turn straight." Mark was rumored to have been in the Philippines, so I constantly checked "The Human Toll" section of The Navy Times to make sure his name hadn't popped up on the death list.)

"Passing out band-aids isn't helping anything," Blake told Maddick. "Can we do some real good now?"

"No," Maddick said. "That's not our mission."

I'd make it my mission to resign my commission as soon as I returned home. Until then, I kept my trap shut while our spooks continued to work the sick, gathering intel on Abu Sayyaf--a far east Al Qaida Cell that was largely splintered and, a year later, "quickly defeated." After Blake and I returned to our stations, I spied Abu Sayyaf in the periphery watching our dog and pony show. They want to kill us, I thought. I kept repeating the words in my mind as I did my good. Their kill face jumbled my perspective. So much so, I *was still frazzled on the convoy back to camp. Halfway through the trip, cutting through town, I looked out the window and saw our Trade Centers exploding on a massive street mural. A few blocks on, I saw teenagers playing basketball in red jerseys that read* Suicide Bombers *across the back, just above their team numbers.* What the fuck?! *I thought. Meanwhile, I had my nine out of my holster, as ordered, with the muzzle pointed down and my finger a hair away from the trigger.*

Just then, a kid motored into my area of responsibility, or between nine and twelve o'clock. What followed next was about as absurd as a nurse with a drawn weapon: "WATCH OUT, RHYAN!" *yelled Maddick.* "WATCH THE KID ON THE TRIKE!" *The kid had a rifle slung over his shoulder.* "SHOULD WE ENGAGE?!" *Maddick asked.*

"Who's this 'we'?" whispered Blake, who had three to six o'clock.

"Nah," replied a cool voice from the backseat. "We don't gotta shoot him."

None the wiser, the kid sped ahead without much ado, thanks to our tinted windows. Maddick had been on high alert because our commanding officer had told us to "shoot at anything that looked suspicious." What DIDN'T look suspicious?! *I'd thought. I didn't have, nor will I ever have, the wherewithal to shoot a child--even if said child were locked and loaded and ready to shoot me in the face. I didn't know it until that very moment.*

Trike debacle aside, I knew what Maddick really thought about the local kids as he handed his boots off to one of them for a shine when we got back. I followed the kid just outside the base perimeter where the child labor took place. I asked the kid why he and his friends weren't in school. They just laughed and snowed me into handing over my boots. But, if they wanted my boots, they'd damn well listen to me preach for the fifteen minutes it took. In the middle of my sermon, Maddick picked up his clodhoppers with a silent exchange (sans tip, the bastard). I slipped them twenty and told them to go back to school. Dumb. These kids were seven or eight, tops. I'd been an accomplice to their truancy. Fuck it, I told myself.

The following week, when we were ready for another humanitarian mission, and the unwashed masses were ready for our Deus ex Machina, *the mission and the machine were suspended just after the Kevlar was fastened and the weapons went to Condition One* (magazine inserted, round in chamber, bolt-slide forward, switch on safe). *Intelligence said an improvised explosive device had been planted along our convoy route. We were not to step foot out of camp from that point forward.*

"Better than turning into pink mist, right?!" said our uber-scary Shoot-at-Anything-Suspicious Army Colonel in Charge--a fate sealed, had our bodies come across a pressure plate. He then proceeded to stack dirt HESCOS around our berthing until the sky was little more than a slit.

I stop writing and start crying.

"You okay, Kari?" asks Miss Dorothea.

"I'm okay," I say.

"Tough stuff?"

"Yes, ma'am."

"You're on the right track," she says. "Keep it up."

"I'm trying."

"I know."

Miss Dorothea heads over to Zeke, Sylvia, *and* Stefano who's bouncing a basketball against our locked double doors. It's his way of asking for an escort to the hospital gym--the huge one shared by hundreds, where pathoses collide one-on-one and, if you're lucky enough to watch, five-on-five. *It's a gas, gas, gas.*

I flip to the middle of the composition book because I'm unsure if what I'm about to write next is more *Balut-ish* or combat-y. Seems right to split the difference if I have any hope of finding out why I'm fucking crying.

I commissioned out of college but, after the Philippines, knew the military wasn't my thing. Besides that, nursing and the military had been cherry-picked for me by Sheryl anyway; she probably had designs on making me a lifelong caretaker, and, two birds/one stone, wanted a carbon copy of her father, the violent patriarch in jump boots. But if Sheryl put me in a uniform to work out her daddy issues, I'm sure she was disappointed; I was no Army paratrooper. I wasn't a scout. I didn't frag my first lieutenant across the throat in the jungle as my dipshit terrain-challenged cousin, Rich Fletcher, often bragged his grandfather had done in Korea. No. I was Sheryl's bleeding heart daughter who was still wondering where her bleeding heart father, Andy, had gone until he wrote a letter. I had just turned twenty-one. He said he was a janitor for a high school in Maryland, and that it was the best work he'd ever done. He said the students liked him so much they put him in their plays. "I'm proud of you," he wrote. I told Sheryl about the letter.

"That no-good cheatin' motherfucker just wants your money!"

"Really? He seems sweet."

"Sweet?! He's a FUCKIN' RETARD! He needs another smack upside the head! He's probably banging the students!" Andy had suffered an accidental blow from a bat when he was five. He and his best friend were playing baseball. He hadn't been the same ever since. Frontal Lobe-ish, let's call it, or poor impulse control. I'd find out years later from his older brother--after my father died at fifty-five from early-onset Alzheimer's--that Andy was always child-like with a sunny disposition.

So Sheryl had chosen my course. Besides, I needed the money; the Tri-State Area hospitals had been on a new grad hiring-freeze since the early nineties. Hello, Navy! Please save me from my Skipper. I purposefully chose a duty station that was three thousand miles away. I'd break free from Sheryl for six sweet years with nothing but Bearcats or Abu-Sayyaf to worry about.

With my Navy commitment completed, and the Philippines history, I'd submit paperwork to resign my commission, but I was

Stop-Loss'ed. The rest was history. The Admiral for the Nurse Corps phoned me and said my ER experience necessitated my forced retention. I'd become "essential" (music to my balut ears). The only hitch was the arts program I was slated to start. There's always next year, I thought, so I called up Boston, tore up my acceptance letter, and drank a fifth of Bacardi Anejo.

I stop writing and speak to the beyond: *War is no mistake, Ms. Madill! War is necessary. Art pales when you have the talent to strip and stick a trauma in less than ninety seconds, clean up the mess, and cry in your fucking pudding. And dear Mrs. Overstreet, I AM backwards! I AM, otherwise why would I fucking be here? I drink. I drink to make it better. I yell to make it stop. I take pills because, maybe one day, I won't wake up. I drink and yell and pop because I feel dead. And there's nothing worse than being alive and feeling dead. I can't get out of this. I can't fix it!*

I'm sobbing. Noah and the Honey Badgers--returned from the gym--are coming over, but Miss Dorothea tells them no. My Canary wants to cut to the chase. *School and war are NOT why you cry, Kari. Keep going.* So I stick to the middle of the composition book, unsure of where I'm headed, but pray it leads me home.

When Stop-Loss lifted, I resubmitted my application for the arts program, but had to change plans once more: Sheryl's second marriage had dissolved by that time. I'd only wanted to move my sixteen-year-old sister in with me. Cassie had been dying on the vine, but Sheryl tagged along because she couldn't do without "the fuckin' child support." She hadn't a pot to piss in after her DUIs, court fees, and divorce. But she wouldn't be like a tag-along spook offering sound advice from the back of a van. No, sir! She'd be the Skipper again, and would control our every movement. There was an unspoken contract: The day I told Sheryl to come live with me was the day I obligated myself to caring for her forever. As a parentified child, *I had no choice but to ensure my parent's wellbeing into the unforeseeable future. And I didn't resign from the Navy, either. No, sir! I promoted to lieutenant commander, instead, as the pay would be enough to support my growing family.*

Goddammit. I head over to the cupboard to get some napkins, milk, and a sweet, but all the peanut butter packets have been pilfered. *Savages.* The Canary tells me to *finish it* so I finish it.

My second deployment landed me in Kuwait, which, post-2008, was seldom more than a dry college campus with a dress code, replete with visiting pop stars and mixed martial arts champions. I myself was duped into singing "Jane Says" at a talent show, but my lack of talent shocked even me. I dropped the microphone mid-song, walked off, and was nicknamed "Sexual Chocolate" for the rest of the tour.

We had one death, an eighteen-year-old soldier who'd been in a motor vehicle collision.

I put my down my pen and refill my coffee cup. It's time to address the real reason I'm here. I draw a line underneath the Philippines and Kuwait. *Those were different.* Nothing can touch Bastion.

Chapter 6

My third deployment landed me in Helmand Province. I was part of a small American medical contingent attached to British-run Bastion Hospital. Situated in a dried-up river basin in Afghanistan's raging southwest corridor, Bastion Hospital had long been dubbed by British media outlets The World's Busiest Trauma Center. *They weren't wrong. Camp Bastion was a short lift from the Sangin Valley, which also carried the dubious distinction of being The Most Dangerous Place on Earth. Still, most Americans hadn't heard of Bastion, and Sangin was about to become worse.*

It's no wonder, I think; Americans are a largely peaceful and oblivious bunch. We eat on the knoll and engage in sheep thoughts (more like ostrich thoughts).

"What up, Kari?"

Julien again. Now there's a wolf.

"Hey," I say while he gawks.

"Julien!" Miss Dorothea says. "Do your writing and leave Miss Kari alone."

"Bitch," he mutters and slinks off.

If Americans *are* sheep, then we're mutton; after returning from Afghanistan, all I've seen--in addition to patient-felons--are a bunch of high-ranking officers and politicians finger-banging the world while we stand by and eat. Sometimes it's consensual and sometimes it's *consenshul*.

I pick up my pen and flip to a fresh page.

We arrived in Camp Bastion in fall 2010. I remember because it was my sister's birthday and the day my grandmother Millie died, but there wasn't time to shit, let alone phone. (Or maybe I just didn't want to think about it.) *Military control over the Sangin Valley was in flux; the U.K. recently turned the Valley's operations over to U.S. Marines. They hit Sangin, and The Valley hit back double. Marines were to flush out the territory to regain control from the Taliban,* but the place was choked with improvised explosive devices: The Taliban would plant them after dark, the terrain windswept, and the Marines would discover them at first light.

Day One on shift started calmly enough.

0730

Trauma Team Two were in a small break room. My corpsman, Rodney, and I were drinking tea and lamenting our lack of coffee while shooting the breeze with a British nurse named Mary. A civilian, Mary was part of Britain's National Health Service and had rogered-up for Bastion four times. In her mid-forties and a mother of one, Mary was an expert seamstress and had a husband who was a traveling heavy metal musician, playing Motörhead and such. She showed me a picture of him, and I told her he looked like Rick Springfield with a Fu Manchu.

"Cheeky fuck," Mary replied. She was about to tell Rodney and me how "shit" her last Bastion tour was when our Team Leader, Tully, busted through our swinging doors and ran past us.

0733

"It's KICKED-OFF! Grab your kit! We're getting a double!"

We run after Tully, who's hauling ass to the communications board in the middle of the ED where he furiously writes, CAT A on the far left side in big bold letters. CAT A, or Category A, were the most severe and sure to die without help. Tully scribbles. His red-cross armband twitches as he stretches to the top of the board.

Just then, a voice comes over the hospital PA:

"OP VAMPIRE…OP VAMPIRE…OP VAMPIRE…."

"MARY!" Tully calls out.

"Hiya!" says Mary, who'd been standing beside him. Mary knows the score and the drill.

"Get DOWN the HALL and GRAB-MORE-BODIES!" says Tully. OP VAMPIRE told us blood was being transfused to the patient in the air and, from the look of things, the Vampire is set to resound again.

Tully assigns me to Bay One, home to our first patient who'd be arriving any minute by chuttering Chinook. The action is just over the mountain range, several clicks from the hospital.

0738

J-Chat, our resident radioman, burst through with a paper for Tully.

"Christ on a bike!" Tully exclaims. "It's NOT a DOUBLE. It's a BLOODY TRIPLE, with a gunshot wound to follow. And there's FUCKING MORE!" Tully scribbles and scribbles. Mary is still getting nurses. Rodney is already back with the shock packs and gloving up.

"What else can I do?" asks Rodney. "I can get more packs. What about litters? Do we have enough? Should I clear the entry? Whatever you need, boss!"

"I'd like you to shut the fuck up," Tully says. "Let me think!"

"Cool," says Rodney, yawning.

I book to the ambulance bay for spare slides. We need the rigid plastic sheets to transfer the casualties from litter to gurney. That's when I heard it. Brits on previous tours said it sounded like the Queen Mother: Polite and firm, yet awfully sorry for the imposition. I couldn't say I knew what the Queen Mother sounded like, and didn't think Helena Bonham Carter counted.

A blare, big as God, reverberates from Camp Bastion's PA:

"STANDBY FOR BROADCAST....

ED STANDBY TEAM...TO ED...IMMEDIATELY....

I SAY AGAIN....

ED STANDBY TEAM...TO ED...IMMEDIATELY...."

Our sister shift, probably in their cots, had just been summoned.

The chutter is faint in the distance. I strain my eyes toward the range and see a little fly beaming right for us. After retrieving the slides, I ready the rapid infuser. The infuser and warmer could dump one unit of blood product per minute into a casualty. It had two pressure bags at the top. Meant for rhythm, the goal would be to alternate to keep a steady clip for a patient who'd be exsanguinating before our very eyes. If the combat tourniquets weren't tight enough, all would be for naught. Unlike psych restraints, the combat tourniquet's magic lay in the squeeze. The tighter, the better. The more they hurt, the more they work.

Team Two dons heavy lead gowns with disposable green butcher smocks overtop, except our British Padre, who hovers in The Sluice--the dirty utility room--and the only vacant spot in the lot. The Padre stands in a designated yellow square five feet from the foot of Bay One, which has an even smaller square beside it for the stave some men-of-the-cloth carry. The squares remind the rest of us that God and Heaven are watching. He patiently waits, holding his hands gently in front of him, while the rest of us buzz and bounce from Bay to Bay. This Padre doesn't have a stave, but he has the whitest hair and saddest eyes I've ever seen.

God save these boys. God save the Green Butcher Smocks. God save Sangin!

I'm sobbing and Foating and snotting. Guttural sounds from God knows where are coming out of my mouth, and I can't keep them in, not even with both my hands over my mouth. Miss Dorothea whispers into the ear of another magenta, and takes the rest of the unit to our next group therapy session.

Miss Dorothea mouths to me, *Keep going.*

Most of the lead gowns have accumulated Sharpie graffiti on their backs. We snatch-up the last gowns: "Sex Bomb" for me and "Jack Sparrow" for Rodney.

0744

Bay One is nearly prepped and ready when J-Chat runs in with yet another piece of paper and meets Tully at the board.

"MARY!" yells Tully.

"Hiya!" Mary shoots back.

Tully jumps. "Christ!"

While Tully had been spinning like a dervish, Mary brought in a motley crew of Ward and ICU nurses, posted them around our eight *bays, and was standing right behind him.*

Tully says he couldn't be bothered with J-Chat and tells Mary to follow him to the ambulance bay to gauge the landing zone. "Let's check on Nightingale," Tully tells Mary. "J-Chat is shit and I'm NOT starting off our first bloody day with a cock-up!"

Nightingale was our landing zone for two distinct entities (among others, but mostly two): MERT (blood-givers), who were a flying British critical care unit with doctors, nurses, and medics (and guns, lots of guns); and PEDRO (the daredevils), the U.S. Air Force medical rescue, who flew Black Hawk derivatives with the slogan "So that others may live." The PEDRO typically don't transfuse, but one of their many talents are skirmish scoop-and-runs. They can pick up a casualty in the middle of battle and provide extra firepower as needed. The MERT and PEDRO were as symbiotic as Laverne and Shirley. More, Cleese and Chapman. Both were fighting against The Golden Hour, *or the time in which is was possible to save the most gravely injured. But, with injuries like these, that* Golden Hour *had shrunk to minutes.*

0750

After a bit more scrambling and yelling, Tully finally hands his papers over to Gemma, a young Scottish nurse with a face-full of freckles. "CLEAN THIS UP!" he demands. Then he and Mary finally book outside to check on Nightingale.

"Well that's a right gob on him!" After appraising Tully's big mouth, Gemma freshens the board so the first line reads: Bay One...CAT A...U.S. Marine...Triple Amp...25 y/o.

Underneath the triple, on a separate line, she adds:

Bay 2...CAT A...U.S. Marine...GSW *(gunshot wound)*/Arm/Chest?...23 y/o.

The casualty slated for Bay Two was especially precarious because GSWs to the upper arm were often notorious through-and-throughs to the chest.

Gemma keeps writing and writing and writing....

"What a goat fuck," says Rodney.

He's right; with fifty more staff set to pounce on our small ED, it was crucial to establish communication lines, which Gemma had scattered all over the board. Today, the players are:

Tully Robertson. A red headed Welshman with an Imperial mustache that curls-up at the ends, Tully is a major in Queen Alexandra's Royal Army Nursing Corp (known as The QARANC, pronounced "quar-rank"). He is our ED Lead, and a big puff with an even bigger temper. He informs me my primary duty, aside from giving blood, is to "clean up dirt and shit." When he bitches or shouts, he sings more than he speaks. I always laugh at him because he reminds me of my Welsh great grandmother, Shorty--matriarch on my father's side--who drove a beat up green Pinto that almost killed seven people and one telephone pole (according my backseat tallies). Tully calls me Head Master of the Lunatic Fringe, and prefers the name Tallulah in casual settings. Anything Tallulah wants, Tallulah gets. Tallulah is a trip. Think Ginger Baker, only gay with an attitude.

Mary Winthrop. Our English civilian punk mother, Mary filters orders from Tully to us. If she were in a cover band like her husband, she'd be a lead-singing Slit (an all-girl 70's punk band who made the Sex Pistols look like Juggalo). The Mancunian saved me from my Foat more than once, which began to take hold mid-tour: "Snap out of it, Kari! There's no time for this!" Mary is also the go-to for injured children--dying ones especially.

Jeff Stanley. An old ER doctor and captain in the U.S. Navy Reserves, Jeff has eight months left on his grueling fourteen-month stint. He walks with a limp and a smile. He wears British boots for the extra support, and only ever flusters when his patients are dying. Jeff NEVER says die. If we are hobbits, he is Gandalf.

Pamela Lange. A trauma surgeon and U.S. Navy commander, Pam is a short-stack with a black bob and big blue eyes. She pulls double duty as the American Officer in Charge, and uses a step stool in the operating room to get at the guts. Bastion is her third deployment. Trapped in her own hurt locker, Pam lives for combat trauma. Basically, she cuts open bellies and clamps off bleeds for a living, but drinks Diet Cokes like it's her job. We Americans belong to her, but the hospital definitely belongs to:

Trevor Stumph. A German-born British doctor and colonel in the Royal Army Medical Corps (RAMC), Trevor is an intense, contemptuous man who wears small spectacles on the end of his nose. He reminds me of my algebra teacher and, during our American orientation (through clenched teeth, no less), he said, "I don't care if you have to resuscitate in your fuzzy pink bunny slippers. When you're summoned by The Call, you must...fucking...move." Taking that one to heart, I sometimes wore a Yo Gabba Gabba shirt--my pajama of choice--to test him. True to form, Trevor never batted an eye. Trevor is pacing back and forth at the moment, making sure we're doing exactly what we were supposed to do. He has a red poppy pinned to his lapel. Americans wear yellow ribbons and Old Glory. Brits wear red poppies (not to be confused with the cash crops of opium poppies that make the Sangin Valley especially dangerous).

Bernard "Smitty" Smith. A doctor and Navy commander, Smitty is the American counterpart to two Bastion radiologists. His purpose, when not frag and bleed hunting in a dark room, is to place a portable ultra-sound against the potentially bleeding belly of every-single-trauma as soon as they transfer from the slide. "Fast scan negatives" are good. "Fast scan positives" are bad. Considering we were to see 200-300 CAT A's per month, Smitty is a dark, busy man.

Mitchell McKay. A Team Two ER nurse and U.S. lieutenant commander, Mitch rounds out Team Two's American officer compliment. He and I are tag-teaming Bay One with two British nurses. Mitch was a prior Navy dive chief, thus salty as hell. Before J-Chat changed our lives forever, and just prior our morning breeze,

Mitch and Tully were having a pissing contest. Tully was an inch away from Mitch's face, smiling like a Cheshire cat over some insult he'd dished.

"They don't pay dentists a lot in your country, do they?" *Mitch countered, deadpan.*

Tallulah, still smiling, and still an inch from Mitch's face, waited. Mitch would walk away to resume reading Quo Vadis, *but not before telling Tallulah,* "My dentist drives a Porsche." (Tully's must've driven a green Pinto.) *Tully and Mitch were a gas, gas, gas and a panacea for what was to come in two minutes and counting.*

Larry Spence. A smarmy U.S. Army major who majors in false smiles and jack coffee, Larry works in the Tactical Operation's Center. When the TOC Roach isn't a litter-bearer from ambulance bay to bed, he's busy making life miserable for the rest of us. He collects commemorative coins from Generals, Admirals, and Heads of State and brandishes them between traumas. Larry plays Call of Duty *all-the-live-long-fucking-day. Larry is also uniform obsessed and is schooling Jeff about his boots while we scramble.* "Sir? You do know *those aren't regulation, right?"*

"No kidding?!" *Jeff says.* "Tell you what, Major. I'll change my boots after you kiss my ass."

Gemma McFadden. A young freckle-faced ER nurse and corporal in the Royal Air Force, the Scot flits from Bay to Bay making sure everyone is solid. She also manages a joke or two in-between. A lady pirate, one of Gemma's eyes scrunches up more than the other whenever she smiles, but especially when she laughs. Gemma thinks Americans are the cat's meow. I tell her Americans smoke between their middle and ring fingers, and do so for months, just to mess with her. Her favorite song is Journey's "Don't Stop Believing," which she spontaneously breaks into four to five times per day. A rabid mountain climber, Gemma is an athlete but she's not very good at volleyball. We play on our off-shifts in the mud-sand outside of birthing. Rather than give the ball a proper bump,

Gemma kicks it. "Reflexes," she says. All Brits kick volleyballs, come to think.

Emma Parke. A statuesque corporal in the QARANC, Emma is a Brummie ward nurse from Birmingham, England's Black Country. She speaks "Yam, Yam," a broad accent similar to Ozzy Osbourne's. Emma is fit, or "hot" in Brit speak. I know this because every time she walks passed a group of British men, someone says "Oh gawd, she's fit!" Though I'd fancy her at first, she is to be married to a bricklayer named Colin after the tour. She says Florence and the Machine are playing at their reception. I asked her who Florence and the Machine are, and Emma called me an alien. Emma thinks ALL Yanks are aliens.

Val Carr. Up from the intensive care unit, halfway between the ER and Ward, Val is a critical care nurse and major "from the north," or "Norf of the River Thames." She is also the self-professed "It Girl of 1985," and has a biting tongue that could put all Bearcats and Wolves out to pasture. She's presently dating a high-ranking younger man from the 16 Air Assault Brigade nicknamed "Dangerous Nigel." Val is every boy's nightmare slash fantasy come true. Think Mrs. Robinson with a whip and a needle.

Benny Ferguson. A ward nurse and jokester with a receding hairline, Benny is an audacious Scot and corporal for the QARANC. He fancies himself "The Most Handsome Man in Afghanistan" and wears a regulation Tam O' Shanter (a fuzzy ball) on his beret. He's rubbing his chest as he strides up to Bay Two, where I overhear his troubles. Gemma and Emma had Veet'ed his chest hairs the night before.

And Rodney? Rodney is pulling out his sheers.

0755

A mob of doctors of varying disciplines is gathered in front of the operating room: orthopedics, plastics, general surgeons, hand surgeons, and more. All waiting for Jeff's word because, believe you me, it's Jeff's World. The surgeons are standing underneath four flags that hang over the operating room's entryway. The smaller flags of Australia and Denmark bookend two bigger ones belonging to the U.S. and Great Britain.

Tully says there's no room for ego, so the blue line running in front of the operating room isn't to be crossed. The Stew and The Way rely on procedure. They rely on sparse staffing. Too much staff and the trauma went to shit. Too little and the trauma dies. Either way, same difference. Listen to Tully and Jeff, or get benched.

The mob waits. Pam's blue eyes match the blue line and the blue scrubs, all itching to jump on the trauma landing on Nightingale in sixty seconds.

0758

Tully instructs half of us to split off and ready Bay Two. I stay in Bay One with Mitch. Rodney hands me one shock pack and Mitch the other. Gemma partners with me on the infuser as it requires two for the clip.

"What's occurin'?" asks Val.

"Huh?" says Mitch.

"What do we have coming in?" Val translates.

"Triple amp," he says.

"Jolly Dee," she says. "Let's spike the blood."

Gemma does the same on our side while Mitch and I gather documentation.

0800

The Chinook's blades are right overhead, loud and unwavering, and, when they slow ever so slightly, we know it has landed on Nightingale. The Blue Scrubs have their arms folded. The Green Butcher Smocks are ready.

Tully and Mary return and the crowd, once abuzz, goes quiet.

"RIGHT!" says Tully. "THERE ARE TWO ON THIS ONE! BOTH LITTERED! THERE WILL BE MORE! BAY ONE IS A TRIPLE! BAY TWO IS A GSW! WHEN THE DOCS COME IN, THE MOUTHS GO SHUT! LISTEN TO YOUR REPORT! THE PATIENT WILL ARRIVE

ON THE HEELS OF THE REPORT! NOW BREATHE! YOU KNOW WHAT TO DO!"

We'd gone to York, England for two-weeks to learn The Stew and The Way before coming to Bastion, but nothing could've ever prepared us for what came next.

0801

The ambulance screeches to a halt outside the ED. A doctor in flight gear has our full attention as we surround him.

"FIRST PATIENT IS 25 YEAR OLD MALE. U.S. MARINE. QUADRUPLE AMPUTEE. TIME OF INJURY 0728. COMBAT TOURNIQUET ON TIMES SIX. ONE ON EACH ARM WITH THE LEGS DOUBLED UP. TWO UNITS OF BLOOD AND TWO UNITS OF FFP GIVEN THUS FAR...."

I don't remember what he says next. I only remember snippets.

0802

One patient. Four skewered puffed-pastries.

A dangler.

A snip from Rodney.

0805

Cold skin.

Brown hair.

0806

"GET THE FUCK OFF ME! I'M FINE! HOW IS HE?! OH, GOD, OH, GOD. DON'T TOUCH ME! HELP HIM! HELP HIM! PLEEEAASE GOD!"

0830

The Quad's in the OR.

The GSW's in a dark room with Smitty.

0844

I'm cleaning up blood and crying.

Mitch wants to talk.

"They're too young," I say. I cry more on his shoulder. He wants to help me clean it up, but I tell him no. I have to do this myself.

Rodney carves a notch.

0902

The Quad and GSW are alive.

I'm bagging their belongings.

A locket from the Quad: One boy, one girl, and one woman. Brown hair.

Oh, God.

"Don't look at it!" says Emma.

"Huh?"

"Bag it, now!" says Mary. "There're more coming!"

0926

Jeff says this is NOT the real world.

Then what the fuck is it?! *I think.*

1003

"You Yanks did well," says Tully. "Now step it up!"

1030

"INTERPRETER TO BAY THREE...INTERPRETER TO BAY THREE...."

A single amp.

A civilian boy. Dark skin. Red hair. Green eyes.

A snip and a cry.

1105

Rodney carves a notch.

I can't remember anything else, but I know what we did. I write on the next page, in the margin, and nearly pierce through. I never want to forget:

<u>*Snapshot - Bastion - Day 1:*</u>

-Quad Amp (U.S. Marine)

-Triple Amp (U.S. Marine)

-Double Amp (U.S. Marine)

-Double Amp (U.S. Army)

-Single Amp (Afghan National Army)

-Single Amp (Afghan Civilian)

-GSW Shoulder (U.S. Marine)

-GSW Leg (Insurgent)

-GSW Head (Insurgent)

-Frag/Shrapnel Face/Neck (U.S. Marine)

-Frag/Shrapnel Extremities (Afghan National Army)

-Frag/Shrapnel Extremities (Afghan Civilian)

-Frag/Shrapnel Chest/Abdomen (Afghan Civilian)

-Dead/KIA (U.S. Marine)

-Dead/KIA (U.S. Marine)

I close my composition book. I have one minute to spare before hauling-ass to *The War Room*, but pause to acknowledge the obvious: My once comforting bedtime routine is toast.

Sheryl was wrong. *Vampires are real.*

BOOK II

BLOODY HELL

Chapter 7

Sure Afghanistan was bad, but The Willows is worse. Cleaning out my memory banks is a little like polishing a turd: the more I write, the worse I feel, the more I want to flush everything down the drain. "Pain is the point," Riza challenged me yesterday. "You're trying to *live* with it, in *spite* of it and maybe, just maybe, *grow* from it."

"I'd rather be dragged away and electrocuted," I grumbled.

"Kari, I'm afraid you'll have to cope with a little *bioburden* from time to time. We can't sterilize your memory."

"Good one," I observed, noting *bioburden, or* the number of bacteria living on an unsterilized surface, was fitting; Riza reminds me every day that my PTSD is a disease, or, at a the very minimum, a dirty field.

I've been here a few days over a fortnight (eighteen goals-worth) and, now, as I choke down this orange water *slash* moll slurry *slash* colon-blow for the umpteenth-goddamn-time, I realize that: one, I know not the first thing about myself; two, Bastion was less of a deployment and more like a crowbar that'd been prying apart my scaffolding piece-by-piece ever since; and, three, Liquid Plumber per rectum *will* hurt, but it *could* work.

If my traumas had been isolated to Bastion, I may've had a fighting chance to withstand the emotional onslaught of missing limbs. Who knows? Different strokes for different folks AND blokes: I keep in touch with Emma, "The Brummie," and her brick-laying husband, Colin, who emailed me about an *un*fallen soldier and friend. The two had been out on-the-town *slash* piss with a former Paratrooper, who'd soon find himself tits-deep in his sixth Spider Bite. The Bite, a lager-cider-black currant-mix, is reserved for those "special" times when a Brit wants to either shag a total stranger or forget *everything*. The Para couldn't forget. *Lest we forget*, as the red poppies warn, but--trust me--none of us do. It wasn't long before the Para lay in one of England's many damp, cobblestoned shambles, calling out "Kill me!" over and over. Colin's email about the situation had been heavy-hearted. *We were gutted*, he wrote, *and I won't forget it in a hurry*. Yet The Brummie never mentioned it; Emma had been privy to quite a few staff and patient breakdowns--particularly my Big One, which occurred on our last shift in Afghanistan. My collapse ended with her consolation, "Come on, Kari...let's get you a nice cuppa tea." I bet my thumbs she said that to the Para as well. Oh, that the tea had worked! As I wished it could've substituted for alcohol, pills, and dalliances. But tea is always much better with mates, who remain too far away.

So, nearly halfway through my sojourn, because I'm still "on vacation" according to dear-mother-Sheryl, I've come to understand I'd reported to Bastion with a shitty foundation--one reinforced by Fear and Blind Loyalty, the ties that bind. My warped framework is now breaking between studs, and the very kind that used to line my apartment walls as a kid. *That* structure is just about down now. *Damn you, Riza!* And God bless.

Still, every time I think of Bastion, another nail, spike-sized and long sunk, cries free from its own release. And, after doing ample time in the *Balut* Room, I now understand why so many service members who "safely" returned home from enduring operations are now in similar predicaments: Though there hasn't been a U.S. draft since Vietnam, the children of struggling (often times, abusive) parents are still profiled and begged to join *vis-à-vis* slogans such as *Join the Navy, See the World* (and here's some money for college if you live).

Grown baluts *training grown* baluts *for bearcats*, I say. The Navy is filled with both. Yet the bearcats are always surprised when a *balut* goes astray after a deployment. A bad one can really upend your BOHICA ability. It's a natural progression, this insolence, and it's exactly what happens when everything you thought you knew turns out to be wrong.

For starters, I'm arrogant: "I've seen the REAL world and you haven't. There're fucking WOLVES out there!" I'm impatient: "Outta my way! I've got groceries to buy and a Kid to ignore!" But, more than arrogance and impatience, I've lost all curiosity. I don't care or wonder about any*thing* or any*one* because nothing compares to Bastion. The world, without The Stew, The Way, or The Golden Hour, holds no interest. I've learned everything there is to learn about the likes of us: We're fucked.

I have a picture on my refrigerator back home of me, minus the Nun, on top of a mountain in British Columbia with a caption I wrote in the corner. *Leave the Navy, See the World (Really).*

My mother doesn't understand my change of heart. "I don't know why the fuck you want to retire, Kari! I mean...you're gonna make captain, *then* it's easy street for us!"

Christ.

"It's SUPPOSED to be fuckin' hard, *commander!*"

Yes, I know that, you goddamn Circus Bear!

"If it were me, man, I'd stay until they dragged me screaming out the fuckin' door!"

What have I done with my life?!

Despite the fury of Bastion, I miss my Brits very much. I consider them close friends, but, unfortunately, they're tethered to my nightmares. I'd tried to visit Great Britain a year after we returned home. I imagined taking a tour, Snake Biting my ass from Aberdeen to Brighton, but abandoned the plan just as I was about to confirm my flight. I saw their faces. Not my friends' faces. I saw Marines', insurgents', and children's faces blasting through their numbered identifiers.

Thus, the Terror by Association forced me to put the Brits in the bin that would contain all sorts of things I'd have to avoid my whole life hereafter and until the end of time. What would happen if I were to see Val, The It Girl, or Tully, The Ginger Tyrant, or even Larry, The Glory-Seeking Cunt? I'd surely remember everything, right?

Just after Bastion, my mother would develop a bundle branch block, which required a lot of cardiac diagnostics. Smitty didn't have the equipment at our hospital to give Sheryl a proper spin. We'd have to go to a bigger military hospital for that. After traveling a few hundred miles, and negotiating the maze of the nearby Medical Center, we trekked through their surgical department where I'd round a corner to see *CAPT Pamela Lange, Medical Corps, USN* on a door plaque dead ahead. I'd heard her schoolmarm voice just inside, scolding someone who likely deserved it. As predicted, I was awash in death masks, so I buzzed ahead and never looked back, leaving my Skipper huffing and puffing behind, though never for long: my mother was-is-and always will be attached at the hip.

Memory-wise, I haven't filed any of my Bastion stuff away. Images are strewn all through my goddamn gray matter. Huge chunks of memory are missing, and those very chunks dictate to *me* when I'll think about *them*. So, along with Great Britain and Afghanistan, I avoid talk pertaining to *even more* countries, like Georgia and Estonia and Denmark--all of whom experienced coalition casualties while I was in Bastion.

Denmark suffered far fewer deaths than the U.S. or Great Britain (or Afghanistan: the civilian death tolls range between 30,000 and 360,000--a nice third world ballpark for a country without birth records). Still, the wounded Danes held a grip on me. Their nurses, camouflaged amazons, stood six-feet tall in their bare feet and hailed from Camp Viking or Camp Price. Camp Price, nicknamed "Camp Nice," had a regulation volleyball court, free guitars to play, and rug merchants, where a three-by-five silk Persian could be bartered down to $300. They also had a fleet of old Mercedes trucks that shuttled the Danes here and there. The beater assigned to Danish medical meshed nicely with their smoking, stature, and long curly hair down to their uniformed asses. They looked more viking than nice, but were a holistic bunch: previous Bastion deployers told me Danish nurses sometimes climbed onto gurneys and hugged their convalescing countrymen, placing the patient's head on their chest to stroke their hair. "Maternal vikings, them," Benny once said.

Jensen, the Dane I knew best, sped over in her beater one day to meet a nineteen year-old Danish casualty, fresh off a Chinook, who "Right-Turn-Resus'ed" straight into the operating room with a GSW to the chest. ("Right-Turn-Resus," a Jeff decree, was declared whenever death was imminent, and when the only intervention left was to crack the chest and massage the heart.) The Mob of Blue Scrubs parted for the patient, filed-in behind, and rallied to save him, but the Dane died. Afterwards, Jensen--though I'd never seen her lie on a gurney--stayed with his body until he was airlifted home to Denmark.

I don't know how she did it. I couldn't comfort or soothe anything in Bastion--not even our stray tent cat, "Cat A." And postmortem care was the absolute pits, if *pits* meant falling face-first into a mustache covered in brains. Mary and I were performing postmortem care on an Afghan Military Police Officer who'd been shot in the head. Mary took the lower part, and I the upper. She would see my early Foat give way to a wobble as I wiped the ooze coming from his nose. It'd been Mary's red-cross armband in the periphery that broke my trance. And, of course, her sweet, dulcet tones: "KARI!" she shouted, snapping her fingers. "Fuck off and put your head down!" Mary handled it like she always did. *Why couldn't I've had an iron constitution like her?* The only things iron on me were my tear ducts, rusted closed after Day One.

Though the gore was goddamn awful, I was more horrified by my controlled lack of compassion and the robot I'd become. How else could I've operated? Something had to give, sooner or later. So, when it started to give, I started to Foat. I was a robot in the beginning, that's for sure, but I was C-3PO at best: Knowledgeable, but neurotic. I chattered away, only I kept it all inside. I didn't want to Foat or faint, but, above all, I never wanted to start crying because, once I did, I was convinced I'd never be able stop. I wouldn't be good to anyone then.

The Danish doctors, however, were a different story. No hair stroking or fainting for them. Major Vestergaard, who'd been on a three-week rotation through Bastion, was slated to travel outside the wire and into the shit. So, to prepare her, Jeff gave Vestergaard as many trauma assessments as he could. She was meticulous: Vestergaard checked the sphincter tone on each-and-every trauma patient who crossed her path. Basically, she stuck her finger up the casualty's ass. If the asshole puckered or the patient protested, then their lower spinal cord was intact. She had a thick accent like the rest, and yelled:

"S-FINCK-TA-TONE-POS-A-TIVE!"

"AHHH...WHAT THE FUCK?!" or some variation always came next--in one instance, from a Marine in Bay Four, who'd been the only injury in a Humvee rollover.

I was in the break room during one such time, eating one Otis Spunkmeyer Blueberry Muffin after another, only to burn the calories in marathon traumas that'd never fail to materialize. The rollover wasn't really my thing anymore because "boring traumas" did nothing for me. I only wanted to move my ass for the worst-of-the-worst because the worst-of-the-worst couldn't talk, cry, or scream (neither could the dead, but the dead were a different story). At least the worst-of-the-worst were living: Bastion's survival rate, no matter the severity, topped 92%. Meaning, if your arms and legs were gone, your odds were better with us than anywhere on earth. Almost all the Marine amputees we'd cared for in Bastion managed to make it back to my parent command in San Diego to convalesce. There were so many amps when I returned that an entire unit had been dedicated to them during the eight months I'd been gone. But I don't pat myself on the back; the more service members we saved, the bolder military strategists became. *Throw the lads in! They'll mend in the Stew.* When our ICU was full, operations were suspended until we transferred the wounded home to make space.

I learned--from the Philippines to Bastion--what medical offensives were like and, though I'd initially failed to leave the Navy secondary to extenuating circumstances, right now I have no problem ripping my ribbons from my chest and calling it quits. Being thankful to the Navy for giving me the opportunity to save lives is like thanking Sheryl for feeding me: Both came with a price.

So, to ease my Bastion fears of talking patients and injured children, I strong-armed Tully and Mary into giving me permanent duty on Bay One--the goriest. It worked for Mary, who much preferred tending to pediatric casualties typically assigned to Bay Three. Mary had a son around the same age as our coalition amputees, and I had a two-year old back home, so we did a deal.

I loved my Bay One. I stocked my Bay One. I kept my Bay One tidy. I counted the blood spatter on its ceiling before I searched my Bay's gurney for "bits" to wipe off, and wondered at night about all who had died there that day.

Then I slept in my Bay.

Some nights dragged. To quell my silent scream, I took to journaling when obsessive cleaning and counting wouldn't do it. I hadn't kept a journal in twenty-five years, but I needed the outlet again. I'd had a diary during the days of Milk and Merits, given to me by my father's mother, Granny P--a Greyhound enthusiast and writer, and the only daughter of Shorty, my Welsh-Pinto-driving great grandmother. The diary had a speeding hound on the cover with its legs neatly folded under its body. But I'd stopped writing in it when Phil, my mother's old boyfriend, pried it open when I was nine. He read it cover-to-cover, apparently, and had a shit-fit after he spied all his nicknames: *Fat-head Phil, Fucker Phil, Fart-Face-Phil,* etc.... So, later, I'd write down my feelings at my own risk.

Was nothing sacred?!

No! The Reptile made sure of that, the Phantom reckons.

But in Bastion, Phil was a distant memory, and Sheryl was a

million miles away, and I hadn't *really* thought about The Reptile in years, but that's where Riza wants me to start focusing today, goddammit.

So, silent and Foating in Bastion, I put in my ear buds, listened to music, and hung out on the ambulance bay steps in-between traumas and wrote and wrote and wrote. I didn't write about the traumas. I wrote about everything else--gags and jokes, mostly. I even wrote about the *bronzing* the British girls did between tents--some without clothes, some doing the "Captain Morgan," a position that enabled all bits and tits to be tanned. Or I'd write about the times I was with Benny and Tully at the NAAFI, a hangout a hundred yards from the hospital. Trivia contests, popular in pubs in and around Great Britain, were the thing, and winning was even better. Tully explained British culture between questions, telling me how many men still wore their sweaters.

"Sweaters?" I asked.

"You know," Benny said, "uncircumcised."

"Gross."

"Oh, but the women love it!" said Tully.

"How would you know, you big bender?" Benny asked.

"I've got sisters!" Tully insisted. "Right Kari, go up to that lot over there and ask them if they play 'anteater' with their men."

"What's that?"

Tully told me, then Benny spat out his tea, "Yeah, Kari! Do it!"

I looked over at Emma, Mary, and Gemma, who seemed to be having an intense conversation, and I figured *Why not?*

"Hey," I interrupted.

"Kari!" said Gemma, "long time, no see. Pull up a chair, mate."

"What's occurin'?" asked Val.

"Not much. Gotta question, though."

"Yes," said Emma, "you're an alien."

"That's not my question." I asked it before losing my nerve. "Do you play Anteater?"

Blanks all around. "What's that?" asked Gemma.

"When you pull your man's foreskin over your nose after a blowjob."

"KARI!" Emma shouted. "Don't be such a disgusting twat!"

"WELL DONE!" Tully yelled from a across the room.

"YOU PUT HER UP TO THAT, YOU MINGIN' BASTARD!" Val shouted.

My journal was full of one-offs like that. Plus it was a good way to pass the time during "OP MAXIMIZE!," yet another proclamation from The Queen Mother: Camp Bastion would silence base-wide email and long-distance phone services each time a British soldier died until family members back home were notified. The British flags where always lowered to half-staff, a tradition never observed by Americans. Some could rationalize Americans had a bigger force with bigger casualties and to adopt such practices would require the flag half-staff at all times.

Isn't that the point?

If I had my way, I'd lower it every time. I would. The reminder would be in 280 million faces every day. *Lest we forget*, but none of us would if I ruled the world. Our flag should've lived there for ten years. It really should've. But maybe it would've bummed a lot of people out.

The Brits lowered their flag. Sometimes every day for a couple of weeks. Then came the red poppies. On one such day, Trevor, our rigid Commanding Officer, rounded the corner of the hospital entrance with his poppy on his lapel, his head nearly grazing his country's colors as he approached. He'd been catching up on business during a lull after one brutal morning. I watched him approach, listening to (oddly enough) the Danish band Mew's "Comforting Sounds":

> *I don't feel alright*
> *In spite of these comforting sounds*
> *You make*

"You journal?" Trevor asked me.

"Yeah. I kinda have to."

"I do, too," he said before marching off.

It'd be the only time he ever talked to me one-on-one, yet I understood completely.

As medical types, Trevor and I, and everyone else working at the hospital, were conditioned from college and, some, from birth to see the body as a temple. Not a temple to CrossFit the shit out of, like Smitty, but a genuine temple to be preserved and cared for.

We were trained to preserve *life*, goddammit. It's no wonder every time a shredded body--friend or foe--and its accompanying "parts" showed up at our hospital doorstep, our perception of the world around us grew more and more slant. *THIS is what human beings are capable of.*

The Reptile is no match for The Taliban, I think.

He's still worse, the Canary tells me.

"Wassup' ladies?! Ya'll want some more Blueberry Rain Douche?" Noah asks, forcing me out of my reverie.

It's Noah's turn to drive the van to Walmart. I begged-off *that* tasker quick: Miss Dorothea takes one patient *slash* freakazoid with her every Saturday afternoon to pick-up snacks, toiletries, and games for the unit. Riza says the trip would be good *in vivo*, a social experiment where Mama could observe my capacity to multi-task and assimilate among sale-hungry customers, but I wasn't about to give Riza the pleasure.

I'd escalate big-time if I went to Walmart on a Saturday, or any day for that matter. Mama's trying to get me to change my mind, but I'm saying *hell no*. Crowds and retail were an acerbic mixture I dodged as if everyone's life depended on it (because it did). Earlier, my family and I had taken a vacation to New York to check out a couple short-run art exhibits. Prior to the vacation, I'd noticed my increasing need to keep to myself. I knew I needed to have one foot in the fire and mix with the general public to stress test myself because, if I continued to isolate, I'd go stark raving mad.

So that's why I started off gradually and focused my efforts on the third largest city in the western hemisphere. We didn't bring dear mother Sheryl, thank God, whose racial slurs would've been akin to a steel poker in a melting pot, *and* would've done oodles for my Kid's cultural education (other than "nigger," Cassie and I had been inundated with a bevy of right-thinking 80's, gutter-class catchphrases like wetback, spic, wop, sand nigger, and dot head).

My family and I had come out of The Brooklyn Museum, and stood in line in front of--what could have easily been--the only food truck in the borough. There was an amalgam of arguing couples, rowdy school children, and pushing passers-by. The Foat came first, as it usually did, but was followed by the Phantom's "GET ME THE FUCK OUTTA HERE!"

Brooklyn, I'm sure, thought me an alien. So my Spouse, bless her, tried to find me sanctuary in the subway by the 2/3 Train. But the subway was even more crowded. I ended up quietly blubbering in the corner next to a puddle of someone's piss. A lady in a booth by the turnstile spied us, goddammit, and looked sad and sorry. But what could she do? My girls just crouched around me. They knew how embarrassed and weak I felt; my positive self-talk for the day had been left in the museum, probably jaw jacking somewhere with the ghost of Basquiat. (I used to be a confident person, or appear so, but even my Spouse admitted I showed up to our relationship wearing a fake mustache.)

So, we ditched the subway, and cut through Prospect Park, where my Kid wandered into the landing zone of a makeshift trick park for freestyle bikers. We didn't see the guy on the bike, nor he us, until he was mid air. "OH, SHIT!" all of us shouted. My Kid balled herself up, waiting for impact, as my Spouse and I ran toward her. The guy on the bike pulled a fantastic move, twisted the apparatus to the side, and landed a few feet from her. "I'm sorry," he said. I was sorry, too. I was sorry I couldn't go anywhere without the Phantom; just as I was about to lay into him, my Spouse diffused the situation with a look. *Don't do it, Kari. Not here. Not now.* Try as she might, my Spouse can't bubble-wrap the whole world for me, nor should she have to. My poor Northern Wind, still lifting me up. One day she'll tire.

Why don't you do the world a favor and fucking drop out! the Phantom tells me over and over, and did so as we walked the rest of the way through the park. *You know your Love is going to flit away, RIGHT?! Have you already forgotten? Sheryl HATES "dykes" AND "faggots!" The bitch is already laying groundwork as we speak:*

"What the fuck's up with you two?!" Sheryl had said before we married. "You're not ugly enough to eat pussy!"

It's just a matter of time before Sheryl has YOU and the KID all to herself again.

After battling Sheryl *and* the Phantom for the last few months, I felt defeated in The Big Apple. A walk in the park had become another lofty goal I'd never reach. I swore off ALL crowds from that point forward and, thus, began holing-up in my house with my mother, the racist, homophobic, poker-wielding Circus Bear. It totally synched with my ever-growing all-or-nothing behavior, learned from Sheryl, who's still holding her heart in her fat hand and waving it in my face like a rancid carrot. Yes, her heart is that shriveled. And, yes, I do feel like a lumbering ass chasing a carrot on a goddamn stick.

Sheryl isn't good *in vivo*; no amount of bear exposure ever rendered a different response in my chest. Even now, Sheryl is breaking my heart: She told the Troll, who'd stopped by my house a couple days ago to check-up on my family, that I'm faking my PTSD. Her nasty confabulations were on par with the Worm's Concubine, who told me a month before my hospitalization, "You're just acting out because you don't want to work, but we ALL have to work, Commander Rhyan." (This after being made to dance and lip sync to Miley Cyrus's "We Can't Stop" by my Commanding Officer. All the executives had to do it. The video was supposed to show subordinates and patients our zany side.)

We all have to work.

The Concubine's remark prompted my first full-on Foat. It's funny: a quadruple amputee and a GSW to the head couldn't fully Foat me, but the Concubine could. I didn't know if I'd cry or kill her, so I fortified my levees, drank-in her vile words, and went to my office without another word. The Concubine also started another rumor in the hospital, telling everyone I gave preferential treatment to gays. Perhaps that's why hardly anyone approached me when I became more erratic. Who knows? My "gay" could've rubbed off on any number of conservative South Carolinians, which many could argue is the only kind of South Carolinian there is, apart from black people. Still, if the Concubine could've seen Tully and me work a few traumas together in Bastion, she would've known that we gave preferential treatment to human beings.

What a country club bitch.

Bastion gave preferential treatment to dogs, too. Smitty, though he's not gay (as if it fucking matters), did a posthumous cat scan on a Springer Spaniel; the spaniel keeled-over seconds after her handler was shot and killed. No cause of death found. "Broken heart," said Smitty.

The Concubine and my Skipper have no fucking clue. *OPEN YOUR FUCKING EYES, PEOPLE! GOD'S SAKES...I'M DYING RIGHT IN FRONT OF YOU!* It's not about sexuality. It's not about deadlines. It's not about rank. *ASK THE CRAZIES WHAT'S WRONG WITH US, AND WE'LL FUCKING TELL YOU!* But no one *really* wants to know. For all the suicide prevention training the military mandates, leadership doesn't want to listen. They're more concerned with numbers, particularly the numbers that say the Suicide Training has been completed and, thereby, dealt with. (One hundred percent completions mean more money from the Navy Bureau for Medicine and Surgery, or BUMED, or "Bu-God." Stay in the black to get more green. That's how it works.)

"Gee...why are people still killing themselves? After all, we have one hundred percent completion on our matrices."

As I sit in this nut-hut, oh Lord, I pray for a cultural shift. Mandates are not enough. Computerized training and Admiral's Calls are rubbish. You want to stop military suicides? First of all, you can't; service members, like other human beings, will do it if they really want to. Until then, there needs to be a conscious shift of concern from dollars to PEOPLE.

My Canary sings all day lately. I think the Troll's canary has been chirping since birth. After Sheryl kicked my teeth in on my front porch, the Troll managed a sidebar conversation with my Spouse after she threw a Jersey Mike's sandwich and Sprite into Sheryl's face. The Troll said hello, and hopes I'm getting the care I need. That was all, and that was enough. Troll is well aware of Sheryl's history, considering she's still "tearing new assholes" every time she picks up the phone to make an appointment for all her huffing and puffing.

Even before emphysema, Sheryl minimized others' woes to prop up her own. Her diseases always take center stage. It's a *Borderline* thing, which is fantastic because *Borderline Personalities* are the most difficult patients to rehabilitate. I couldn't coax my mother to see a shrink to save my life--not even with VIP status as the Director for Mental Health. A fruitless pursuit, it was as successful as an ED nurse with PTSD managing a bunch of manipulative shrinks.

"Oh, I tried that shit," said Sheryl. "It doesn't work!" I knew what it really meant, though: "It's a disease, Kari, and I'm helpless. Besides, I like being this way. And it gets me stuff, so fuck it!"

It's total bullshit. I have *Borderline* features (as opposed to the whole shebang) and I hack at them like they're a bucket-full of snakes, but Sheryl *likes* being Skipper. Meanwhile, I'm trying everything I can do to stop drowning myself. I think that's why *Rational Recovery* is resonating so true; the text debunks each of AA's Twelve Steps. We're not helpless! We're not sheep! We're strong, goddammit! *Rational Recovery* is gritty but hopeful. That's me in a nutshell (I can tap, too). I don't want to knock AA. If it works, then hallelujah, but I believe the last thing any trauma victim should do, willingly (or unwillingly, depending on the group), is to assume a position of powerlessness to alcohol, God, or anything. And, besides that, I haven't seen my clan's efforts bear any fruit whatsoever. All I see are a bunch of rotten bananas.

Speaking of bananas, my fear and impatience still prevents me from going to The Willow's cafeteria; the sandwich man is too slow and clumsy. He leaves the fucking line to fetch exotic ingredients like bread, cheese, and turkey. You ask for a little salt and the bastard takes a smoke break. He pisses me off so much that, if given a chance--and because I can't shoot him--I'd love to take a Sharpie and easel to The Willow's Human Resources Department, where I'd map-out a watertight action plan that would turf his ass to the Linen Department before he punched out for the evening.

Break his back! says the Phantom. *You're good at that shit. Put 'em in the wash and spin him a few times!* Instead, I just pick myself and wait.

Honestly, a turkey sandwich could make itself quicker.

And don't get me started on ice cream. How can you fuck up a scoop? He can. He's gifted with incompetence like my cousin Teddy (Shandy Fletcher's middle son and brother to Rich, the Hog Outlaw with the *fuck you* mouth). Teddy was the biggest motor mouth, gold-brickin' son-of-a-bitch I'd ever met (and I've met many). Though eleven years my senior, Teddy's IQ was rumored to have been low (Shandy called him a dumb motherfucker pretty much every day). Bully for him he wasn't handicapped like his younger brother Shane, born with wide set eyes, a small mouth, and a big tongue from too many Kamikazes *in utero*. (Shandy began having babies at fifteen, right after she started drinking.)

Noah wants to know if I want Sour Apple Douche, instead.

"I hear it's gentle on the minora," he says.

"Appreciate the concern, but no."

No more daydreams for Gilligan, the Phantom, and the rest. *This kid is relentless.* I'm pretty sure Noah only wants to buy feminine products to mess with the cashiers' minds. A lanky white kid and an old black woman with a bunch of tampons, vinegar, and cash? Now that's a party. Pity for him there's only two of us women and neither of us need "cotton ponies" either (thank you, Noah).

"Get jigsaw puzzles," I tell him.

"And a box of peanut butter cups," says Sylvia, handing over a twenty.

I follow suit and give Noah my debit card and PIN, but every cell in my body wants to snatch back the plastic because it's been recently revealed that Noah spent six thousand dollars on power tools while on an Ativan bender just prior to The Willows. A last straw of sorts, he'd filled up his apartment with so much Husqvarna and Makita his roommate threw him out.

Rodney had been in a similar quandary before being admitted. His doctor put him on a spectrum of meds to subdue his temper and control his sleep. Trouble was he tended to binge shop when gorked, and never remembered what he bought until it showed up at his doorstep--a trend I'd hear about during a morning phone call.

"How you doing', Kari!"

"Hanging in there," I told him.

"Oh, that's great!" he said. "Hey, did you send me a package?"

"What?" I replied. "No, I..."

"Fuck!" he interrupted. "I did it AGAIN!" He bought a $200 limited edition Michael Jackson album and an adult Incredible Hulk costume last week. He told me between yawns; Rodney yawns all the time now. I think it's related to his medication, but he says he does it just to stall "cuz I can't remember what I just said." His short-term memory is wasted.

"I'm coming to visit you guys," he tells me.

"When?" I ask, and he tells me next month.

Rodney visits me every season for weeks at a time. I don't ask him to. He just does. It's a four-state flight away, but I guess he needs the company. I'm sure he would've visited his sister if she'd been alive. I often wonder what Rodney was like pre-9/11. Rodney--ever since I've known him--can best be described as clingy. He'd recently taken a shine to my Kid, since I'd been emotionally inaccessible. My take was that his *collateral damage* from Iraq was really getting on top of him, and this was his way of making amends. My Kid played with him and kept him in the here and now, instead of the way back when. It was cool because I can't engage with her anyway, and my Spouse was always working and my Skipper was always bitching. He was saving the Kid, in a way. It was normal, I told myself, because I knew what "normal" was, right? Rodney mostly talked of politics and glassing Afghanistan.

Rodney is unstable at best.

Here at The Willows, I can just picture Rodney in *The War Room* yawning and talking about how the world owes him. And maybe that's true, but this *Balut* is drowning. Misery may love company, but I got at least two raving lunatics to deal with--three, if you count Sheryl. That's all I can handle.

"Sure," I tell Rodney, when he calls. "Come visit whenever you want."

Goddammit. I don't talk about war when I'm at home, but I bought a revolver and was keeping a switchblade on me at all times. The Kid asked, "Why do you have a knife, Mommy? No one's gonna kill you." She said something similar about our dog Arnold, "He barks at everything, Mommy. When's he gonna know that no one wants to hurt him?"

I wasn't talking about war, but I was still at war.

Noah doesn't talk about war, either, but he did well in *The War Room.* I'm proud of him. Turned out he's a spook and, as we watched him fidget and cry, he divulged all the information and actions he was made to keep secret, but not before Rule One was reiterated and the meeting commenced: *What's said in The War Room stays in The War Room.*

108

The War Room is quite a thing. Riza previously downplayed it, "It's a room just like this one and blah-blah-blah...."

Yeah, right! I thought you were gonna shit yourself!

(Kiss my ass, Phantom.)

The War Room's walls have no accolades, awards, or degrees, but it's vibrant. There's artwork: bottomless pits, covered eyes, covered mouths, covered ears, guns, blood splatter, and tombstones. It's all remarkably bad and beautiful. Then there was the ever-present quote by Calvin regarding *the battle within*.

Lucky for Noah he doesn't have to read an autobiography in The *Balut* Room like Sylvia, Tommy, Brian, and I do. Noah's wounds are strictly combat-related. He was part of Psychological Operations, or PSYOPS. When he wasn't witnessing interrogations, he was low-riding in Humvees, blasting Little Mama's "Lip Gloss" or AC/DC's "Thunderstruck" or MC Hammer's "Too Legit to Quit" during Muslim Call-to-Prayer. No family traumas for him. No sir, unless you count being the only son in a houseful of sisters.

The solely combat-screwed are Noah and Zeke, while *Baluts* only include Stefano and Julien. The rest of us have war and family traumas, both.

Daily Goals begins again.

"Hi, I'm Kari."

"Hi," says everyone.

"My goal today is to find the bastard who keeps nicking all the peanut butter packets."

Giggles sound off around the room, but I'm not fast enough to catch who.

Next time, bastards.

"That's okay," says Sylvia, "Reese's are on lock."

"Good," I say. "I'll be sure to stick'em up my ass." I'm squirreling them, goddammit.

"Now what's your REAL goal?" Miss Dorothea asks.

"To write ten pages in my Autobiography without fail."

We dish our daily goals until it's a wrap. But, before I get back to my childhood woes, we have to vote in a new President for the Cuckoo's Nest. The inmates have an election when the previous one discharges or is dragged away to The Eff U. The President's primary duties include doling-out chores, following-up on said chores, and browbeating lazy bastards.

The previous President, Juan--a staff sergeant in the Army-- talked with Zeke before discharging this morning.

"I'm jealous," said Zeke.

"Don't be," replied Juan. "I got a lot of work to do when I get back. Like kicking my best friend's ass, for one."

"Why?"

"Because he's fucking my wife."

Zeke grins. "You want me to do it?"

"What?!"

"You know...beat up your friend."

"Nah," says Juan. "I don't wanna pay anybody to do that shit."

"Oh, you don't gotta pay me!" Zeke shoots back. "As soon as they jump me out of this shithole, I'll call you."

"I'm not worried."

"Oh, yeah? Why's that?"

"I know where to find you.'

"You from Alabama?!"

"Nah. You're still gonna be here when they bring me back."
Served.

So, as I slump in my chair, I wonder: *Who should I vote for?* Brian would be good. He has two weeks left and seems to be over the hump. Zeke and Noah are no-go's. Miss Dorothea would never go for it because the only things Zeke and Noah excelled at were naps and flatulence.

Sylvia! She's a good girl. All the guys listen to her. I listen to her, too. Very nurturing, that Sylvia. I cast my vote for her.

Miss Dorothea counts. "One vote for Sylvia and...*seven* votes for

Kari!"

"What the fuck, man?! Ya'll KNOW this ain't my bag! NOT NOW! I'M ON VACATION, GODDAMMIT!"

"Good choice," says Miss Dorothea.

Laughs fade to snickers and I want to put four in a headlock, two in a Full Nelson, and murder the last. Julien wanted to "hang-out" with me on the smoking deck earlier. I told him no, and now he's giving me the stink eye. He doesn't like boundaries. *Tough shit.* It's a nice warm-up. One must start with an Ass Clown and work up to a Circus Bear (who's been free of the whip for *far* too long).

Chapter 8

In 1981, I was obsessed with On Golden Pond--an elderly-coming-of-age story whose couple would double as my pseudo-grandparents in times of need, much in the way rock stars on MTV doubled as my Mom and Dad. Granny P, my father's mother--and daughter to Pinto Shorty--took me to the movie when I was eight. That's when I first noticed her subtle resemblance to Katherine Hepburn's character (from the Keds on her feet on up to her perfectly coiffed silver bun). She laughed her head off whenever Hepburn called Henry Fonda, "an old poop." Granny P similarly laughed when watching old British TV shows, "Are You Being Served?" and "Coronation Street."

Though I only recall Granny P in small fits and starts, what I do remember is warm--much like the movie. Pond's matriarch, Hepburn, was a comfort to her husband whose body and mind were failing. Granny P equally loved her husband (the "insurance man"-come-loan shark with a bad ticker). Obviously, my father's side of the family was not without its share of dysfunction, but their boundaries were always healthy and their love seemed limitless.

Unfortunately, that well dried-up when Andy, my father, closed shop, and the memories of On Golden Pond, and Granny P for that matter, became forever polluted by The Golden Dick--a medieval joke practiced over and over again at a giant mud puddle dubbed the Fletcher Family Ranch, or the Fletcher Family Freak Show, as I came to call it.

In the summertime, when the beach wasn't an option and PWP Camp was between sessions, I was shuttled over to The Freak Show where cussin' and stealin' were permissible--encouraged, actually. They also loved a good knee-slapper, telling dirty jokes all day long. The Fletchers likened their brand of humor to Eddie Murphy's because "that nigger was funny." Twins, Sheryl and Shandy, would practice jokes and punch lines over and over. The Golden Dick, a *family favorite, went something like this:*

A Jester gives his Princess a basket with a set of instructions. "Hello, my fair lady! The Prince wants you to use this while he's off conquering the world."

The Princess opens the basket and is shocked to discover a Golden Dick inside. "Oh, my! What ever am I to do with this?!"

"Well, my dear, when you are randy just say 'Golden Dick, fuck me.'"

"And what happens then?"

"Why it fucks you, of course!"

The Princess used it that night and, sure enough, whenever she asked it to fuck her, it did. The entire castle didn't get a wink of sleep that night because the Princess, in her ecstasy, moaned from the bone until sunrise. Afterwards, one of the guards approached the Jester and inquired about last night's commotion. The Jester replied, "The Princess, my good fellow, was given a Golden Dick by the Prince, and it fucked her all night."

But the guard didn't believe a word. "Pfft! Golden Dick, my arse...."

At which time, the Golden Dick rushed from the Princess's chambers and went straight up the guard's ass.

Funny, right?

I was eight years old and somewhat wise to the ways of the mud puddle, yet I STILL didn't get it. Nor did I get it after the joke was practiced ad nauseam *by good ol' Sher and Shand that summer, and recorded by Rich with his clunky video camera to be replayed to endless hilarity.*

Cousin Shane and I had been seated on the carpet, watching, and drinking Acme Bo-Bo Cola. Shane, well trained, laughed on cue with Rich and Teddy during the punch line every single time. His happiness, like mine with Sheryl's, was tethered to his brothers' and mother's. I just stared and drank my Bo-Bo. The blackberry flavor was my favorite. It went great with my Bo-Bo Sneakers. Sheryl was between jobs and in-fighting with her mother and uncle, so my kicks were Woolworth specials--white pleather and mesh with maroon accents and fat olive green laces. But the only way I could've truly elevated them was with a blowtorch.

So what's a disenfranchised kid like me to do?

Rock the Bo-Bo and listen to a bunch of morons try to speak posh, that's what. Their shitty English accents were worse than Dick Van Dyke's, for chrissakes.

"How was that one, Kar?" my mother asked.

"The accent sounded weird."

"STOP FUCKIN' CUTTIN' HER UP!" Shandy told me.

To re-iterate (or reacquaint), Aunt Shandy had three sons: Rich, a twenty-two year old hog felon with a fuck you lip; Teddy, a nineteen year old pock-faced motor mouth; and Shane, a mentally handicapped seven-year-old whom Shandy had dubbed her "Cross to Bear." Shane also constantly gnawed the base of his left thumb. I may have been a picker, but Shane was a chewer.

Unlike my second cousins, the titty-loving television repairmen, my first cousins were rabid. Sheryl called Rich and Teddy "streetwise." I called them redneck assholes with muscles and town accents. (I didn't know the extent of their trashiness until years later when I showed my college friends some old family photos. "Holy fuck?! THAT'S your family?!" said my roommate. "It's like Cops!")

The two brothers beat the shit out of each other from one end of their marijuana crop to the other. Rich and Teddy fought ALL the time, but Rich always won. The Fletcher Ranch sat on five acres, but Rich and Teddy insisted on growing marijuana just off Shandy's property line, and in the field of an old black farmer named Gus, who'd machete the weed down. Rich and Teddy would then rotate the crop to another clandestine location on Gus's property, and the pattern repeated.

The Fletchers' dining room table was an old cable spool. The cable table always had mounds of marijuana on it. So we ate meals in front of the Atari in the living room instead, and under dangling fly strips with cheap glue that dropped flies into my Bo-Bo Blackberry every now and then.

Bo-Bo Blackberry, have you any glue?

No, sir. No, sir (and I'm tired of drinking flies, goddammit!).

The brothers would weigh, bag, and fistfight their way through their day, and, at night, record Mama Shandy and Auntie Sheryl telling dirty jokes and laugh and laugh and laugh.

One day, walking past the cable spool, I asked, "What's all that stinky green stuff?"

"You're too young to understand," said Teddy.

The Fletcher Freak Show had pigs, dogs, and horses--all of which were neglected. Shandy had adopted a black lab. The lab's name was Tigger, but Shandy renamed him Nigger, and proceeded to ignore him day-in and day-out. Tigger was confined to a twelve foot by twelve foot yard, which would become a dirt pothole filled with turds in a month's time. He was never walked or allowed in the house and, save for Shane's and my all-too-brief affections, never petted. He was lucky to have been fed (or unlucky. Personally, I'd have chewed my own leg off and bled to death after the first week).

I tried to walk Tigger, but he was so strong and starved for stimulation that he pulled me all over the cornfields and got away from me three times. When we returned home, and the dog eventually showed up, I'd pick all the tics away from his eyes. After that, the dog was mine. He didn't care for Teddy, that's for sure, who'd kick Tigger every chance he got. Teddy wasn't what you'd call an animal lover, though I suppose his brother was; Rich had a Rottweiler named Mr. Growly and the beast actually took down the Fletcher pony, for chrissakes. Call me crazy, but I think Mr. Growly made him proud.

The pigsty out back was a mess. But I don't mean the conventional mud and slop. It was bloody. The sow, Squeakers, ate her litters--twenty-one piglets-worth. I'd watch from the side of the pen each time and cry and cry.

The Fletchers had a stud horse named Cherokee, and it had a perpetual erection that nearly hung to the ground.

"What's that?" I asked.

"You're too young to understand," said Sheryl.

The Fletchers would have huge bonfires with other hog outlaws. Beer bottles were drunk and thrown by the caseload. Shane's foot, on one particular night, was cut open while he walked to the bathroom, necessitating an inebriated drive to the ER. Shane's tongue was too big for his mouth, and his eyes were nearly blind. Though he sounded like Scooby Doo and looked like Mr. Magoo, we understood each other perfectly. And I cried and cried when they wouldn't let me go with them.

"Why can't Shane talk?" I asked.

"You're too young to understand," said Rich.

I was too young to understand a lot of things. Like why my Aunt's new boyfriend, an upstanding businessman, would ever want to date the likes of her. Shandy had ditched her husband for him after they met in AA (oh yeah, that's why; chockfull of people who make excellent choices). AND Shandy was still seeing Dr. Sutton on our living room couch (a few loose ends to tie-up, I guess). The businessman lived up the road with his son. The son was the same age as me and we'd pal around with Shane and get into all sorts of trouble--the good kind, like racing horses through cornfields, making concoctions from kitchen ingredients, planting whoopie cushions, and playing Asteroids and Pitfall and Space Invaders until the sun came up. But, when the businessman and son weren't around, it was crop-pickin' time:

Still considered an initiate to The Freak Show, I wasn't allowed near the marijuana, but Shandy had other plans for me. The sons, Shandy, and I drove all around south Jersey's farmlands in Shandy's Pontiac Bonneville. Once they found a field to their liking, Shandy and Rich booted Teddy and me out of the car with burlap sacks to pick tomatoes and eggplants and cucumbers.

"Why are we stealing vegetables, Aunt Shandy?"

"You're too young to understand. Now shut your fuckin' trap and fill it up!"

They cruised up and down the rural highways and byways, while Teddy and I picked and picked and picked. I got sick of it after an hour and, during the last run, decided to wait on the side of the road for the Bonneville with my sack. I saw Shandy's car coming down the road with another behind it. Foolishly, I waved my Aunt down. When the Bonneville approached, I was met with Shandy's: "GET THE FUCK DOWN, YOU STUPID BITCH!" as she sped away to lose the car behind her. Fairy Godmother Shandy had spoken, so I rushed back down into the drainage ditch, found a row, and filled my last sack.

Back at The Ranch we celebrated our booty by smoking and drinking and shooting the shit. Teddy was an expert on everything, including drywall. I guess that's why the seams on Shandy's wall looked like crevasses. I wouldn't have been able to traverse them with cramp-ons, for chrissakes.

Shandy gave me a Salem. I'd heard menthols made your lungs bleed, but I smoked it nonetheless. And their beer tasted like shit, so I spat it out. They laughed and laughed.

Later in the evenings, I would listen to The Beach Boys and play Atari in the living room with Shane, while Rich and Teddy would blast AC/DC, weighing and bagging their weed in the dining room. One day Rich had his Bob Segar bootleg cassette blasting. (I could never make out the lyrics because all I heard was Rich hooting and hollering, saying "FUCK YEAH!" and "WHOO-HOO!" and "HOLY SHIT, THAT WAS FUCKIN' AWESOME!") He and Shandy saw Segar in Atlantic City with a double-brick-sized recorder stashed in Shandy's purse.

When they were all Segar'ed out, Teddy would put on AC/DC's "Love at First Feel," and sit next to me.

"Why did Rich hide the recorder?" I asked

"You're too young to understand," said Teddy moving closer, reeking of alcohol, which was his drug of choice. The song, "Love at First Feel," was about a man's crush on a teenage girl, but I didn't think Bon Scott ever intended it to be a love anthem between a nineteen-year old man and an eight-year old girl. Apparently, I wasn't too young to understand Teddy's needs and, not long after that, the joke.

The Canary claps.

The Phantom flaps, *Shut the fuck up! This isn't a goddamn performance! Once she reads this shit to the other* baluts, *they'll treat her like she's dirty. YOU'RE TAINTED, Kari!*

"I know."

She's brave, says the Canary. She's kept it in for far too long.

But it has NOTHING to do with Bastion! says the Phantom.

It has EVERYTHING to do with Bastion, the Canary counters.

Drudging up *The Fletcher Family Freak Show* is nothing compared to the spelunking I'll have to do for *The Big One*. Talk about your dark and twisted. I've been dreaming of that day ever since, though the Deer Dream is slowly taking over the Vampire and mucky blood.

It's part of the program and part of the problem, I remember. I had the Deer Dream again last night and, though it's always absent blood and guts, save the hint of the blood-colored scroll, it paralyzes me every time. Between the doe's yellow eyes and the buck's charge, I don't know which frightens me more. *In this world there is no Kari Rhyan.*

It's 0930 and I feel like I've been awake (or asleep) for a hundred years, so I close my notebook and pull away my "ear buds"; I haven't imagined a volume yet that could neutralize such images. I go to my room and drop the shades. My pillow is drenched in no time from crying and sweating. If I had my revolver in my nightstand, as I did at home, I'd eat it. I would. My heart is pounding out of my chest worse than ever before.

I can't breathe.

NO ONE WANTS TO HEAR YOUR SOB STORY, KARI! YOU'RE A BLUBBERING PIECE OF WHITE TRASH! YOU JUST WANT FUCKING ATTENTION! LIFE IS HARD, COMMANDER RHYAN, AND WE ALL HAVE TO WORK! CAN'T YOU GET OVER IT ALREADY?!

I'd eat it. I swear I would.

"Kari?" Miss Dorothea is at the foot of my bed. "Come to the lounge," she says. "We got you a puzzle."

"I'm sleeping," I tell her.

"The unit needs a President. There are chores to assign..."

"Bullshit. Leave me alone."

"I can't do that."

"GODDAMMIT, DOROTHEA! LEAVE ME THE FUCK ALONE!"

(I knew it would never work. It didn't work when Zeke wanted to sleep forever, either. "GET THE FUCK OUTTA HERE!" he told her. "I'VE KILLED NINE FUCKIN' *MOOSH* AND I COULD KILL *YOU* IN A HEARTBEAT!"

"Okay, Zeke. You have five minutes to get yourself together and join the group.")

"Okay, Kari. You have five minutes to get..."

"Oh, for fuck's sake! Give me a second!"

"Good," says Mama.

Mama is just like my Spouse. Neither one lets me isolate for too long. Being President feels familiar; I have responsibilities. I can't ignore them the way I've been ignoring my Kid, and--God willing--I'll stop ignoring her when I get home if Rodney grants me passage. Responsibility and accountability are just the things to keep me in the game. And ownership isn't just for the blue-haired rebellious teen on a campus bench. No. It's for me, too. I need to own my actions. I need to own my feelings. I don't want to fade away. But I'm so afraid of telling Rodney and Sheryl what I need.

"Here ya go," says Noah.

Noah, bless him, meets me in the hallway and gives me a puzzle of a purple teddy bear holding a bunch of balloons. That kid saves me every time whether he knows it or not. I'd told him earlier about how embarrassed I'll be when I return to my command. He said I needed to concentrate more on self-acceptance. I'd read the same thing in *Rational Recovery*. Like Noah, I need an AA group like I need a few more Bearcats and Skippers breathing down my neck. *No thanks.* I'm slowly finding out the universe provides in spite of the second law of thermodynamics: *The universe tends toward disorder.* Noah, goddamn mess that he is, delivered me just the thing: I'll take *this* Teddy over the other one eight days a week. With Starbucky back in the box, I'm psyched to solve this 250-piece puzzler. *Christ, this'll keep me busy for two goddamn seconds.*

After dividing the booty, Noah retreats for a nap while the rest of us head to the big gym. Dorothea lets him rest--a reward for a job well done. Brian and Julien are in sessions with their therapists, so Sylvia, Tommy, and I follow behind ballers, Zeke and Stefano, to watch another one-on-one comedy show. Miss Dorothea has allowed Sylvia to take her box of peanut butter cups (*yes!*), and hands us off to another magenta so she can reassume her place on the unit.

Stefano coaxes Sylvia onto the court for a game of HORSE starting at the free throw line. Sylvia bounces the ball a couple times to ready herself:

PITUNK, PITUNK....

"Your zip tie broke!" shouts Stefano. Our plastic ties substitute for laces, also bagged and tagged and far away.

Sylvia looks down. "No, they aren't, ASSHOLE!" and quickly resets herself.

"You got a booger on your face!"

"SHUT THE FUCK UP!" Zeke says.

"Okay, okay...." says Stefano.

Tommy and I open her Reese's and I suddenly lose what little appetite I have left. The peanut butter cups are Wounded Warriors inspired. My treat has *Honor, Courage, and Commitment* dusted in edible text on top. I can't get a break. Tommy gives me a *What gives?* look as he tears into his second package.

"I'm not hungry," I tell him. "I'm pissed off."

Tommy nods his head and keeps eating. I almost want to let him eat the whole box just to see Sylvia lose her shit. She's about an inch away from it as Stefano keeps riding her ass.

"SHOOT THE J!" he shouts, before Sylvia misses her "O."

"Imma kick your ass, Stefano!" Sylvia says. "Just you wait!"

As usual, Tommy doesn't say much, but I swear we're talking anyway. It's like it'd been with Shane; no matter his disability, Tommy and I understand each other perfectly. Tommy, my Ginger *Balut*. He's just like some of the other enlisted *baluts* back home. Yes, I'm a commander and, as such, shouldn't fraternize with the younglings. I should play golf with stodgy senior officers instead, like the time I played golf with a senior female officer who had called black people "a bunch of Leroys" (how do these people find me?). Still, a drama-loving *balut* like me, trained in the fine arts of manipulation and boundary-crossing, is never going to lock it up when it comes to fraternization. It's like telling my Kid to choose between Barnes and Noble and Chucky Cheese. Chucky's gonna win every time. It's how Rodney and I got close. We were never romantic, just buddies (though, as of late, I've been wondering what his intentions are). I don't know if Rodney is a *balut*, but *the computer says yes*. He never cared if he died in Iraq or Afghanistan, as long as he had a group to belong to. He's trying to belong to me, but I don't want him. I'm too busy figuring myself out. One only has to take note of the cross-pollination from *The Balut Room* to *The War Room*. It's all there. I don't know what Rodney's deal is, but you'd think I'd know by know.

I give Ginger *Balut* a few new words to look up and use every day. He found out I was a senior officer when I showed up and, therefore, thinks me smart. I don't think he thinks I'm smart as much as he thinks himself dumb. So, he asks for words--his way of wanting to speak without saying so. Something happened to Tommy when he was boy. Something similar to what happened to me. He was six and the boy twelve. It doesn't make it any better. Kid-on-kid abuse is just as bad.

Tommy was raped by the boy for over a year. It was around that time he lost his ability to talk or, rather, didn't want to. His older sister spoke for him and communicated all of Tommy's needs. Tommy never so much as referred to the abuse, let alone addressed it, until he had a freak out in the barracks and was sent across the country to The Willows. He'd been drinking and hitting the ecstasy in hopes of burying it. Though I'd been journaling since Bastion, I didn't address any of my stuff, either. Tommy may've been drinking and pill-popping, thinking himself stupid, but I'm almost twenty years older than him and doing the same damned thing AND dancing around my issues with a poker-wielding Circus Bear.

I never could face my fears. Not to mention the journal I poured-over in Bastion (now that I've reread it a hundred times) is just a bunch of porch-rocking bullshit. I wrote about anything and everything, but left my real issues alone. That lock won't be picked again by Phil or Riza or anybody. Nope, I never talk or write about my shit. Neither did Tommy until now.

There's something else Tommy doesn't talk about, or may not realize: once a child has been touched in such a way--even if the child escapes abuse--without therapy, he or she is likely to be abused again: Perverts can smell it. That's the reason Julien tried to get Tommy to warm up to him the week before I arrived, and eventually tried his hand with me. They *know*.

Case-in-point: My Slime Ball Navy colleague from San Diego, during the days of Admirals and Bearcats, had approached me just after my first marriage ended. He wanted a three-way between him and his married girlfriend. I said no, and his girlfriend accosted me a week later to ask again. I was used to the drill from bi-curious straight girls, so, once again, I told her no. Then came the reply: "But there's *something* about you, Kari." The Slime Ball would eventually threaten my life, thinking I'd take her away from him. *Where does the Navy get these people?!* I thought. Everywhere. If I've learned anything while I was being passed from a Circus Bear to a Bearcat is that gutter class values are pervasive. The Slime Ball scared the shit out of me so bad I left a message on his machine, begging him not to hurt me. *I had a kid, for chrissakes,* and this clown was the closest thing to Teddy that I'd ever seen before, or since. Prior to finding out he was psychotic, we'd talked about our daughters. I told him I hoped my Kid grew up to be happy, and he said he hoped his didn't turn into a cock whore. *Jesus....*

Then there was the time I sought spiritual guidance from a female Navy chaplain. I asked her how she reconciled the church's opinions on homosexuality. "Do you think it's a sin?" I asked her. "No," she said, ordering drinks. We were at a bar for a Navy fundraising event, so I presumed it okay. She'd eventually down six more beers and ask if she could have sex with me that evening. She asked me a half a dozen times, then drove home blitzed, though I tried to take her keys. Slime Ball and Preacher Lady, granted the abuse both must've endured, were predators.

Tommy was raped again, thirteen years later, by a fellow Airman. Tommy freaked the next day and now he's here telling the horror to us. It took forty-five minutes to tell a story that could've taken one. And, as with Noah in The War Room, I couldn't be more proud of Tommy. When I have to read my shit, it'll be Tommy I tell it to. That's the only way I'll be able to get through it.

Teddy, The Reptile, was my only victimizer, unless you count Sheryl and the rest of The Freak Show. After The Ranch, I withdrew and stopped grooming. I started picking my thumbs and moved to my face. As a teen, I had a face full of acne. I wanted to be ugly. I watched television day and night and never left my house. If there were more perverts out there, I'd never give them the chance. The behavior carried over to adulthood. I think I must've been the only person who went through four years of undergrad and had one sexual encounter (oddly enough, with a gross soccer player named Skip, who'd later be nabbed for rape in his senior year by a girl who wasn't so *balut*).

Nope, Tommy doesn't talk. Tommy thinks he's stupid. He thinks I'm a smart *balut*. But he's wrong. I'm great at faking my smartness. I used to be great at faking my heterosexuality, too. The Navy cleaned up my face and clothes, and then I became "cute," though it never mattered. The second I was approached by a man was the second I faked interest. As I did with Mark, the SEAL, I'd have to fake everything if I wanted to live a "normal" life: marriage, rank, acceptance, etc.... I couldn't be gay; I'd be fingered by Defense Directive, *Don't Ask, Don't Tell,* and, worse, by Sheryl.

Sheryl's high tolerance for my current Spouse is odd. I was sure she'd blow-up and storm out once I told her I was marrying a woman. There's still an undercurrent of disgust (more of an overcurrent, but I'm trying not to think about it). My Spouse remains close-lipped about the whole thing, but I know Sheryl's shit is wearing thin.

It wore thin on Ms. Madill, too, when she noticed my grades failing halfway through the fifth grade--the final year of The Reptile's advances. I started writing stories in class. They manifested there because I couldn't write about it in my diary, where I was just about to confess the abuse (as if *I* were the assailant), but then Phil got a hold it and that was that. The stories I wrote in class were dismal, but not yet confessional. That, coupled with my D's and F's, forced Ms. Madill to have a parent-teacher conference with Sheryl.

I had no idea it'd even taken place until Sheryl came home and slammed the door. "Don't you *ever* fuckin' talk about family business with that bitch teacher of yours again!"

"What did she say?"

"That you were *sad* and you couldn't *sleep*," Sheryl replied in a mocking tone. "There WON'T be a next time. You get me?!"

"Okay, Mom."

It was true. I was sad, and I couldn't sleep. Teddy always woke me up in the middle of the night at The Ranch to take care of his needs. So my body, by that point, was never able to relax--at The Ranch or otherwise.

I give Tommy his words: *corollary, parse, and Rubicon.* He'll use each of them in a sentence over the next couple days, and each time I'll give praise.

Don't coddle him, says the Canary. *You aren't his sister.* Riza and I had a discussion about Tommy during our scab-picking session yesterday.

"But he's just a little boy!" I cried.

"No," said Riza. "He's a man. He has to grow up, and you have to give him the space to solve his own problems."

How could someone hurt him? I'd thought. As sweet and vulnerable as he looks right now in this place, I can only imagine what he must have looked like as a child.

Exactly like you, says the Canary.

"COME ON, 'E'!" says Stefano.

Sylvia chucks the ball at Stefano, but he catches it in one, swift motion, and shoots from the three-point line.

Swoosh.

"FUCKING ROBBED!" shouts Zeke.

Stefano was scouted as a high school sophomore in Chicago, but devolved into gang activity and Baby Daddy-dom, having three kids with three different women.

"Damn," I'd said when I found out. "What the hell?!"

"I don't know, you know?" Stefano said.

"Hell no, I don't *know*. Keep it in you pants or put a condom on, for chrissakes!"

"Haha...ok, ma'am."

Kids today...

I eat the peanut butter cups because they're good, goddammit, and think about my Deer Dream with the scroll and its message. Then

I stuff a couple Reese's packets in my shorts pocket for Sylvia and wait for a magenta to walk us back to the unit.

Chapter 9

We've just finished watching the documentary *I Am*. It was supposed to be uplifting. I'm sure the star--a former Hollywood director--wanted me to feel a warm-fuzzy after he saw the light and left his multi-million dollar home and occupation in exchange for a doublewide residence in a Malibu trailer park, just down the road from Pepperdine University where he had become faculty.

"Oh, he's REALLY roughing it!" I blurt.

Zeke laughs. My, how the tables have turned! Like sands through the hourglass, so are the days of our displacement.

"Come on, Kari...you don't think he's trying to tell us he's in touch with what really matters?" asks Riza.

"He'll be in touch after he puts a leg or two in a burn bag," I say. It's true and if I could punch something and get away with it I would. But I don't feel like going to The Eff U today. Not now and not ever.

"It was a Rubicon of horseshit," says a small voice a few seats to my right.

Very good, Tommy.

"Why would he have to put a leg in a bag?" Riza asks me.

"Because YOU civilians," I point, "live in La-La Land! It's not reality!"

"Who says it's not?" Riza asks.

"ME! OKAY?!"

"Damn right!" says Zeke.

"And you'd want *us* civilians to see the things you've seen?" Riza asks me.

"For starters."

"Okay everyone, let's break for a minute. Kari, I want to see you next door."

"Ooooo," says everyone.

Whatever.

We walk from the lounge to the same empty group therapy room where we first talked twenty-two days ago. The clock is still a bastard and Riza's still picking. I've never stopped; my thumbs are bloody as hell.

"Have you been writing your Combat Timeline?" Riza asks.

"It's not combat," I mumble.

"I'm sorry?"

"My stuff isn't combat."

"Not this again," Riza mumbles.

"Yes, this again."

"Why would you say that?"

"It's irrelevant, since I'm not going back."

"Back where?"

"Back to *The War Room*."

"You will if you want to complete the program."

I tell her I never had a gun in Bastion.

"I'm sorry?"

"I NEVER HAD A GUN IN BASTION!" I slow my breathing and reset. "They locked our weapons in a Conex Box. They told us we didn't need them."

I look down at my thumbs, and there's blood collected underneath my middle finger, the one I use most. "It's the same but it's different," I say, picking, then strike gold. The thumbs drip.

Breathe, says the Canary.

"Kari?"

"You don't understand...it's NOT combat. I have no right to be in there. None!"

"You're right," she says, "I *don't* understand."

"I haven't *killed* people, Riza! I haven't given orders to kill. I haven't seen my best friends die. And, look! I got my arms and legs. See?!"

"Then what would you call it?"

"Unlucky."

Riza stares. I stare back. Fuck Foating. I'm not running from this one.

Which one? asks the Canary.

"Riza," I say.

You're going back, the Canary croons.

"I'm *not* going back," I say.

Yes, you are.

Riza scoots her chair in a bit closer. "Kari?"

"Huh?"

"When did you last write?"

"What?"

Riza has taken the same even pitch I used on Millie, my tone-deaf tooth-grinding grandmother who had a heart paced to absorb just about anything and everything, but my own chest burns. Riza sounds like she's underwater. "How long has it been since you stopped writing?" Riza asks.

Yeah, says the Phantom. *How long has it been since your last confession?*

"A day," I mutter.

"In your Timeline?"

"Nine," I correct and Foat away to La-La Land myself.

"Kari?"

"Oh whaaaat?! For *chrissakes*...."

Riza tells me she's clearing the rest of my day. "You need to focus on Bastion. I don't care if it's a page or ten or a book. You need to sit with it. You need to sit and write."

She gets up and heads toward the door. "I'll let Dorothea know," she says without turning around.

"Yay." *Goddammit. Screw them AND their lousy double-team. They don't fight fair.* I straggle behind Riza, and back to group where the noises settle. I'm ignoring the other muggles straining for eye contact; they want the gouge, but they get jack, except Tommy, who gets a wink.

Riza addresses the group. "I'm going to tell you about war..."

"Pfft!" says Zeke.

"...as it was *hundreds* of years ago," Riza clarifies.

"Riza was in The Crusades," says Noah.

"You're stupid," says Sylvia.

Riza's countenance lightens a little, then hardens at once. "Let's start with a question. Does anyone know why it was commonplace for kings and queens to keep their armies at war?"

"They wanted to conquer," replies Noah. "Expand territory."

"Why else?"

Blanks all around, except Julien, who's sleeping.

"They couldn't bring them back," Riza says. "They kept their armies fighting because they were afraid of bringing them back to civilized society. They considered the soldiers savage."

Riza looks down and fiddles with her fingers for a second. When she looks up, I see a glimmer of someone else. There's an ache. She looks like my Spouse, one hip out, head leaning slightly to the side, and eyes blinking back one endless upwelling. So, when her eyes float over the room and finally settle on me, I feel like I'd just chucked a Blu Ray at her sandcastle. "The armies," she resumes, "were never brought home. The men never came back. They were abandoned to greedy causes, Kari, which is more savage than ANYTHING that could happen in war."

"I understand," I say.

"We don't have to see what *you've* seen to understand that."

"Yes, ma'am."

I lean forward to get a little air before explaining what I've tried to explain to Johnnie Walker during our endless late morning sessions. "I'm sorry, Riza. I know you mean well, but all I'm saying is...in order for civilians to *truly* understand, they need to experience what we've experienced."

"Yeah," says Noah. "Maybe next time they'll think twice about supporting dipshit kings with bogus causes."

"Shut your fucking mouth!" We all turn and lean to the side of our high-backed leather chairs that don't swivel, but still take prisoners. Zeke doesn't have his arms folded anymore, but his fists are clenched. "You little shit," Zeke says too quietly. (I'd rather he yell, quite frankly.) "You think my friends died for nothing?"

Zeke's jaw relaxes but his knuckles whiten. He glares at Noah. This is the first time I've seen Zeke's kill face. It's an eerie, yet tranquil face--a paradox I'd noticed on the mugs of the *Abu Sayyaf,* who eye-fucked us in The Philippines. *He wants to kill Noah.* He keeps staring. I get up. To do what? I don't know. Slap Zeke's face.

"Let'em sort it out," Sylvia whispers, putting a hand on my shoulder.

"Zeke's going to charge," I whisper. "I know it."

Noah Foats, refusing to engage. Zeke glares. It's dead silent.

"Come on, Zeke!" Sylvia breaks the tension, but it's no use.

"Whatever, Sylvia," Zeke says and gets up to face Noah. "You got anything else clever to say?"

"Leave him alone!" Sylvia shouts.

Noah Foats and squeezes a packet of peanut butter into his mouth. *I gotcha!*

"LOOK AT ME, YOU LITTLE SHIT!"

"ZEKE!" Riza pleads.

FUCKING GET TO IT! The Phantom eggs me on. My chest burns. *I DON'T NEED LEATHERS TO TAKE HIM DOWN!* I move to stand again, but a voice pipes up from the back.

"SIT DOWN, EZEKIEL!"

Brian takes off his sunglasses and locks eyes with Zeke, and now Zeke listens.

"Our friends didn't die for nothing," says Brian. "No matter the reasons for being there, our friends died protecting *us.*"

Riza motions for Brian to continue.

"I want to go back," says Brian. "I do. I want to see my friends. I want to have a purpose. I want to do important things. That's what they told us we'd be doing. *Important things.* But now? All I want is to laugh again. I want that more than anything. I miss them. I miss laughing *with* my friends. I want to live, but I don't know how. My friends died so I could, but I don't know how."

"I still don't know how," says Noah.

"At least you're trying," Zeke manages.

Riza steps to the bookcase in the corner opposite the television, where a mini-library of self-help books have gone largely ignored. I spy the spine of the one she grabs, *The Post-Traumatic Stress Disorder Sourcebook*.

Riza flips the book open and cuts to the chase. "Obviously," she says, putting on her reading glasses, "we do things differently nowadays." She clears her throat and reads, "The entire society bears the warrior's wound," and snaps the book closed.

That's it? It was a good tactic; maybe now some of us will actually read the book.

"We bring you back," she says. "We *want* you back. So DO come back. PLEASE come back. Come back to THIS reality and tell us everything you've seen and done. We want to know it all. We want to learn. Your loved ones still wait. You aren't the only ones torn apart by this pain. You MUST know it. You MUST *see* it."

Noah Foats. Sylvia Foats. Brian puts his sunglasses on and pushes them back to the bridge of his nose. Zeke folds his arms over his split knuckles. Stefano chews on a toothpick. Tommy leans over and looks at me, and I--after appraising my defeat--submit to Riza, The Cuban, who is pointing at the movie's credits, but looking at me.

"THAT man in the documentary shouldn't *have to* see what you've seen to be in touch. He searches for what's important in the only way HE knows how. His path is NOT yours. Your path is NOT his. I doubt that he, or any other civilian, wishes this kind of pain for you. So don't wish it on him."

"He's free," I tell her. "And I'm fucking jealous. I'm not like him. I thought I had choices, but I don't. Other people have them. Not me. I feel like I'm dying and, some days, feel like I'm dead already."

"But you're alive," says Riza.

"Then I wish I wasn't."

Riza's eyes are red and watery. Tired or sad, sad or tired, I've wondered all this time. I feel like an asshole. The tears start trickling down Riza's face. I haven't felt this bad since I was seven when I called my friend, Leshawn, "a boy." I hadn't a clue of the connotation. I just called him a boy the same way he would call me a girl if I'd acted like a Nancy. A black teacher, Mr. Givens, overheard and took me by the hand and banged it on his desk with each successive syllable: "HE'S-NOT-A-BOY! HE-IS-A-MAN! HE'S-NOT-A-BOY! HE-IS-A-MAN!" Leshawn hung his head and cried because he thought I was in trouble. I know. I was young. And maybe the teacher was wrong for assuming I'd know the ins and outs of black struggles, but the truth was I'd only been trying to keep my head above water. Like I'm trying to do now.

My homespun traumas blunted me, perhaps, but this Crank Vet Syndrome fucking blinds me. My Spouse, Riza, and Leshawn may as well be the same person. I want to breathe with them, to come up and share air. I don't want to take them down. I don't want to take Pepperdine down, either. He teaches. I could teach a thing or two. I could teach my Kid to help a drowning person without going down herself. I really could.

I could teach my Kid that war is a mistake. War is an anchor. And Sheryl, weighing me down AND dunking my head every time I try to come up, is just like the military leadership who weighs me down with more directives and deployments and denial. But I won't be under for much longer. I'll float instead and swim back. I miss my Spouse and Kid. I want to come home.

I look at Riza's face and see her pain, and I finally see my own pain for what it really is--an excuse to stay broken. Riza isn't afraid to cry like the rest us slunk in our beige recliners like dumb animals. Riza has cried for forty years.

"My husband came back from Vietnam talking like you," Riza says to me.

I hear a "shit" from the back of the room. I assumed, like everyone else, that Riza's husband died in the war. I don't ask how he died, and she doesn't tell us. All we know is that Riza loved someone, and now he's not here.

"You aren't dead," says Riza. "But you must cut through your traumas to live."

My vision flashes red. I'm in fifth grade science class, the year I told Teddy, The Reptile, to stop putting his mitts on me. "The universe tends toward disorder," Mr. Winters says. "Any motion is potentially reversible...Kari?"

I can't fix this.

"Kari?"

I can't.

Tommy nudges me. Riza waits for an answer.

"Huh?"

"Will you try?" she asks me again.

"I will."

"Will you try, Zeke?"

"I guess."

"How about you, Tommy?"

"I want to."

"Brian?"

"Of course I will."

Riza takes a deep breath and encourages us to use our time wisely. She takes her notebooks filled with *us* (and, no doubt, our whimsy) behind the nurses' station to chart. We all disperse to our corners and do what we think is most wise: Brian reads, Sylvia calls home, Noah naps, Zeke stands next to Stefano who's bouncing a ball up against a wall, Julien watches *Ridiculousness*, and Tommy plays Sudoku. I grab my composition book and sit with the purple puzzler, which is far too simple to keep Bastion away.

I open up my composition book and see where I've left off.

Ah, yes: a page full of casualties.

Each line shoots a pang through my eyes and down to my Domino. My Domino has a small lacquered snapshot of Joel Tudor on a wave that I cut out of a surfing magazine; we made them in Art Therapy yesterday. I'm supposed to rub it when I get anxious, so I can spare my thumbs. No wishes, though. If granted, however, I'd request a bye on my Combat Timeline. I wish it ended there.

In a way, it has; I can't remember anything that happened between my first shift in Bastion and the last. I can't. I've been rubbing Joel's nipples for a good ten minutes and I can't think of one thing to write. I retrieve my Bastion journal from my nightstand to jog my memory, but it says nothing. It has funny stuff, jokes and conversations, but it doesn't have the meat. There aren't even any dates. I'd been trained to write nothing. What if someone read it? Well, turns out that someone is me.

This bitch is crazy.

(Kiss my ass, Phantom.)

I sit. I Foat. The tears come. I can't remember. I can't remember months. I know they happened. I came to know my workmates over three seasons better than I knew most of my family or friends. I know we ate together. I know we talked outside of our tents on sunny days (so, most days). I know we laughed and laughed. I heard about their loved ones back home. I knew their routines, good and bad. I knew their strengths and weaknesses because, in Bastion, you saw both.

But my first day and my last day, it's all I got. Thirty minutes have passed, and I can't remember the traumas. We're supposed to leave all the bad stuff behind, but I can't remember the middle. *Goddammit, I can't!*

How could you? the Phantom accuses. *How could you forget?! Is this all a lie? FAKER!*

I get up. I pace the hallway. I'm trapped. I can't understand how. I think and think and...*nothing.* Riza wants me to do this, but it's not clicking. I'm not rational, and I'm not recovering. If there were rum, I'd slam it. If there were Percocet, I'd pop it.

First day and last day. First day and last day....

I'm not ready! I tell myself. *I'm not ready for* my Big One. *I'm not! I'M NOT!*

I'm hyperventilating. If I go back to my room, Miss Dorothea will find me and drag me out. I saw them; she and Riza talked. Conspiring. Mama is behind the nurses' station looking at me right now, and looking at me in that way.

"I'm not going to let you fall."

She's getting the leathers! says the Phantom.

Mama somehow traversed thirty feet in one second because she was behind the desk and now she's here right in front of me.

"Sit down, Kari. Have you eaten?"

"No. Why?"

"You look like you're gonna faint, is all."

Mama takes my vital signs and my blood pressure is a little low, my heart rate is a little high, and I've gone totally bonkers.

"What's going on?" asks Miss Dorothea.

"I can't remember Bastion. Only parts."

"Well," she pauses and finally says, "think of it as one *looong* day, and go from there. Start in the morning and end in the evening. See where it takes you. It isn't for the record. It's just for you."

I suddenly know what I have to do. My mind isn't letting me think about the *between*, so I'll have to attack from the sides. I'll take the rooks and kill the knights. I want to come home.

A few deep breaths later, I grab my pen and step off.

My first twenty-four hours in Bastion set the stage for the entire tour. Filled with all the sound and fury a fortified hospital could have, from the helicopters that landed on Nightingale morning, noon, and night to the screaming and swell from the casualties and Queen Mother, I reflexively slipped into TV mode, as I'd done as a kid, to mentally escape all the chaos and aggression I couldn't physically avoid. Instead of sitcoms, however, I'd end up watching a bunch of bawdy Brits take the piss out of each other every single day.

During slower nightshifts, when there was nothing left to do but think about all we'd done, my cohorts and I would amputate the legs of leftover gingerbread cookies sent from home. Tully even stepped on a stool just like Pam did to get to the red icing, or guts; *Mary razzed a young English corporal at the cafeteria for mistakenly sending a foot-in-boot back to Germany with the patient's personal belongings ("Aye, yous one a sandwich short of a picnic!"); Benny wheeled a Taliban from the Ward to the OR for surgery on Christmas Day while wearing an above-the-knee silver dress and Santa hat; and Gemma danced at the NAAFI to "Cotton Eyed Joe" after a brutal New Year's Eve filled with sloughed off back skin and exposed nerve bundles.*

The last day in Bastion brought with it my Big One: the trauma that came when I thought I'd seen everything, the trauma that made me forget the between, the trauma that upended my Balut *values and, what I firmly believe, is STILL the only reason I'm here.* (But I just can't go there. It's too soon.)

Cut through it with tin snips, says the Canary. Little by little. Ready? Steady. Go.

I'm dozing off in Bay One, groggy from the roar of the air traffic that accompanied a busy night. Our berthing was farther away from Nightingale, but, in the tents, it always sounded like the Chinooks and Blackhawks were landing right on top of us as we slept. As I wait for the next wave of casualties in the Bay, counting the ceiling splatter for the last time, Benny runs up from the ward and stands at the foot of my gurney. He squats with his arms overhead in the shape of a V.

"The new lot's here!" he yells, and then farts. "Oh, and I saw you on telly again!" Our group, after three seasons, was set to lift off to our respective homes in two days. We'd make way for the new crew tomorrow. They flew in directly from HOSPEX, the training evolution that took place in York, England. They're fresh from a

crash course on *The Stew* and *The Way*. As for the TV quip, I'd been standing in the background of a HOSPEX training video, which finally aired on British television. Trevor was being interviewed while I looked hungover in the background. (Which was true. In fact, the last thing I'd remembered from the night before was Val wearing rabbit ears and dancing in day glow at a York nightclub called The Reflex to a song called "Love Plus One" by Haircut 100.)

"Is this your victory dance?" I ask Benny, still with his arms over his head.

"No. Ring-tailed lemur." Benny did impressions. This is Benny's first animal and, just like that, he jets off before I can call him a knob. He was always crop-dusting his gas, never bothering to 'cut the tail.'

I stand up from my gurney and straighten in time to see three junior naval officers walk through the bays with their heads on a swivel.

Rodney rushes past them. "Where the hell are my SHEERS?! GEMMA!" He runs through the OR's double doors. There goes Rodney, fucked beyond belief.

A young lieutenant named Abi introduces herself and tells me she wants to take a hospital tour. She'd dropped off her sea bag by my old cot and motored over to ask questions.

"Have you seen much? What kind of stuff? Is it hard? Do you get used to it? I hope I don't kill anyone. We're all so nervous, but we're so excited. You know?"

"I didn't fart," I tell her.

She shrugs off that one and resumes. "What's the best advice you can give?"

"Get a deployment wife and be faithful," I say. A deployment wife is your ear on tour. It needn't be a sexual or cordial relationship, so long as the person's there for you. It's like a pillow; you cry and drool on it. I was lucky enough to have two: Gemma and Emma.

Abi is smiling ear-to-ear. "I'm glad I'm finally doing what I was commissioned for. That admin crap back home is the pits."

"Totally...."

Tully runs in. "All of you out! You'll have the bays to yourselves soon enough. Now fuck off, please, and come back tomorrow." He scribbles on the big white board with his trusty marker, like he always does, filling the bays and making assignments. The junior officers scram. Guess he showed them. I didn't want to dish the dirt anyway. Their smiles hurt me, deep down, where Jesus lives.

Triple Amp, Tully scribbles.

"OP VAMPIRE...OP VAMPIRE...OP VAMPIRE...."

The MERT, our flying oblong double-rotor trauma bay, is giving blood, so Gemma and I grab a rapid infuser and prep for the triple. The blades chutter, and the Green Butcher Smocks and Blue Scrubs are synched. The patient transfers from the slide with no danglers. Smitty says "fast scan negative," so we get to pump up the patient a little before Blue Scrubs have their way. Us blood molls are motoring and almost finish our second shock pack when I hear a POP and SPLAT. Gemma had taken a pie in the face. She'd forgotten to unclamp the infuser after a quick bag change, causing the fresh frozen plasma to burst.

"What do we do?!" she says with the donor gold dripping off her lips.

"Crack on," I tell her.

I'm laughing my ass off as I say it, but we keep the pace while the triple amp fights for his life an inch away. I keep laughing as Gemma mumbles about all the diseases she may or may not have contracted.

"You winding me up!?" asks Tully standing over my shoulder. "I will slap you two into the middle of next week! Stop laughing and get back on task. Kari, I love you but, next time, you're getting gripped."

I lock it up quick because this is MY Bay. I throw Gemma a towel and glance at the Padre in his yellow square. His lips are moving.

His eyes close. His eyes open again. (Pray for me, too, Father.)

British press is in attendance. A cameraman stands on one of our metal trashcans lined with Bay One's biohazard bags. He wants a bird's eye view. I'm pretty sure if I had some "parts" in hand, I'd have pushed him off the receptacle, put the piece in the bin, and probably laughed more. I would've and, what's more, I wouldn't have missed a beat with the resuscitation. This has become our dance, practiced over and over, hardwired and hardboiled.

The triple makes it to the OR, where the surgeons hope to preserve at least one elbow and (God willing) both knees. It's all about muscle preservation. How much tissue can you save, thank you very much! *Pam steps on her stool to get at the guts, and I pass the baton to another nurse so I can head back to the ER and clean up Bay One.*

I take a detour outside so the KBR cleaning crew can hose off the gurney.

"STANDBY FOR BROADCAST...

OP MINIMIZE...OP MINIMIZE...OP MINIMIZE...."

Flags are lowered on Bastion as word travels to Britain. I come back to Bay One and clean up the blood. A British General is Foating in the sluice by himself.

I shake off the Queen Mother and General Tearful and lend a hand in Bay Two, where Val--It Girl, 1985--is adjusting the urinary catheter of an intubated Afghani with a massive head wound. He's to transfer to Kandahar--a bigger military hospital with neurosurgical capabilities. But he's to go to the ICU first to free-up our gurney.

Val's hand is moving about his lower half to secure the tube.

"Wanking a patient in his hour of need, I see?" says Tully as he backs into Val.

"Oh, piss off, Tallulah!"

Tully and Val jockey for Funniest Brit on Tour, a crown Tully would've surely ripped from Val's bun, tied back just enough with hair wisps the size of nymph fairies running down her neck--not at all like my shrews that hang in my face. Val owns her sexuality AND her wisps. Not me: Tully called me cute after I tripped and farted during a trauma, mid-tour. "Cute like cancer," I'd told him.

Val has the patient sorted, so I hustle to Bay Four and help Mitch transfer a Gurkha to the Ward for Emma. On Day One, I asked Emma about Gurkhas while pulling duty as the token American for their NAAFI trivia team that battled it out for a free pizza on "Man Love Thursdays," a term for the affinity some Afghan men showed each other just after hump day. I don't know about any Man Love Thursdays--different people, different customs--but I do know that I'd go on to lose trivia games for my team more than once. My questions were Oscar-related and I always answered "Oprah." Pop culture wasn't my thing by that time, but all the Brits thought Americans knew Hollywood and I figured "Oprah" would eventually be right. Brits said being with us was like walking around in a movie. If we Americans were TV tropes, I remained Gilligan, the gullible numbskull.

"You know we've got tanning beds and ATVs by the flight line now?" said Emma after one Trivia loss.

"No way! You guys think of everything," I said.

"Good God, you alien! Of course I'm not serious."

I believed any and everything they told me because they had the same voice as The Queen Mother, and she NEVER joked. I was Gilligan, that's for sure, and Gilligan noticed the dark group of men who kept to themselves outside of the NAAFI.

"What's their story?" I asked. The men had slanted eyes and strong arms and looked mega cool.

"They're Gurkhas," Emma replied.

"Why don't you guys hang out with them?"

"Because they're Gurkhas, Kari."

They were part of the Queen's army, Nepalese warriors who excelled in hand-to-hand combat. They had mini machetes called

Kukri *strapped to their waists and I, after imagining their kill faces, kept away from them too.*

Mitch and I transfer our Gurkha to the only vacant bed in Emma's Ward. The Gurkha glances through the partition and sees one of the injured insurgents we were keeping along the front wall. The insurgents were always shrouded behind curtains with a guard assigned to each. I nod at one the Marines standing watch over Tali Alley. He's reading Razzle, a British skin mag that sells like hotcakes here in the sand.

The Gurkha keeps staring. "Uh...," says Emma. "Let's move him over here. This one's just discharged."

"He discharged already?!" asked Benny sailing past with a bed pan.

"He discharged himself. He left a note. 'I feel better. Thank you. Afuk.' He was a lovely man, Afuk."

(Awww...farmer Afuk.)

"NO FLOBBIN ON THE FLOOR!" shouts Emma.

The insurgent spits next to the Gurkha, prompting the Marine to toss off his Razzle and jump to, so Mitch and I get on it, and move one stone cold killer away from the other. After the melee, Mitch and I push our empty gurney past Benny, who's now arguing with Gemma over who's the rightful owner of an autographed Mark Wahlberg photo. Wahlberg visited Bastion, as did Prince William, and The British Prime Minister before him. I'd gotten a photo with Wahlberg in the ICU. (I was too late to catch him in the ER because I was always on the can, storing up my anxieties and "expelling" them between traumas.)

"You've missed him," said Jeff with a limp and a smile.

"Fuck that," I said and trucked down the hall, pushing through the line that'd formed in the ICU. I tapped Wahlberg on the shoulder of his black leather jacket, and asked for a picture. His eyes were red and watery. Tired or sad, I cannot say, but I could guess after appraising our wall of Marine and Afghani amputees. Larry, The

Glory-Seeking Cunt, was there (of course), so I put him to good use. He snapped a blurry picture of the star and me from afar, but I'd gotten my proof. I booked back to the ED with my autographed picture and told an Army kid sitting in the hallway to "Go to the ICU if you want one of these," but he was blank. Vacant. Turns out he'd just left Smitty, who'd been the bearer of bad news about his friend. (Smitty found pieces. He never picked them up.)

By the time Prince William stopped by the following week, I was so unaffected I went to my tent instead, and ate a "cat's asshole" (meat wrapped in pastry) and slept until The Queen Mother woke me again; after locking eyes with the Army kid in the hallway, I'd be ashamed of my own enthusiasm. I was a TV kid and actors were God, but God never visited Bastion.

Still, an autographed picture is a hot commodity, as Benny tries to snatch a Wahlberg *out of Gemma's hands.*

"It's mine, and you know it!" he says.

"Don't be such a puff," says Emma.

"Well, I'm not made of wood!"

"Come on, now," says Emma, "give him back his eye candy."

Gemma relents and gives the Wahlberg to Benny. He wanted to surprise his girlfriend. I'll give mine to my sister Cassie. "Kari met stars and saved lives. Isn't she the greatest?!" Yeah, great like gangrene.

We're needed back in the Bays, so Gemma, Mitch, and I hoof it back to the ER, where a six-year-old Afghani girl is slated to come into the ED with second degree burns, only to be corrected to third degree a few moments later.

"Get with Mary on Bay Three," Tully tells me.

"Uh-uh. No way. It's a kid, and I'm not gonna take…"

"You will, you prat! Stop your wingin'!" (Pronounced like "engine," but with a W and a handlebar mustache.) *"Everyone is busy, and we need another nurse. Take medication!" he says and hands me the keys to the med refrigerator.*

"I need them to put up with this shit!"

Tully speeds off to torture J-Chat for giving us shaky details. It wasn't J-Chat's fault; the reports from the field were always in flux, and no one knew what was coming until they landed. And I didn't want to see this one. It was a kid, and I couldn't handle a kid.

"One more," says Mary. "Come on, for old time's sake." Mary isn't mad at me anymore. Earlier, I stole the last tea bag out of the stash next to her bunk. I thought she'd kill me. I'd replenish her supply ricky-tick and am now back in her good graces.

Mary hands me a Meerkat with a diaper. It has my rank and name on it because I shit myself in the Sluice once. She gave me a coffee cup, too, with the same critter on it. The Kat said, LCDR Rhyan...Saving Lives, Simples. Cute, I say and take the gifts to the break room and hustle back to Bay Three. The blades chutter. The kid is here.

Mary motions to Bay One and says in my ear, "Best not be in there."

Val is charting behind Bay One's lectern. She's standing rigid and red-faced, trying really hard to cope; the patient she's scribing on is one of her 16 Paratrooper peers. It's not her boyfriend, Dangerous Nigel, but a guy she knows well. He's been shot. I wouldn't know what it would be like to see one of my friends on a gurney. Val taught battle care to 16's Combat Medical Technicians. She's gonna lose her shit, I think, but remembered she runs on a steady stream of coffee, V8, and Rip It. If there was shit to be lost, I knew she'd lost it already and was well in control this late in the game. We all are. I guess that's why my chest is on fire.

I stand on my tiptoes and get a gander at his vital signs on the monitor at the head of the bed. The CMTs did well: her friend's vital signs are on the low side of stable (rock solid around these parts).

I've never seen Val cry. I've never seen Mary or Tully cry nor Mitch, Benny, or Gemma. I've seen Emma cry once, after cradling a Para who found out he'd lost his foot. "I HATE THE FUCKING

TALIBAN," he bellowed.

I get my yellow tackle box of meds out of the refrigerator, containing pain and paralytic agents. It's all the tools of the trade for a rapid intubation; if this kid has burns like they say she has, she'll need a remedy as soon as her flesh hits the gurney.

The ambulance screeches. Syringes are full. Trevor is hovering. Jeff is there because Jeff is always there, limping and smiling. PEDRO, the Air Force rescue, comes in and places a bundle of blankets before us and begins his report. "OK, WE HAVE A SIX-YEAR-OLD CIVILIAN FEMALE WITH FOURTH DEGREE BURNS..."

"WHAT YOU MEAN, FOURTH?!" yells Tully over the blades.

"IT'S DOWN TO THE BONE, SIR. HER UNCLE SAID SHE AND HER FRIENDS WERE PLAYING AND SHE MUST'VE GRABBED A LIVE WIRE."

I've never seen a fourth degree burn, but children were always getting bombed-out. Their playgrounds were battlefields. Most injuries like this never made it to the helo, children being useless pinions in a war machine--not to mention, nine times out of ten, they're dead before PEDRO swoops in. If a grown man wearing battle-rattle in the prime of his life barely survives, then these kids didn't stand a chance. Grown men also wore blast pants, or double knitted silk shorts that somehow kept their private parts from getting fragged.

As we untangle the covers, I see a small girl with big brown eyes staring at us. We pull the blankets down further and see a black glove, from wrist to fingertips--a black glove of skin covering a small dead hand, thin as flypaper. My eyes drift up. From wrist to shoulder is bone. Not a single shred of connective tissue or muscle or fascia remains.

And she wouldn't cry for anything. She's in shock, I think (and I Foat and think more). Seeing blood is not a problem, but bone and gray matter have always been...hard.

"SNAP OUT OF IT, Kari!" Mary has already started the IV.

I suck it up. I go through the motions. I don't look at the girl, but she's looking at me.

"SHE'S SHOCKY," says Jeff. Pam and Jeff and Trevor argue over what course to take with an electrical burn.

"WHERE'S THE EXIT?!" asks Pam.

"WHERE'S THE EXIT?!" asks Jeff of PEDRO.

"WE DIDN'T FIND ONE!" The PEDRO is a tall, black medic with a deep, gravely voice. He walks off to refill his cache of pain meds so he can lift off again. PEDRO usually returns to the bedside one more time before lifting off to field leftover questions. The blade noise recedes.

He never came back. Poor bastard.

Trevor and Jeff and Pam are mind-melding at the foot of the bed.

"We can't do anything heroic here," says Trevor.

"Cooked on the inside, I'm guessing," says Pam.

"The kid's toast," says Jeff.

"How much morphine?" I interrupt.

"Five," Jeff says, "and keep it coming. Follow it up with some Versed and Sux."

Versed makes her forget. Sux, or Succinylcholine, paralyzes her for the intubation. Once I give the cocktail, she'll never come off the tube. She'll never wake up.

A British Pediatrician runs in and takes a look. She'd reported last week. This is her Big One.

"What have we done thus far?" she asks in a too-measured voice. She's gonna lose her shit.

"Putting her under," I say.

"Go on, then," she replies, snapping out of the Foat. She talks with Pam and Jeff while placing the dead hand and bone back underneath the blanket.

I'm giving the meds as the kid stares at me. I finally look into her eyes because I know I'm the last person she's ever going to see. I can't handle this shit, *I think, but her eyes are so wide in my periphery and I just have to look up. I stare into her eyes as I push my last syringe. I get close and tell her it's going to be ok.*

"Bye, baby," I say as her eyes close.

The kid is taken into the OR to find the exit wound, and the Pediatrician follows behind. We don't need to transfuse her, so they don't need Mary or me in the OR.

We clean up Bay Three. Mary says nothing. Jeff says nothing. I say nothing until the Pediatrician comes out of the OR. She says the electricity traveled down her center and exited through her anus.

"Cooked," Jeff says and the Pediatrician cries.

"If you're going to do that," I tell her, "then leave."

She beats it out of Bay Three and Mary stares at me.

"What?" I ask.

"Nothing," she says.

Trevor is in Bay Two by himself, Foating his ass off and snaps back to reality when another ambulance screeches in. A Dane with a GSW to the chest blows by with CPR in progress.

"Hey Jensen."

"RIGHT TURN RESUS!" yells Jeff, and the patient and his Viking head straight into the OR with the Blue Scrubs.

<u>*AM Snapshot - Bastion - Day 184*</u>*:*

-GSW Leg (U.K.)

-GSW Arm (U.K.)

-KIA (U.K.)

-GSW Head (Afghan Military Police)

-Frag/Shrapnel Face (U.S. Marine)

-Triple Amp (U.K.)

-KIA (Denmark)

-Burn (Afghan Civilian)

-Double Amp (U.S. Marine)

-Frag/Shrapnel Legs (Insurgent)

-GSW Head (U.S. Marine)
-Closed Head Injury (Insurgent)

I close my composition book. I'm inching closer my Big One as I hold my guts in and breathe while another nail cries free from its own release.

Chapter 10

I played war when I was a kid. Though, granted, I hadn't played with the boys in the neighborhood who'd already formed little block militias by the tender age of ten. I couldn't run with them by that time; Skipper Sheryl and The Fletcher Family Freak Show had whipped me into shape, so I didn't play as much as I drifted in and out of games-- hopscotch, jacks, and double-dutch--like a lost ghost. One minute I was there, and the next, gone. I played with ants instead, or *warred* with them. I hadn't learned to "make like nothing happened" yet or become Gilligan, the faithful servant. The kid in me, or my little Canary, had to die first. I'd banished her to a holler when I discovered I was helpless to defend myself. And, even though Teddy had nearly killed my spirit, it'd be another six months before the final transformation took place.

There were huge anthills between the cracks of the sidewalks in front of our apartment that'd given way to tree roots. I'd always pick on the anthills, too little and insignificant to fend off my advances (I'd later play alligator slalom on Parris Island's golf course just prior to this hospitalization--buzzing by them with my leg dragging off the cart). I believe the urge to step on an anthill is intrinsic, but especially to me, having been stepped on for years. It's not the urge itself that's concerning, though. A stomp, however, is a huge tell. Give the hill a little nudge with the toe of your Bo-Bo Sneakers, and you're a scientist. Jump on it, and you're (in all likelihood) a sadistic son of a bitch. I gave the anthill a narrative first ("Little did Bob know, a pink spaceship was approaching...") and then ran over the mound with my Huffy. After the ants scrambled, I'd kill each one with my front tire. "Bob's running for his life! He's gonna make it!"

Squish. (Almost.)

I'd do this for hours. So, what's that make me?

"Kari!" yells Zeke. *Act of Valor* is on the tube, and he wants me to sit next to him. I've forgiven him his kill face, and he has forgiven me for almost smashing his face. *Go team!* The flick, Zeke's choice, is little more than a glorified recruitment tool, but, "Hey, they blow shit up!" The alternative would've been *Spartacus*, but we're not allowed to watch simulated sodomy when Miss Dorothea's around. "Lord, have mercy."

I'm excited to see the movie, I must admit; we can't blow our tops at the The Willows without risking a trip to The Eff U, so *eff it!* We'll live vicariously through *yet another* SEAL movie, instead. *Good times.* Noah comes out of his room, sees what's on, and goes back to bed. Across the lounge, Stefano is arguing with one of his baby mamas on the community phone, so Zeke turns up the volume to drown him out. "Ain't listening to that shit."

Tommy is on the other community phone talking to his sister, and puts one finger in his ear and keeps chatting. I look around for Sylvia, but her ride came; she discharged today, and we'd said our goodbyes earlier. *I'm gonna miss her.* I guess that's why Zeke wants me close; the kid's got mommy issues, most likely, what with the need for constant female companionship. He even wants to teach my Kid how to fish; just another clan leader with no clan, says me.

Don't treat them, Kari.

Brian is in the second row of recliners, writing on the *balut* end of his notebook. Brian was slapped around as a kid, and his therapist thought it would be a good idea "to just go on ahead and tackle that, too." *It's part of the program and part of the problem,* as Riza put it a lifetime ago. Brian's almost outta here, and he's still writing and still Froggy. Six weeks isn't long enough, but all the therapists tell us The Willows only stands us up. We're responsible for dusting ourselves off. Don't dust yourself off, and you become Rodney. Don't even stand up, and you're Zeke. Stay down and....

I should've brought my sunglasses, I think. I wear *Ray-Ban Aviators* because I'm a pretentious asshole, but I'd sooner crush them now. When I first commissioned, I'd gone to the Miramar Officers Club, of Top Gun fame. It was a novelty trip. "*Awww*, come on!" my roommate said. "You gotta do it once." A group of Navy pilots came over to our table as soon as we sat down, and started jaw jacking. The pilot sitting next to me was wearing aviators.

"You're a nurse?!" he asked.

"Yeah," I said. "I work the oncology ward at the Medical Center."

"Oh, that's great! I have this pain right here," he said, grabbing his genitals. There was a female pilot sitting across from us. She was drunk and laughing. Real charmers.

I'd worn my sunglasses every chance I got in South Carolina because I knew my eyes put people off. I see them whenever I spy myself in the mirror, and I look like a lunatic. Since returning from Afghanistan, I've had a perpetual pained expression, which always begged the inevitable question: "You all right?" In Britain, it's a greeting. The American translation? "So, uh...you taking your medication?" Yes, copious amounts.

I've learned a lot in the last four weeks. I'm nearly home. *And then what?* Who knows? I may as well kick-off the remaining two weeks with a war movie. None of the nurses think it's a good idea (or good morale), of course, but it's Sunday, and even The Molls rest between doses on Sunday. Besides, war movies are easy; there's good guys and bad guys and a SEAL I'd mistaken for dead.

"Holy shit! THAT'S MARK!" I shout.

"Which one?" asks Zeke.

"That one," I say and point through the flames of the opening campfire scene. "And Sam!" (Mark's buddy, Sam, jumped from my duplex roof into a community pool with my cake, and had sex with one of my friends in a crawl space. Real charmers.)

"Must notta been that good a friends," says Julien, "if you didn't know they were in a movie."

"That's because I thought Mark was DEAD, asshole! I never watch shit like this anyways."

I sink into my recliner and take note of the shock and awe. Noted. *This sucks.* Good choice, Zeke. He's watching the booms and blood and is happy as a clam in high tide. *He's playing war,* I think. How am I here while he's there? Am I weak? Am I a pussy?

I can't breathe...I can't breathe....

Don't get me wrong, I'm glad Mark's alive, but he's on screen killing people and getting popped and screaming! He's injured. NO! It's not real! NOT REAL! None of this is real. I feel like I'm going to be sick.

I remember Mark. I know who he is, but I don't know who *I* AM. *I Am.* I'm somebody who's supposed to be enjoying this shit. Pump more blood! More blood! Into their veins, and in my eyes! I AM! Where's my fucking sunglasses?!

I bet Larry, Bastion's Glory-Seeking Cunt, *loves* Valor. He played *Call of Duty* on the other side of the ambulance bay while we pumped and pumped and pumped. America is watching this shit while we pump and pump and pump! Larry and Mark are killing people on screen while we pump and pump and pump!

Snap out of it! the Canary tells me.

"I don't wanna," I say.

Giddy-up, says the Phantom, *the best part's is coming!*

It's only a movie, says the Canary.

It's real enough, says the Phantom. *It's got all the sound and fury. There's even a funeral. It's real.*

Funerals. I went to those. The Brits called them vigils. Two rounds of cannon fire. I was there. That was real, right?! RIGHT?! All those Bastion bits.

"How am I here and he's there?!" I yell.

"It's just a movie," says Zeke.

"It's man-made," I say.

"What?"

Never mind.

It's not your path, the Canary says.

"I'm a weak piece of shit."

"You're crazy," Zeke mumbles.

In this world there is no Kari Rhyan.

◆ ◆ ◆

"Wake up, Kari."

I open my eyes and raise my head to see a figure standing over me with no arms.

"Where'd your arms go, Miss Dorothea?"

"Kari...," she spreads her arms, levitating and unattached.

I blink my eyes a few times and see that Miss Dorothea's arms are, indeed, attached and I am, still, without marbles.

"How often you have flashbacks?" she asks.

"A few times a week."

"Most of them like that? Missing parts?"

"Yeah. Arms, usually. Sometimes legs."

"The phones are free," she says, changing the subject. "Go on. It'll do you good." I call home at a set time every day. I talk to my Spouse for a good thirty minutes. She and the Kid are doing well. "We love you so much, my darling."

Oh, how I miss them.

Oh, how I've hurt them.

Sheryl's drinking more now than ever. There's boxed wine in the fridge, just like old times, with no AA in sight. I remember when I'd initially moved her in all those years ago I told her the only reason I'd ever ask her to leave was if she started drinking. But she took it up again after I came back from Afghanistan and started drinking heavily myself. How could I fault her when I was just as guilty? As with her therapy sessions that didn't work, neither had AA. *It's all my fault.*

My Spouse also tells me Base Housing has been sending emails about Sheryl's dog. It's crapping all over the neighborhood. My magical thinking deludes me to the point that maybe, just maybe, the dog has a hex on Sheryl. That must be the reason Sheryl is so unreasonable, until I realize that she's always been unreasonable and her dog is just another household possession. The small, anthropomorphized mutt has become her third husband. The dog hangs the moon, and I hang myself with its medical bills. Don't get me wrong, I love animals, but the Skipper wants her Schipperke to live forever. She probably figures, *Why clean up the mess when the world owes me?* But the world doesn't give in to such demands, so she takes it out of hide, my hide. Those rare times when I don't acquiesce to my mother's demands is when she puts the mad shitter on a pedestal: "I love Skippy more than my kids!" she'd say. "His love is unconditional." *No,* I'd think, *a dog will take all the bullshit in the world for some Pup-Peroni and a cuddle.*

My Spouse says Sheryl can be really supportive at times. I told her those were Sheryl's *moments of clarity.* She has them like the rest of us have moments of weakness. So, now that I know she's drinking, I tell my Spouse to be careful and not let Sheryl drive the Kid anywhere. I can't accommodate my mother anymore. I'm a lousy Gilligan; denial and optimism never managed to get me off the Island, but I'm set to swim.

Miss Dorothea says I have another call, so I hang up and talk to Rodney. Rodney says he's moving to the same town where I plan on retiring in a couple years. My Spouse, prior to our marriage, purchased a small home in an isolated town, and we openly discussed moving there after I retired from the Navy. He changed his mind about New York City. "Too many ghosts," he said, referring to his sister.

"I'm sending you a list of houses on the market," Rodney says. "I need your opinion."

"I don't have an opinion on that," I tell him. "It's your call."

Rodney yawns. "Well, you know, I thought that you'd know the area, and everything else, and know where to steer me."

"I don't," I tell him.

Rodney yawns again like he's trying to scratch his tonsils. "Well, I'm going to send you a list and, if you change your mind, and everything else, tell me which one to buy."

Then he says the two things he always says before we sign off, which takes forever with the yawning and "you knows" and the "everything else's": "You're my best friend, you know that? You're my sister."

I tell him he's my best friend, but he isn't. I tell him he's my brother, but he's not. My boundaries are still porous; I can barely fend off Julien, so how can I fend-off "friends" and "family?" I have to grow some balls. Riza's harping about the *Resiliency Bucket* again. Apparently, it's still overflowing. It must be, because I'm still Foating and letting people walk all over me until the Phantom comes. The Phantom hasn't come out for Rodney or Sheryl though. *They need me.* "If your bucket wasn't so big," Riza told me, "then maybe Sheryl and Rodney would've hit bottom a long time ago and straightened themselves out. They are adults, Kari, not children."

Meanwhile, Rodney is topping my off my bucket with his dust. He hasn't brushed himself off a millimeter. Neither have I. So, we developed a history after retuning from Bastion, a mutual relationship born more out of utility; Skipper Sheryl told me there were only two reasons to keep a man around (besides procreation). One, every woman needs a punching bag. The catch is you have to take his pops first, but it's the perfect excuse to hit back. But I don't want to fight like Sheryl and Rodney: not too long ago, Rodney showed up unexpectedly with a kill face on my doorstep after a couple of days of unreturned calls and several three-minute yawning voicemails. "You better answer the phone when I call," he said too quietly. "Bullshit," I muttered and closed the door in his face. I wouldn't talk to him for three months.

It's always been easier to turn my back on a problem than address it. So what's his problem? *Shit if I know.*

Rodney will eventually return to my island. I know this. He thinks my boundaries are "hang-ups," so he treads lightly for now like the Circus Bear who has been standing on my neck for thirty-nine years. Rodney yawns and says "sister" and "best friend." Rodney is afraid of being alone. Thirty-seven-year-old-Rodney says he doesn't know how to make friends. My Spouse says he practically wets himself when I walk into the room. She says he's harmless, but I'm the last of his friends who can tolerate him. I'm sure Rodney's Marine friends wouldn't be so keen on him spending so much time with *their* kids, but maybe their kids aren't being ignored like I'm ignoring mine. Rodney likes to control everything and everyone, and I let him. Rodney dumps in my fjords, but he isn't like Worm and Concubine, who want to dump and run. Rodney and the Skipper prefer to dump *and stay.*

The second reason to keep a man around, per Sheryl, is to put them to good use, or "make them do shit around the house." Whenever Rodney visits, The Skipper makes him feel needed and wanted in between insults. So, I let him do stuff--projects I'd wanted to do myself, and projects that'd help *me* stay sane (like mothering). Rodney thinks smothering the Kid keeps him focused. I say the Kid, and his constant encroachment upon my life, keeps him from doing his own internal work. It's Day 110 for him over there, so what does *that* tell you?

My Spouse, newest to the family, has kept her mouth shut, but it's getting to her; Rodney calls my house every day. Rodney is always there, and now Rodney is moving to our small community. War will never leave me.

Rodney gets money from the VA. A lot of it. He also gets Combat-Related Special Compensation from time spent in Iraq. He has enough scratch to go to school, find a new vocation, and buy a house wherever he wants. But he wants to be near me and the Kid and talk about war and not go to school and not get on with his life.

"Okay," I tell Rodney. "I'll take a look at the list."

I get off the phone and start picking my thumbs. *They're picking me clean.* And Rodney isn't the only Rodney. There are tons of lost souls back at my command looking for war and all too eager to bring me and everybody else right along with them. We've had four suicides in the last two years at my command. Were they the pickers or the pickees? That's what I'd like to know. I see an insidious pattern: all vets, from the great wars to the not so great wars, eventually come home. They are growing neurotic children. That's what happens when a parent has PTSD and doesn't address it, like I haven't, or like my grandfather hadn't. My Kid's already nervous, but I'll be damned if she turns bad like Sheryl. Then again, I'm not a war-mongering racist like my Grandfather. I may be a Phantom, but I'm not the devil. And sometimes I can't tell the difference between my grandfather and my "best friend."

Rodney brings the war back with encroachment and anger and the hijacking of precious moments. I bring the war back by not talking about it. I'd rather come home to my bed, drink and pill-pop, and pick fights on Facebook. Rodney couldn't carry on the charade at work, but I can. I'm STILL the Fixer.

No...I'm not. I was The Fixer. But who am I now if I'm not my brother's keeper or a Yes Man or a Gilligan or even a nurse?

I go get my composition book, sit down next to Kinkade, and flip to my autobiography because I'm dying to find out.

Monsters are real. Sheryl got that wrong, too. Monsters and Vampires are as real as baby teeth and growing pains. Sheryl didn't want to hear about my woes. She didn't want to hear it from my teachers. She didn't want to hear it from therapist, either. I told Sheryl about the molestation when I was eleven. I didn't tell her, really. I just squirmed in my bed with the covers over my head for three days straight when she finally asked the question.

"Were you touched?" she asked with a lacerating sharpness in her voice, like she already knew the answer. After I told her yes, I had been, she talked with her twin, Shandy.

"Well, at least he didn't bust her," Shandy reckoned.

"WELL, THEN WHAT THE FUCK DO YOU CALL IT?!" demanded Sheryl. Shandy wouldn't talk to my mother for two years. Shandy was always forcing my mother to make choices and,

eventually, Sheryl would always choose Shandy and the Reptile, who constantly called me a dick tease. He never went all the way with me because, every time he tried, I cried really loud-- uncharacteristic for such a quiet child (an otherwise ideal choice for Teddy). He always stopped short, but I still bled; the Reptile would've made a grown mother of three cry and bleed. Then he'd stroke my hair and say, "Good girl." I figure Teddy must've been scared of waking up his older brother, Rich. Rich may've been a disgusting human being, but he'd have beat the shit out of Teddy if he'd known. Or so I thought. My guess is that he DID wake up, he DID see, and said nothing (to the authorities, at least).

So, years later when I was having chronic panic attacks, The Twins both decided it would be a great idea if I went to see Dr. Sutton, Shandy's fuck buddy, for some therapy. It's no wonder then, when I went, he was squirming more than I was. I didn't understand it at the time. (I didn't understand it until a couple minutes ago, actually.)

Of course I saw Sutton! He'd been diddling Shandy, the Reptile's mother, for years. I can only imagine what Shandy must've said, "Sort the little bitch out, Carl, or I'll tell everyone about the strap-on, you fucking faggot!" And, just in case Carl couldn't sort me out, she banished Teddy to Pennsylvania for seven years until the statute of limitations expired.

During Teddy's hiatus, Shandy decided to relax her harsh treatment and told me I could stop crop-picking her neighbor's goodies. Instead, she made me stuff the lawn lambs she sold by the truckload at craft shows. Tri-State residents love fake lambs on their front lawns for some strange reason.

But the lambs didn't help, so, during our first session, I told Dr. Sutton I was a monster because I was probably doomed to hurt other children just like Teddy had hurt me.

"No, honey," Dr. Sutton said, "that's not your way."

"But that's what's supposed to happen, right? Shandy said

Teddy hurt me because he'd been hurt."

"Not true. Most people believe it happens that way, but it doesn't. Not always. Teddy's sick, Kari."

Dr. Sutton prescribed Buspar for my panic attacks. I still didn't believe the bit about other kids, so I kept to myself. After my Sutton Sessions (all two of them), Sheryl asked: "Why the fuck did you like going to The Ranch all the time then?!" If she had read between the lines in my diary, she could've guessed. "Out with it!" Sheryl said. "Why did you like going over there all the time?!"

"Because I loved Shane," I told her. This probably confused her. Sheryl never understood what love was. Shandy said the same thing: "Your mother isn't right because she wasn't loved enough."

So, my traumas never slowed Sheryl's. I saw her hog-riding boyfriends: pop her in the face (broken nose); peel away as she was stepping off a cycle (broken femur); break pictures over her head (a few stitches); and many other atrocities. I'd called the cops a few times, and had seen the wrestling matches that would ensue between them and her boyfriends (and sometimes with Sheryl in the middle). After calling the cops on one such occasion, her boyfriend looked me dead in the eye with a kill face and said, "I'll never forgive you for this. EVER!" I stayed hunkered down by the kerosene heater, filling it up when dry, and kept watching TV.

Family outings were even better. We bounced off a median one time while Sheryl was under the influence. The Pat Benatar tune, "Hell Is for Children," was playing on the radio, and I believed her. We weren't buckled and I was scared shitless. My head hit the passenger window first, and then a second time when Sheryl's head crashed into mine from the centrifugal force.

"Stop crying!" she said, getting her bearings. "I'm all right! I'm all right!"

I wasn't.

We went to a wedding, which ended with another soused drive home. At a four-way stop, she kicked in the radio because she hated

Stevie Nicks: "Wait a minute baby, stay with me a while..." BAM, BAM, CRUNCH! Sheryl stepped out of the vehicle after and lay in the middle of the road in her dark green sateen bridesmaid dress. She screamed and kicked her legs all over the place and I could see her underwear through the gaping holes in her pantyhose. All the cars at the four-way stop watched. It was better than TV for them.

And I never told her about school, not that she ever asked. We'd moved away from the city and close to the suburbs where Sheryl had been husband-hunting. It was a rich school district. A.I. DuPont Middle School was adjacent to Westover Hills, an all-white community full of mansions and double-flipped Lacoste and oxfords. I was being razzed big time because of my Bo-Bo sneakers and quiet ways.

By seventh grade, everyone was picking boyfriends and girlfriends, and I didn't bother to get close to anyone. Not that I could; I didn't want to hurt anyone. I just kept to myself and decorated my paper bag book covers with "Ozzy" and "AC/DC." My classmates thought me satanic scum. Good, I'd thought. They should be scared.

Then my nightmares started. In this one, I'd always wear a little red one-piece swimsuit with yellow stripes up both sides. It's the suit I'd always slept in at The Fletcher Family Freak Show, and the suit that was always stripped off me by Teddy. Only, in the dream, he would escort me out to Cherokee, the horse with the long dong, and make me ride bareback. Seated in front of Teddy, still in the suit, I was being touched from behind. The businessman, Shandy's husband by that time (poor soul), and his son were on another horse, watching Teddy and me trot by from Gus's farm, the one on which marijuana was being grown. The dream would flash to a tub in Sheryl's apartment. I'd be in the bath with Shane and it would be black from us sitting in it. I was filthy. Then Sheryl would burst in and call me dirty bitch and say "Let's go shopping, Sexy Momma! It's Martin Luther Coon Day!"

I close the notebook. *I'm gonna be sick*, I think.

I haul ass to my room and throw up in the toilet. I return and keep writing.

What made The Twins and Company so evil? I'd heard all the stories about my grandfather, but was he really all to blame? If so, then I should be a slut, an addict (check), *or dead after a childhood with Sheryl. But I'm okay, I think. Or am I? If I had it to do over again, I'd have run away with the circus, but the circus found* me *instead. I wanted to matter. I wanted my pain to matter to Sheryl.*

I met Sheryl's father once. He came over to the house alone. My grandmother, Millie, had been divorced from him for ten years and was remarried to a better man. My grandfather was old and feeble, huffing and puffing from emphysema. I said hello, and he stared. He asked Sheryl where the closest liquor store was. I corrected her, and he shouted, "DON'T YOU FUCKING DO THIS TO ME!"

Okay, *I'd thought.* Find the store on your own, and I hope you die trying. *The Twins must not have minded how loathsome he was, because Shandy had named her firstborn after him and Sheryl invited him into her home for a spell. She said she hated his guts, but put him in the twin bed next to mine. Looking back, I felt like bait. Thankfully, though, he and I didn't much connect. I wasn't his kind of gal because I didn't shrink from fear (at least on the outside). I was great at remaining expressionless. I stared back at him; the Foat had been there the whole time.* I'm still alive, *I'd thought,* and I'm gonna live longer than you.

Sheryl used the Daddy Excuse all the time. "I'm doing the best I can! Look how I was fucking raised! He beat the shit out of me, Kari!"

Oh yeah, well I've been traumatized by more than one animal for as long as I can remember, and I still have a soul!

So?

I close my book and collect myself.

"Your mother is *Borderline*," Riza said on week number two.

"She's got connection issues and feels she's not worthy of love."

Whatever, I thought. *You can put that shit next to your Bucket and Sandcastle.*

Riza also called me on my shit earlier today after group. We had a *Kumbaya session* where a paper was passed around the room for every patient. Each had to write one nice thing about the other. We were given our papers at the end, and were instructed to read each other's comments. My accolades included: *good listener, smart, nice smile,* and other positives. But, when it was my turn to read, I made up my own comment to read aloud: "Kari has a nice ass." Everyone laughed, which was good because that's why I said it. I hated myself so much I couldn't even read the good things. I'd rather be a joke. Later, Riza's student sidekick came up to me and said she was really sorry that someone had been disrespectful. I told her I made the comment up. She straightened and said "interesting," then ran to Riza, I presume, because, during our next one-on-one session, Riza told me I'm worth more than my physical attributes.

Time for some peanut butter! I think, and go to the kitchen and, once again, come up empty *(fucking Noah!).* I mope back to my table and sit with Mr. Kinkade. The jigsaw, once completed, will render a small cottage, with a post and house number. It will be spring, and the flowers will be pink, purple, and blue. The background will have rolling greens and a clear sky.

So Walmart lovely.

◆ ◆ ◆

After Miss Dorothea horned-in on my skies this morning, I checked my email and saw a message from an old college friend, pregnant with her third kid. *She's brave.* I'll never bring another kid into the world. My college friend is one of the doe-eyed ones or, better yet, a sheep. The Sheep-Wolf scenario applies. Children are lambs. And what other animal but a sheep would be foolish enough to bring a lamb to the slaughter? Sheepdogs don't really help, either. They're on TV and in movies and writing books, while the wolves are running our country and telling our Sheepdogs to go to other flocks and kill lesser wolves.

A few months before my breakdown in South Carolina, I was selected to go to the Pentagon to take a class on *How to Be a Joint Surgeon* (or how to be *A Big Maddick*--our lead medical officer in The Philippines with the itchy trigger finger and shiny boots). I walked into the Pentagon and saw long faces and leather briefcases. After filing into the classroom, comprised mostly of ring-knocking-full-colonel Air Force Academy alumni, we all introduced ourselves. The two-star general who ran the class jaw jacked with each of my classmates (his voice sounded like a box of rocks) and then he ended with me.

"Hello, I'm Commander Rhyan. I'm a director from Parris Island." (I'd said Parris Island, a Marine Corps Recruit Depot, and much more identifiable than Beaufort, a Lowcountry small town just above Savannah, GA. *Everyone* knew of Parris Island.)

"Okay!" he interrupted. "Let's get started."

He didn't care. Parris Island rang no bells. Oh, he knew the place, but an Air Force general inside the beltway (the I-495: a freeway that encapsulates D.C. like a cyst) doesn't care about such *hors d'oeuvres*. They'd rather chuck the *balut* and get to the meat.

I lived on Parris Island. I drove past recruit graduations regularly. Once they were recruits. Now they'd become Marines--some with their own Circus Bears huffing and puffing behind them on the way to the parade grounds. I always wanted to shout out of the window, "GO BACK!" Run away from this place because there is something far worse than being a *balut*, and that's being a *Balut* in Uniform. If you thought your ass was owned at home by a family full of chain-smoking, Fox News-watching, racist, oily, weather-beaten assholes, then you have no idea the perverted proportions your indentured servitude will assume once you're handed over to The Cyst. That is, until you see a body ripped apart, and then are expected to make like nothing happened.

Or maybe that's just me....

Yep, my college friend is brave. Smart, too. She aced Western Civ, which wasn't easy because our professor, Mr. Abernathy, a cranky Vietnam Vet (not to be confused with *Crank Vet*), was tough. He used one book, Howard Zinn's *A People's History of the United States,* to preach the truth, way before Zinn enjoyed more mainstream popularity in the nineties. And we listened, too, because Mr. Abernathy had a prosthetic leg. He was a former Marine Corps captain who hated war. Hated, hated, hated it. He said the only good thing that came out of the war was meeting his wife, a former lieutenant and the Navy nurse who cared for him. Mrs. Abernathy was my sophomore year nursing instructor. I trucked over to her classroom every Monday and Wednesday, right after her husband's class let out. *I can join the Navy like she did,* I'd thought. *I could maybe even meet the love of my life.* Amazing how the prospect of love outweighs a missing limb. The Navy it was! Sheryl wanted me to go in the Army, as her father had done before me (and as Teddy did eventually), but *no way.* I chose the Navy because The Abernathys turned out "okay." I ran into them in the hallways a couple months before graduating and told them I was to be commissioned.

"Oh...." they both said somberly. Mr. Abernathy broke the silence. "You're gonna do great things, kid."

"Take care of your patients," Mrs. Abernathy advised before looking at her husband and walking away.

"Food's here!" shouts Noah.

We ordered P.F. Chang's. I get the bill. I pick up the tab a lot because I'm the highest-ranking officer and make the most dough. "Rock-Paper-Rank" gets me out of most shit duties, especially as President, so I spoil the juniors. Good food is good morale. I sign the bill and notice an extra sixty-two dollars worth of Crab Wonton.

Savages.

Chapter 11

I rant all the time on Facebook (yeah, I'm one of those people). My posts and comments have been so nasty I've been booted from two (or ten) friends' lists so far. I'll make a joke out of almost anything and will try to mindfuck anyone if the mood suits me, but I really only end up mindfucking myself. If Foating or Phantoming doesn't work, then I'll Facebook. It's my *Golden Dick,* a schtick I return to over and over. Only I'm not some white trash talking storyteller with a shitty dismount. Shandy and The Fletchers unknowingly grew themselves quite the formidable raconteur, one with razor-sharp timing.

You're no hero, the Phantom observes.

No shit. And I don't wanna be.

I haven't been firing on all cylinders since *Act of Valor.* Which is to say I'm on a tirade, lashing out against all sorts of patriotic propaganda. It's pretty easy, actually, seeing as how all my Facebook friends are social and fiscal Navy conservatives: they fancy themselves Sheepdogs, but they're all a bunch of sheep. How does the saying go? *We're here to defend democracy, not to practice it.*

Just this morning I read a post about how great *American Sniper* was: *The man was a warrior and was called home to his Lord when his duty was complete. He's an example of what loyalty and honor are all about.*

It was too good to pass up, so I cracked my knuckles and commented: *No one, dead or alive, should be revered for taking another life--let alone 150 of them. Nor should anyone boast about his kills. It's in poor taste, quite frankly, as is this post. And, by the way, you're a fucking idiot.*

The Worm loved it (being that it was his post).

You're a troll! he wrote. *The movie wasn't even about his kills.*

No? Then why in the hell was the movie made in the first place?

Stop being an over-sensitive liberal. Here's a life jacket. Swim back to the ship!

That's a good one, I wrote. *Ever been to Iraq or Afghanistan?*

What's that got to do with it?

I rest my case.

You're still a Troll! he countered.

And you're still a fucking Nancy! I told him, before signing off. No biggie--just a couple field grade officers acting like turds in front of the whole world. Tax payer dollars at work. But Worm and those like him are too banal to pick on now. I'd rather pick on ants. At least ants clean their dead off the sidewalks. My comments, my missives, my *kills*--because the Phantom thinks them so--are strewn over everyone else's newsfeeds. It's insidious, and it's sad, and it accomplishes nothing. It's just the gnashing of teeth. POP, RAKE, POP, POP.

I used to be like Worm with all his patriotic bullshit, dispatching all sorts of *wisdom* when I first returned from Afghanistan: *While you enjoy this Memorial Day, don't forget to say a prayer for all who died to keep us safe.*

Not too provocative, but listen:

While you enjoy this Memorial Day...Translation: While all of you are eating on the knoll...

Don't forget to say a prayer...Translation: Pray! I don't care if it's to Jesus or the ewe you're beer-goggling. Please, God, don't forget to pray...

For all who died to keep us safe...Translation: For me. You don't have to think about the dead because I dream about them for you every night.

Since returning from Afghanistan, I'm so encumbered by fear and hate, the thought of the world going on without me is just too much to bear. Alive nor dead, I've transitioned to a world in between--where the Kid follows me around the house with a wine glass because she knows her mommy needs it--some parallel that's so awful it makes me wish for death. I've woken up, goddammit, and I'm disoriented as hell. *I need a long sleep.* After my period of canned patriotism, I morphed and lashed out, hating this *new* world, and damning it for all it ever was.

Fry the bastard! I'd posted about an Army soldier who lit up a village, killing a bunch of Afghani women and children. I received Likes and *Hell Yeah*s, but the one comment that provoked me more than the initial media blitz was:

Come on Kari....

I hadn't heard from Mary in a year. *Hello, Mary,* I replied. *It's the kids. You know....*

But all this anger? she wrote. *It's not your way.*

It's unforgivable, I insisted.

He's ILL, Kari. Omnes Honorate. HONOR ALL.

She wrote the same thing when I posted, *Private Reward for the Heads of the Boston Bombers* and, my favorite, *Modest Meat Source Proposal by McDonalds after Child Porn Verdict Convicts Seven.* The Canary was right; Teddy was worse than Bastion. Mass murders aside, every time I read posts about child molesters and child murderers, I spin up so much that the only thing that calms me down is calling for blood. I'd read a story about a man who raped and strangled a five-year-old and dumped her body on the side of the highway in a pile of roadkill.

I HOPE THE INJECTION BURNS! I commented.

Omnes Honorate, Mary relied.

Yeah, yeah, yeah, I told her.

How's the little one? Mary asked, changing the subject.

Happy and healthy. (I assumed, since I can't tell a Brit I'm stuck in the clink. Not them.)

It's Day 31, and I'm really trying to turn the amplitude down on this "new me," who's acting more like a fifteen-year-old than a woman. I have no filter. I'm like Millie with her SNAP, CRACKLE, and POPS. I'm like Rodney, only I'm not bitching about the five dollars the bank stole from me. I'm like Zeke, who got hauled away to The Eff U last night, but I ain't a puncher. No, sir. I'm never goin' by way of the Window-Licker. I'm not "distructful" as Sheryl calls me.

I'm working my Kinkade Cottage, instead, as Miss Dorothea decides to stand next to me and help. We've gelled the last few days. She'd told me about an incident that happened when she first worked at a trauma center "ages ago." I'd kept my eyes on Kinkade, grunting every now and then.

"I worked in the ER just like you. Not in the military, but right here in Tampa. Began working there a few years after I got my nursing pin. I saw the run of the mill stuff. You know, belly aches, chest pains, and scrapes. Every once in a while, though, you get a bad one. Not the kind *you* saw, but it just about sucked the life outta me, the first one."

Grunt.

"Young man came in with one leg okay and one leg not. He was in a real bad car accident. I was taking off his clothes. Turns out his legs were the least of it. Guts were all over the place."

Grunt.

"I put a wet dressing on the belly and looked at his leg. Mangled. I tried to remove the splint. It wasn't tied that good anyway. So I pulled on it, but it wouldn't budge. I kept pulling and pulling until the doctor came up behind me and told me to stop. I'd been pulling on the poor man's femur."

I look up from my cottage and into Miss Dorothea's eyes, but she's staring off into space.

"Femur didn't look human. Looked like a big wood splinter. You know?"

"I do," I say, then offer "It sounds like you did your best." Riza says that we have to give people positives, or genuine compliments, because it helps to fend off our own negative funk. I may as well start with Miss Dorothea.

"Anyways, after that I was transferred because...I suppose I just checked out. Stopped talking for the rest of that day. Then a week went by. I was barely holding it together by the end of the month when they moved me. I couldn't stomach the blood and guts. Not for *one* day. You managed to do it for *months*! The way you feel now. Where you're at now, in this place. It's where you're *supposed* to be. You're a strong woman, stronger than me. So, now that I've said that, when you gonna let your guard down? I ain't the boogey man."

I'd been fiddling with a piece of my Cottage and didn't know what to say, so I say "soon" because it's only one word, and it could be the truth.

"You're doing good, Kari. Real good, and I'm proud of you. The nurses, you know, we all talk and we all wager, and we wager you're gonna be fine."

"Thank you, ma'am. I hope so, too."

"But Imma keep gettin' on you about Walmart! You keep to yourself too much, and that's no good. Trust me, I tried that."

"I'll go next time," I mumble.

"Good! And open that notebook. You been carrying it around all day. Haven't seen you write one thing."

Miss Dorothea walks away to retrieve old "Mr. Faithful," her vital signs machine, and calls each one of us over. She informs me that she'll be calling on me last, so I take her hint and crack on with Bastion. I glance at my Snapshot full of morning casualties. I note the last patient, *Closed Head Injury (Insurgent)*.

I remember him.

After the little girl with the burn...died, we received an insurgent with a bonk on the head. He'd been captured after planting the IED that blasted off a Marine's legs, the Double Amp currently being resuscitated by Gemma, Mitch, Jeff and six other Green Butcher Smocks.

I take the insurgent with Mary. I didn't treat the insurgents differently; my robot ways prevented me from emoting most of the time. That was how Bay One became mine. But, this time, I was on Bay Five. Boring. The insurgent had been cold-cocked and wouldn't be waking up any time soon, so we stripped, stuck, and monitored him until we could get him to Smitty.

The Double Amp comes out of CT and is wheeled into the OR with the Blue Scrubs for muscle salvation. I get a good look at him (the Marine, Brian's friend, with the red suede Nikes who buzzed in on a Segway. Jesus...Red Blazer).

Finally, it's the insurgent's turn for a spin in the CT and, to do it properly, we need at least four bodies to transfer the patient from the gurney to the platform. An American doctor takes the head to manage his C-Spine because we always operated on the assumption that all patients had a spinal injury until it was ruled out.

Mary takes the upper body and I get the lower for the transfer. The doctor counts off. On three, Mary and I roll the patient, while Benny gets the transfer slide underneath him. When the patient is on his side, the doctor jiggles the head. Bobbles, actually (perhaps lethally).

Mary, Benny, and I share looks over the patient. And, after we complete the transfer and the doctor walks away, Mary and Benny approach me.

"Did you see what he did?" asks Benny.

"What?"

"What he did to that patient's neck!" Benny whispers. "It about made me sick!"

Mary cuts her eyes at me, waiting.

"I didn't see nothin'," I mutter and run to the bathroom to throw up. I come back in time to transfer the patient from the CT back to the gurney. Mary is at the head of the bed this time, counting for the transfer. After we have the patient back in the Bay, she tells Benny to buzz off.

"I don't understand, Kari."

"Neither do I." (I'm a fucking coward.)

"It's small, it's round, it bounces on the ground, it's your mum!" Benny has shifted gears already, and is serenading Emma, who's up from the ward helping Mitch transport a soldier from the Royal Irish Guard--he's got appendicitis and laughs so hard he hurts

himself.

"*Wanker," says Emma. "Kari?"*

"*Huh?"*

"*Have any chocolate?"*

"*No," I say. "I won't have any five minutes from now either."*

"*Cheeky fuck."*

As soon as Emma and her patient leave, Benny and Gemma begin prepping Bay Four for another head injury--a Marine. J-Chat says it's just a concussion from a rollover, so I balk.

"*You guys can handle this, right?" I say.*

Gemma asks me to stay because "What if J-Chat's full of shit again?" which seems to be the case because CPR is in progress as the ambulance doors open. The Marine is white as a sheet. Larry pushes through to see the action like he always does, but this time he pushes me. It isn't a nudge, either. I'm sent into the storage cabinet and almost fall on my ass.

"*Fuck this shit!" I strip off my Jack Sparrow and march outside.*

"*Don't go, Kari!" Mary yells after me. "We need you!"*

"*YOU DON'T NEED ME!" I yell as I walk out the door.*

I throw-up in the gravel and yell more between heaves. "THIS IS A GOAT FUCK! THAT BASTARD *PUT HIS HANDS ON ME!* I CAN'T KEEP DOING THIS SHIT! I CAN'T! YOU GOT ONE ASSHOLE OVER HERE CRANING HIS FUCKING NECK, AND ANOTHER OVER THERE CRACKING'EM!"

Early on in the tour, Larry was giving me the vibe and I, in turn, told him I was gay. "Oh, I understand," he said. "I took Psych 101." Larry said in the same breath that he could tell a gay from a mile away. I told Val, and she dubbed him a Reprehensible Glory-Seeking Cunt. It made sense to me. But, all bullshit aside, that was My Marine he pushed me away from. That's how seriously we took our assignments. The Stew and The Way had been breached.

"*He was MY MARINE!" I say between heaves.*

Mary watches me vomit for a second with her hands on her hips.

"I know, Kari. It's fucking mad, this."

I wave her away. "THIS?! THIS *IS FUCKING MARS! IT'S A FUCKING JOKE! NOW LEAVE ME ALONE!*"

"Take your time. Collect *yourself. I'll be back in a bit, yeah?*"

"Yeah. Whatever..."

Tully, Gemma, and I "Hot Wash" during lunch at the Scoff House. A Hot Wash is an after action *meeting (formal or informal), where members of a trauma team do a quick wrap up. Areas for improvement are typically discussed. Not us, though; no need. Instead, Tully has one eyebrow raised and is checking out the soldier in the front of the line. But Tully isn't a sex pest, like I'd be if I weren't such a Gilligan. Being single on tour, I should be.* Where's the love of my life any goddamn way? *I should be shagging left and right, but I'm "too odd to pull," according to Tully.*

One of our British general surgeons, a short man of Indian persuasion, is also a weirdo, but he's got the confidence factor. I'd been looking for him earlier to consult on a hand trauma.

"Have you seen Plastics?" I asked Tully.

"Yeah," he replied. "He came in with a pashmina wrapped around his neck, hugged a couple of girls, and left. Randy bastard."

You do what you have to. Get your kicks where you can. I don't judge. It's none of my goddamn business. I'm not the matrimony police. Some, like Plastics, only need a hug or two to get by. Some need a shag like Larry. And some, when they're not on call, need a nip of vodka in the chapel. That's what Gemma and I did; I'd gotten a package from an old friend in California I'd met prior to my move to South Carolina. Chuck was an old Vietnam vet from Marine 1/9, or "The Walking Dead," who'd lost all his friends. So, every Friday for thirty-plus years, he'd been visiting the Marine patients on the ward.

I should've known something was up when Chuck's package clinked. "I say we put the kettle on in the chapel," said Gemma, "cuz' no one EVER goes in THERE."

She was right. God wasn't part of the mix. He really should've been, but he wasn't. All that praying stuff would've just fucked up our robots. And so we drank. Not enough to get drunk, but plenty enough to get warm. In the chapel we talked about everything but trauma. I'd asked her:

"So, when you watch the Olympics, aren't you REALLY watching just to see what the Americans do?"

"What?! No."

"Come on, 'the whole world has 'eyes on us', right?"

"Rubbish," she said.

She told me NASA had called Great Britain and said we Americans weren't the center of the universe. Funny, because Larry had once referred to Great Britain as "America's Retarded Little Cousin."

Tully, Gemma, and I get our curry and sit at an empty table by the tent's exit flap. Abi comes up to the table, and I let Gemma and Tully field the questions. I feel so goddamn sorry for her, but I can't look in her big blue eyes and see that big blue optimism. So, I look over her shoulder and see, next to the bug juice, or Kool-Aid, a corpsman I knew from Kuwait. Petty Officer Wilson was eighteen when I met him and wanted to get into the shit, but there was no shit to get into in Kuwait. He kept complaining about how bored he was, so I sent him to the ER where a kid lay dead, having been in a high-speed motor vehicle accident on a Kuwaiti highway. A young nurse corps lieutenant was in the ER, doing the postmortem care by himself (he'd been training for the Chaplain Corps, so the dead were his bag).

I insisted Wilson join him. Wilson wouldn't be the same for the rest of the tour, growing more quiet and isolated. The young lieutenant chastised me for blindsiding Wilson.

Now, I call Wilson over. We get to talking, and I apologize.

"No need to apologize, ma'am. It taught me a lot. It bothered me then, but it doesn't bother me now."

"*Just back from Sangin?*" *I asked.*

"*Hell yeah! I'm in the shit now, doing all sorts of stuff. I'm using my wits,*" *he points to his temple.* "*I'm starting cricothyrotomies and placing chest tubes. I get inventive with kids. I mean...they're dead if I don't.*"

"*How many times you deployed?*"

"*Four, second time here. Went to Iraq once, but Afghanistan's different. You know?*"

"*I do.*"

"*It's funny because I feel like I'm just getting my groove, and now we gotta go home. Already making plans to come back, though. My chief's gonna hook me up.*"

"*How's your family?*"

"*I'm divorced.*"

"*Seems like you should be one rank higher,*" *I observe.* "*What happened?*"

"*Got busted down.*"

"*How are YOU?*"

"Honestly, ma'am, I don't know." (Wilson would tell me years later that failing to save a life in the field was the worst pain imaginable, "but," he said, "I'll be damned if I'm going to miss out on all the beautiful shit in this life.")

Wilson has a lot of beautiful shit in his life, a daughter for one. Friends, for another--not to mention breathing, which is in and of itself an art.

I say goodbye to Wilson and we make our way back to the hospital for the afternoon session. On the way we pass a group of Royal Air Force string musicians playing the Beatles' "Eleanor Rigby" in a circle, under a tent, next to a group of Gurkhas, who are smoking and listening.

"*My mum loves that tune,*" *says Gemma.*

PM SNAPSHOT – Bastion – Day 184

- KIA U.S. Marine

- Appendicitis (U.K. Royal Irish Guard)

My Big One's about six hours away, but that's enough for today. We've got Art Therapy and I'm ready for another domino; I lost my "Joel." We head over to Patchouli, and back to our U configuration. There's no more Sylvia, so I'm left alone to handle Stefano. We're to make papier-mache masks that represent our inner strength.

By the time we're done, among us are The Green Lantern, Batman, Hulk Hogan, and a little girl with freckles and shrews in her face. Her eyes are gray, and the ends slant down, and she's wearing glasses, and she's crying. Her lips are red. The red is a closed zipper.

Patchouli says we have to name our piece.

I write *OP MINIMIZE* on the sloughing newspaper behind my eyes, and head to my room for a quick lie down.

On the way, I pass Brian's room. He's taping up another picture of his wife Jessie and their three children.

I peek my head in. "Beautiful family," I say.

"Thanks," he replies. "They're my life."

BOOK III

JESUS WEPT

Chapter 12

Like a pit viper, the voice stretches out of the phone. "Yell-O?"

"Hi, Mom."

"HEY!" It's one in the afternoon, and Sheryl is three sheets to the wind. "Ain't *I* the one that supposed to be callin' *you?* Happy Birthday, kid!"

"Thanks."

Sheryl asks me how it feels to be forty. I tell her it feels like fifty. "Oh, don't I know it! And it only gets worse, believe me."

"I heard the Comptroller came by."

"Oh, yeah," she says. "Him and his wife. The wife is *sooo* attractive. Not like us average girls."

That's *interesting,* as Riza's student sidekick says: Sheryl can't give another person a compliment without "cutting herself up," but neither my mediocrity or maturation (Sheryl's version, at least) are on my agenda today. "Thanks for the package," I offer.

"Package? Oh, *she* did that. Not me." (My Spouse sent peanut butter, Kid photos, and a red velvet cake.)

If things had been "all good" at home, I'd know it. But Sheryl's "yell-o" was all I needed; my survival depended on reading my mother's cues. Cake or no cake, I knew all hell was breaking loose in Cackalacky, and I needed a window in. If I confront Sheryl right away, I'll be cut off and dressed down. I can't have that: I don't want my Spouse and Kid to take the brunt of the load.

No, in this instance, the conversation needs to meander; Sheryl often says she never knows I'm fighting with her until she starts to feel stupid. Gilligan meets The Nutty Professor, but I'm tired of mincing words, and I'm raging so fucking bad right now I could leap through the phone. My reasoning is gone. Kari has left. I want to bash Skipper's face in with a conch shell and choke the living shit out of her. Sheryl, I've been informed, hit my daughter last night. The Kid was in the kitchen talking to my Spouse. After the slap, my Spouse pushed Sheryl away, and Sheryl, in turn, slapped my Spouse on the side of the head. *Sheryl loves the headshots.* When I was six, she pounded me on the head over and over after I'd wiped her spit off my cheek. She'd been screaming in my face for "cutting her up." I hadn't been trying to defy her. I just didn't want spit on my face. Try telling that to a lunatic. Sheryl hit me so hard, for so long, I just surrendered as usual.

"I saw stars," my Spouse said. "I felt the hate loud and clear."

So the motive *was* there after all; my Kid was being punished for having had the audacity to bond with another woman, now her adoptive mother. Though my Spouse had been "the cause" of *the* Kid being slapped, I can only imagine what Sheryl would've done to the Kid had she provoked Sheryl for another reason, and my Spouse hadn't been around. My Kid isn't like me. She's got something special: righteous indignation, call it. The Kid doesn't cower from Sheryl. *The Kid cowers from me.*

Sheryl's loathing of others, whether in my life, or the Kid's, had been there from day one (except for Rodney, who "does shit around the house"). The Skipper even got snarky with the Filipino nanny I hired after my soon-to-be-ex-husband left. Sheryl was fresh off her *Blitzkrieg* in Florida, lighting up "nips" left and right, so, when the time came, she snatched the Kid out of the nanny's arms as soon as the door opened. "I'm here now. You can go," she said, waving her away. "You're no longer needed." Admittedly, I was thankful for the restraint Sheryl showed (one of my ever-present bogus silver linings: *Well, it could've been worse,* I'd thought, *so go ahead and give the nanny a nod and be sure not to thank her for all of the love and care and instruction*). So, I'd nodded and done just that. The nanny looked at me as Mary had when I told the Pediatrician in Bastion to stop crying, and as Gemma had after I admitted I was lonely as hell. That look said: *Kari is in trouble and there's nothing I can do to make it better.*

Riza had given me a book, *Trauma and Recovery,* to demystify Sheryl's control. In it, Dr. Judith Herman details a subterranean coping mechanism displayed in chronically-abused children. Doublethink: *Though (the abused child) perceives herself as abandoned to a power without mercy, she must find a way to preserve hope and meaning. The alternative is utter despair, something no child can bear. To preserve her faith in her parents, she must reject the first and most obvious conclusion that something is terribly wrong with them.*

Sheryl requires constant attention and submission from everyone, but I'm the only one who gives her what she wants day in and day out. This is my fate. My Spouse and nanny were punished just as I'd been punished--in my case, for wanting to learn about my father (and, now, for marrying again). The trouble is my Spouse thinks I'm worth more than a meal ticket, and that the Kid is more than "a little bitch," as Sheryl calls her. My Spouse says *I'm* beautiful and kind and honorable--the good kind (not the insta-honor the commandant confers with military rank and file).

I love being loved for who I am, whatever that is.

I'm gonna kill my mother. I shift in my seat, listening to Sheryl's rundown of bullshit events. *I'm going to shoot her.* Fitting, as I recall, the last question I'd always ask before falling asleep was whether or not she'd live forever. She lied so I would sleep. Sleep that'd been interrupted by a monster and, now, infected by vampires. *At least Teddy didn't bust her,* Aunt Shandy reckons. *At least it's not combat,* as Big Navy confirms.

Sheryl updates me on the *The Sons of Anarchy* and *The Biggest Loser* while I reach back for evidence: This is the first time Sheryl has hit the Kid, though I wonder, because I'd taken my four-year-old to a pre-school physical after returning from Bastion, and the resident who performed the exam told me the Kid displayed the social mannerisms of a two-year-old. (Not to mention, I'd utilized scare tactics, "Let the doctor see the roach in your ear." I've used fear to subdue my child since she was born. Why? Because I'm scared shitless of *everyone* and *everything* myself.) The Kid wouldn't let the doctor come close to her, and she wouldn't talk. Instead, she balled herself up in a corner on top of the exam table. The resident advised me to watch the behavior as I beat back the possibility that Sheryl had been abusive.

But now I knew for certain. "How's the Kid?" I interrupt.

"She's fine, but the little bitch won't give me a break! I was trying to watch my shows, and she kept sneakin' back into the living room. I threw her ass back in the bedroom and told her to go the hell to sleep."

Poor little girl. I'd been sleeping with the Kid since she was born. I'd been petrified when I found out I was pregnant with a girl. After her birth, I kept her close around-the-clock. *No one will ever take this one by surprise,* I told myself. They'd have to get past me. Me, who keeps a switchblade in my pocket and a gun in my nightstand. Me, who wonders why I ever entrusted the Kid to Sheryl in the first place. Me, who's still stuck in a nut hut with a red velvet sugar rush, having devoured my blood-red cake with its bone-white frosting. The cake-- All Saccharine with Zero Triggers--was gone after ten minutes. *Savages....*

I broke my Kid of the big bed after I met my Spouse, but the transition was tough going up until my leaving for The Willows. One of us still had to lie with her in her twin bed until she fell asleep. I feel guilty to this day because it had been my doing. It was my hang-up. It was my fear that had gotten to her.

"Stop calling her a bitch," I tell Sheryl.

"Why? I call you a bitch, and it doesn't bother you."

"It bothers me. You just never asked."

"Stop being so damn oversensitive."

"Stop hitting my Kid, and maybe I'll think about it."

Sheryl gasps like a clogged vacuum because Sheryl always gasps whenever I backtalk or cut her up or stick up for myself in any way, shape, or form. Luckily, I'm not within spitting distance.

"Oh, *she* told you that, huh?! Well, she's a fuckin' liar just like your bitch sister." Cassie, who stopped taking Sheryl's whimsy a few years back, forwarded me an email she received from Sheryl, in which she complained about my Spouse and called both of us lezzies and dykes.

"And, besides that," Sheryl says, "I've been this way all my life, so what's the big fuckin' deal?!" She laughs, but this joke isn't funny anymore.

"You are so hateful."

"Oh, gimme a break. You're the same damned way. I've seen the shit you post on Facebook. You're a commander! Have some respect for yourself! Stop being so distructful!"

"You don't know anything."

"No one MADE you go over there, Kari! That shit came with the job, and now you're bitching and moaning."

"Like my molestation came with The Ranch?"

"I-didn't-molest-you! How many times do I have to tell you?!"

I refuse to allow Sheryl to derail me. "If you're going to remain in the house," I tell her, "you must treat others with respect--including the clerks at the hospital." (Gasp.) "My PTSD is real, by the way. I know you've been spreading rumors to the contrary." (Gasp.) "How long have you been hitting my Kid?"

"Pfft!" she says. "*Your kid...*"

"I'm sorry?"

"All you do is fuckin' ignore her!"

"Because I'm in FUCKING PAIN!"

"Well BOO-HOO! I had it way worse than you! And I'll call you a DYKE if I want to because that's what you are, so what's the big fuckin' deal?!"

Thud. Rage: blind rage so powerful I want to rip out the phone and whip the stiff metal cord against the drywall. I'll chip out a crevasse and peel it away with my fingertips until they bleed down to my macerated knuckles. I want to tear the shit-shack down.

"You know what you are, Mom?"

"This should be good," she says.

"You're a white trash piece of shit who takes absolutely no responsibility whatsoever for all the nasty things you've done and I'M TIRED OF FUCKING PAYING FOR IT!"

"KARI RHYAN!" shouts Miss Dorothea.

I hold up the phone and cup the receiver. I take a couple quick breaths, but breathing isn't working. "I'm sorry, I'm sorry, I'm sorry!" I tell her. I don't like to make Miss Dorothea mad. I don't like to make anyone mad, but these days I'm finding out that, to take back my life, some people gotta go--people who say they've always been there for me, people who use words like *daughter* and *friend* and *sister*, and people I'll see on their deathbeds one day. But *I'm* the one in a death throe; Skippers and Rodneys and Reptiles have been gnawing at my bones, but they can't have my marrow. *YOU CAN'T TAKE IT ALL!*

"Jesus' sakes!" Miss Dorothea says. "Who you talking to like that?"

"My mother," I say.

"*Child*...take that dirty talk down ricky-tick. You better than that."

I tell her okay and put the phone back to my ear and get nothing but a dial tone. It feels good to be forty and all grown up, *but not really*. There's no joy in taking it back. My life always belonged to Sheryl, and I'm not convinced I can live without her. Sheryl is my world, and she's told me since birth that the world "out there" was far worse.

I believed her: Just after I was commissioned, during the few years I'd escaped from my mother's clutches, I'd met another female officer. She pursued me for six months and became my first girlfriend, but she left me after a year, saying homosexuality was a sin, and that we were *wrong*. I felt worthless. And, yes, I felt *wrong*. She stayed in my life, though, calling me whenever she needed a boost. She toyed with me for a decade. It was around the time of the break up that Sheryl's marriage fell apart. I guess Sheryl and I were both lonely. I guess I am complicit in my own abuse. I may've wanted to get my sister and myself out of Sheryl's nasty nest all those years ago, but after being dumped and called wrong, all I wanted was my Mommy. I'd kept the relationship a secret from Sheryl because she said "dykes are confused." And I was confused as hell. Scared, too: *Don't Ask, Don't Tell* was still in full swing. So, I swore off all women until I was thirty-six, just before Bastion, when I'd eventually come out to Sheryl.

"I'm gay," I told her, sobbing my eyes out.

"I know," she said, crestfallen.

Riza says I have to take back my life. "Do it, Kari. The joy comes later."

I don't know about any joy. As of late, I've been daydreaming of lining-up Sheryl, Shandy, Rich, and Teddy execution-style. I don't use my switchblade or my pistol. I use a bat. I start with Rich because he's Shandy's first born and "The Christ Child," as Sheryl calls him, jealous for even her twin's twisted affections for her son. "Shandy threw rocks at me when we were kids," my mother told me. I'll be damned if I ever vie for the attention of someone like that.

So, my Canary asks, *why are you vying for Sheryl's?*

She's done with that shit, the Phantom figures, because I'm going for The Christ Child's knees. *Ting! Ting!* I use an aluminum bat to gauge the sweet spot. *Ting!* That's it. *POP!* He wails. I breathe twelve breaths per minute--no more no less. I leave the dog where he lies.

Then Teddy. *Ting!* That's the one. *POP! POP!* His kneecaps, cantilevered to nothing, float. Teddy screams. I breathe. Then a ground rule double to the head--just enough to get him supine. I need him vulnerable. I need a clear shot. Here comes the pitch...and...BAM! It's a triple to the cock! It's more than enough to make him cry and vomit and beg me to stop. *Look familiar? SOUND*

FAMILIAR?! I prop him against a wall because, let's face it, my bases are loaded, and I'm going for the grand slam. I'm going to explode. *YOU HEAR THAT, TEDDY?!* The Phantom is screaming. *IT'S YOUR TURN TO BLOW!* I get in the batter's box and I keep my eyes on the ball, or, in this case, the boil on his left cheek. *Ting, Ting...BAP!* The cheek gives. Twelve breaths. Blood pours from his eyes and ears and boils. I consider the blood spatter on his hands, still grasping his genitals. *Not dead yet,* I think. "Do I still have my dick?" he manages, blood gurgling. I remove his hands and unzip his pants. He's swollen and bleeding and I go at it with the bat so hard, and for so long, that it resembles a split hot dog on a campfire spit. I chuck conscience. *Bye, Bye Birdie.* I give Teddy one final whack to the head, and turn back toward the living--one wailing son and two sniveling motherfuckers--scared to death and all alone. "We're all alone," Teddy would tell me. Not anymore.

That's enough. I don't know how I'm going to kill the others yet, so I finally hang-up, silencing what has become a busy signal. I make way for Stefano (Baby Momma Two), and head across the lounge to beg Noah off the computer so I can email my Spouse at work. I write the instruction: *DON'T leave the Kid alone with Sheryl.*

It's Day 34 and *I've GOT to get home,* I think. I've got to frag my Skipper. She needs to walk the plank, along with her collections of bells, spoons, and souls. *And her little dog too!*

Maybe then the Deer Dream will stop. Riza tried to tell me earlier, but I didn't get it until today when I confirmed Sheryl's abuses. Sheryl is the doe with the slanted yellow eyes. I hadn't believed Riza--not even as I trolled over my Facebook posts and began deleting those from the Phantom et al., until there it was: the connection. The Deer Dream arose out of a story I'd posted, calling for the head of one child killer, Mario Andrette McNeill. He'd been found guilty of raping and killing five-year-old Shaniya Davis after purchasing her from her drug-abused mother. McNeil dumped her body on the side of the road among deer carcasses.

"Your mother is the doe in the bedroom," Riza had said. "She's always there, and always watching."

"Who's the buck at the top of the hill?...McNeil?... Teddy?"

"Teddy is the simple answer," she said. "Though I suspect it's something more." But Teddy made sense--a buck charging a bunch of helpless children. *In this world there is no Kari Rhyan.*

"It means I didn't die," I tell Riza. "I should be thankful."

"Maybe," Riza says.

I consider the buck as Big Navy and it fits like a glove. "I'm scared of dying and never mattering," I said.

"Bingo," said Riza. Shaniya Davis, dead and gone, mattered to me, and does still. Now, I want blood. I smell it when I zone out and taste it in dreams.

After sending off the marching orders for my Spouse, I head over to the Kinkade Cottage where Zeke sits. He always comes in on the tail end of the puzzle because he says it's easy and he doesn't have to think so goddamn much.

"So..." he stalls, "I have to do the autobiography thing now."

"Yeah?"

"Yeah. Two trips to The Eff U, so my therapist says I have to." Zeke got in a fight with Stefano, one that Zeke instigated. Stefano, in his slouching trousers and insouciance, is always an easy target for hard-asses like Zeke.

Miss Dorothea steps over to us. "You coming to the gym?" she asks Zeke while holding a basketball. He glances at Stefano, by the door with his back towards us.

"No," says Zeke. Miss Dorothea turns and walks away, and Zeke mutters, "I'm done with Nigger Tree Hockey." Miss Dorothea slows her pace for a beat, enough for me to gauge she's heard the remark, and proceeds to the gym with the others.

"*African* Tree Hockey," I correct, "and don't say shit like that."

"I call a spade a spade. There's a difference between black people and niggers. Stefano is a nigger."

"What does that make you?"

"What the fuck you talking about, ma'am?"

"You shoplift from Walmart." I spied him in the outdoor section putting something in his jacket yesterday. I'd been fixated on a small old lady with tremors. We'd had a week of torrential rain, and she was picking out an umbrella. As I watched her fumble with the mechanism, checking for functionality or holes (or whatever trembling old ladies check for), I was gripped with fear, thinking, *This world is too violent for people like her*. I wanted to scoop her up and take her away and rub her hands and make us tea, just like I'd wanted to do with my grandmother Millie the last time I laid eyes on her. She was in a nursing home and didn't know who I was and couldn't hear anything. She just started talking to me about how she, the oldest of seven, would trudge through five miles of snow to buy the pie her mother loved.

"She was always taking care of babies and I wanted to take care of her," she told me. *POP, PLUNK.* "I love the little babies, too."...*PLUNK.*

Millie was a housekeeper in the very hospital where I'd been born. She cleaned the nursery back then, and the staff allowed Millie to hold newborns, especially the sick or abandoned ones. Millie couldn't save her own babies from her monstrous husband, so I imagine she found the experience therapeutic until it wasn't; she'd hold the babies every day until they died. She must've held one dying baby too many. She was forcibly retired. Millie's boss told my mother, "I love Millie, always have. She's done her job without complaint." (Millie had been dubbed The Cleaning Ninja because of her silence, speed, and attention to detail). "But something's changed," her boss said. "She's not making sense. She's having outbursts, and it's scaring the staff. She needs help." Millie died the day I landed in Bastion. As the nursery was Millie's domain, so too was Bay One for me. We tidied and cleaned our spaces among the dead and dying. Yes, this world is too violent for sweet old ladies and babies. *You stay here, love, where it's warm and safe* while I watch this goober nick a fish-finder.

"Oh, that's just for kicks!" says Zeke. *Bullshit.* He'll hock it for pills when he gets out. Opana, a mega-narcotic, is all the rage with the kids back home. *Poor Zeke.* I can't blame him for it, with all the bad stuff he's seen and the friends he has lost. He's an angry, prejudiced little shithead, but I have a soft spot for the kid. I have to believe he can change, otherwise all hope is lost--something no *society* can bear.

I shake my head, and he changes the subject, "You still writing your autobiography?"

"Yeah. Almost finished, thank God."

"What kinda stuff happened to you?"

"My older cousin molested me for a couple years. Can't remember much of it."

I raise my eyes to meet his. "I'll kill that motherfucker if you want," he says.

"Thank you, but no. It's not that I don't want Teddy dead. I just want to do it myself."

"Just putting it out there. I'd kill Julien, too, in a heartbeat. Nasty bastard."

"Oh, come on," I say. "His negatives outweigh his positives."

Zeke grins, "Right."

"You have family trauma?" I ask.

"That's what they say. It's what my sister says too, but she's nothing but a hooker."

"For real?"

"Nah. She just likes getting in my business all the time."

Julien's mother, come to find, was an actual hooker. "A stupid fucking whore," as Julien put it. I sat in on his autobiography before he left for his court martial this afternoon. His mother made him wait outside in the cold while she brought in her tricks. He said he listened to her fuck all night, man after man, so she could go out and score meth. It was the same thing every day for four years until Child Protective Services intervened when he was thirteen and sent him to foster care. Had Julien been a girl, he may've been a Shaniya Davis, sold for meth. It's my theory that when Julien raped the thirteen-year-old girl he was probably raping his mother AND, in a way, himself. It doesn't make me understand Julien, or those like him. It just makes me a little less afraid of them. I may've wanted to smash in Julien's face during the days of Starbucky but, deep down, the little girl inside of me was curling up in a ball waiting for his instruction. And now? I just shake my head, much like I do with Zeke, and much like Miss Dorothea does with all of us.

Still, whatever horrors Shandy dished on Teddy, I can't shake the rage I feel towards him. And I can only guess what Shandy put him through. Teddy goes to therapy and AA, so he's "better now," per Shandy, who's still hoping for a family reunion. Sheryl may be my mother, but Shandy is the Grand Dame. "Can't you just get over it?" she always asks. "My dad put his hands on me and *I'm still standing*," she'd say, breaking into Elton John. Then I'd invariably Foat (on one particular visit, in my twenties, on the back porch next to Teddy's shoes. Evidence he was still living with Shandy, and, quite possibly, was even hidden away in the house).

Can't you just get over it?

Not long after my confession, Teddy did a stint in the Army and got married to a woman who had a six-year-old daughter. Shandy showed me pictures of Teddy with his new family. The girl looked...*muted. It continues.* Teddy, shortly after, divorced and is now a truck driver (soliciting underage lot lizards, I presume. But who's the real Reptile?). *It continues.* Teddy exposes my younger male cousins to pre-pubescent girls getting raped online, as I was recently informed. *It continues* and NO ONE is doing a goddamn thing about it. Teddy tells his younger cousins that he's a Navy veteran. He's trying to build ties with lies. *It continues.* It continues like war continues. Talk about it and you're labeled hysterical or a coward. There's nothing too egregious to glance over or too horrible to stay silent about. Can't I get over it? Fuck no, I can't. And, even more so, I won't.

Early in my career, I sat in as a jury member for a court martial. It was a molestation case so, while selecting the jury, the defense attorney asked if any of us had a molestation history. *Yeah, like I'm gonna admit that* amidst peers and lawyers. I never even admitted it to anyone outside of Sheryl and Shandy. *Go figure.* So, I stayed in the box and watched the pedophile's mother cry and carry on. She was small and sweet and said, "Everyone thinks my son is a monster except me." I sat in that box and cried because I felt her love for him. If a mother could love a monster, then was I something worse? The guy got three years (time served on a re-trial, unbeknownst to us he'd initially gotten nine years, and I got drunk for five). Julien hates his mother. I hate my mother, too, but I don't go around trying to fuck little kids. And, last time I checked, I'm not a racist asshole, either.

"Everybody thinks they know what's best for me," says Zeke, "but this is just a bunch of hokey bullshit."

"Zeke, you are ill. Keep repeating that to yourself," I tell him. "Now go apologize to Miss Dorothea."

Zeke says "Whatever," then goes for a smoke. I watch housekeeping prep Julien's old room for the next wolf or *balut*, and I thank my lucky stars I'll never have to see Julien again.

I stride up to a med moll and tell her I'm ready for my slurry as Zeke walks by and asks another magenta for an escort to the gym. I don't know if he'll apologize, but at least I called him on his shit. It's good *in vivo*.

After the slurry, I revisit *Rational Recovery's Grand Illusions* while seated in my beige recliner. *Grand Illusion One: Recovery from substance addiction has something to do with attending meetings where people talk about themselves.*

Ain't it the truth?! I think. But Riza says talking about trauma helps. Is that part of the Grand Illusion, too? I feel like I'm in an AA meeting whenever Rodney starts talking about war. Since that's true, then war is a drug. *Illusion One* goes on: *Many stay in AA because they are desperate for anything less frightening or disappointing than their own lives.* If that's true, too, I'm doomed to Rodney's circles and cycles for the rest of my life. Just a couple of cranky, dusty vets chasing their own tails.

Well, the Canary says, *fuck that.*

◆ ◆ ◆

We have an hour of pool time every afternoon. I'm never too keen on getting down to my bathing suit--not with the cloud that hangs over all of us, from basic insecurity to genuine fear. I hang my feet in the chlorinated water instead and am careful to mind the sun.

Brian sits next to me. "Sorry I won't be here for your Timeline," he says.

"Discharging today?" I ask.

"Yeah, finally. Longest ten-weeks of my life."

"Ten weeks?"

"It took me a little longer, too," says Brian, cocking his head toward Zeke at the other end of the pool.

"Sorry I wasn't there for your autobiography," I say. (I was outside jumping off a piling at the time. The Willows has a *Confidence Course*. It wasn't a problem for me because I'd leap off every time, half-hoping my harness would break.)

"It's okay," says Brian. "Same story anyways."

Brian opens his notebook to the center. He takes a bookmark and turns over a dirty brown patch. There's a horse's profile in the middle with *Martinez* written in black Sharpie in the upper-left-hand corner and *O Pos* in the upper-right. He hands me the patch. *Good to have met you, Brian Martinez.* I wish I could've said something cool like that. I wish I could've said anything at all. Instead, I'm squeezing the patch, looking down, and watching the tears drain off my bifocals into the pool.

"Thank you for taking care of my friends," he says. His buddies, warm transfers, were passed from him to me--*balut to balut.* He leaves so I can cry in peace.

I eventually put the patch in my pocket and wipe my tears away with a t-shirt sleeve. It's high noon, and I'm a ghost, pale and Foating. I change location to a patio chair with an umbrella. I open my composition book and write about my friends.

I loved my Brits, and they loved me. That's what we told each other in our own ways on the last day, or the day I've distilled from one hundred and eighty some-odd days in The Stew. I'd been accepted the day I met them, and was therefore deemed "somewhat" normal.

I stop writing and consider: Even now, after my online tirades, they accept me. *She's lost her head again,* but it's okay. Meanwhile, my command doesn't want to touch me with a ten-foot bearcat; they haven't called me, and I no longer expect them to. In the words of a recently retired Marine Corps general: *We need to come home like veterans...not characterized as damaged, or with disorders, or with syndromes or other disease labels...we should deny cynicism and giving-up simply as forms of cowardice.*

Right....

My command thinks I'm a malingerer, and those who don't, doubt their own better judgment. And although I know I have a problem--one I'd chew off my own thumbs to cure--my command's lack of interest is painful. The unkindest cut of all, it's far worse than labor pains and broken bones, worse than being molested, and worse than bagging once perfectly good twenty-year-old arms and legs. The pain of being labeled *weak,* overtly or otherwise, is killing me. *Perception is reality,* an old Navy captain once told me, and what I see in their eyes tells it all: *You're a crybaby and a coward.* Yes, I doubt my own illness. Even my mother thinks I'm faking, so I must be.

If I related this to my Brits, they'd tell me it's rubbish, but they're thousands of miles away, and I'm here writing about them. It's unfortunate: the most stable relationships I've ever had, other than with my Spouse, were in Bastion. Sometimes I wonder if I love my old teammates *because* they're so far away (except Rodney, who's up close and personal). My Brits, though, live on in nightmare. The Vampire dream always starts off in the chapel with Gemma. We're drinking just enough vodka to feel warm, as we really did drink in Afghanistan. (What's worse than a coward? Being a coward who drinks in the chapel. If I'm expected not to feel, then I'm going to drink. It's why I did it then. It's why I do it now. It's probably why I'm going to do it when I get out of here. I'm not normal, and the only people who make me feel normal are probably getting pissed as newts in some cobblestoned shamble even as I write this.) In the nightmare, I always walk out of the chapel and into a sea of blood with vampire teeth and torsos floating around. There's no Gemma. There's no Bastion. There's just me and them. And the blood. Always the blood.

After returning from lunch with Tully and the rest, I hop on the computer. There's Big Navy email traffic: Don't Ask, Don't Tell *has been lifted. I read the message to Tully.*

"Well it's about bloody time," he says. The Brits had openly accepted gays for the last ten years.

There's also a message from the head of security at my command back home (or the medical center from the days of Admirals and Bearcats). *My colleague, The Slime Ball, the one who approached me for a three way and, later, threatened my life, has been accused of rape. Security wants me to give a statement because the person he allegedly raped was his (still) married girlfriend. I wrote back and told the head of security that I'd handled the issue at the lowest level and didn't want to talk about it.* (I'd later dish all the details after more prodding. Later still, Rodney, during one of his visits to my workspace post-Bastion, rimmed Slime Ball's Nebraska coffee cup with his anus in the staff bathroom. *Good old Rodney.*)

It continues, I thought to myself, yet again. We tend to amputees and burned children, and it continues. Despite my statement, I'd be solicited for sex again by both when I returned from Bastion. Separately, of course, as their mutual fuck-fest had already bitten the dust. I was something they couldn't have. *Is this fucking Mars?* Well...yeah, and it has been for long time.

I get my make-believe headphones and hit shuffle:

> *Back when we were kids, we would*
> *Always know when to stop*
> *And now all the good kids are*
> *Messing up*
> *Nobody has gained or*
> *Accomplished anything*

I look up from my email and see everyone has donned Kevlar. "What the fuck's this?!" I ask.

Pam, hustling past, says "Might be an IED in the OR!" Something was lodged in an insurgent's knee, and Smitty can't make head or tails of it.

"EOD coming?" Tully asks her.

"On the way!" Pam shouts as she books through the OR double doors.

"Get your Kevlar on," Tully tells us. I refuse. Instead I walk right in and see the surgeons and nurses in helmets and vests working. One of the nurses, also in battle-rattle, is in a neighboring OR suite sloshing up blood from an amp now in the ICU. His upturned leg is in a yellow bag. The foot and ankle are ashen. The digital cammie uniform, shredded, begins at the calf and ends in a blood puddle pooled at the bottom where his hip would have been.

"Rhyan! Get your Kevlar ON!" Pam says.

"Why?" I say, staring at the leg, my robot flailing. "All the gases in here, we'll be blown sky high. This should've been done in the field! He's an insurgent, anyway. A dirt floor and rusty spoon are good enough for HIM!"

"LIEUTENANT COMMANDER RHYAN!" snaps Pam.

"QUIET!" says Tully, standing behind me. He holds up a hand to Pam, but addresses me. "He's a human-fucking-being!" he says,

leaning in. *"Now get your fucking Kevlar on."*

I blow him off again, and head out to straighten Bay One. Ten minutes later, Pam comes out with a PVC pipe and holds it up. *"No explosives."*

"Joy," I say.

Emma pays us a visit from the Ward. *"Coming to the vigil after work?"*

"I can't go," I say and make up some bullshit excuse. I can't take another, even though it seems like the whole of Great Britain showed for every single one, lining up in perfect formation for their fallen countrymen. I'd heard about the ramp ceremonies for U.S. KIAs but, as the dates and details were seldom passed, the ceremonies weren't largely attended. British vigils, however, remained events. After the bagpipes (if Scottish or Irish) and tribal dance (if Fijian), two rounds of cannon fire ushered their dead into the next world. It was so loud, the whole formation always startled a little with each blast.

"Come on," says Emma. *"It's the last one. We need an American. It's good morale."*

"Okay, goddammit."

"Kari!" yells Tully.

"Off you go," says Emma.

I turn around, and Tully says I have a phone call from my Kid. On the way back to the break room, I hear a Muslim wailing. His oldest son, a civilian herder, died in a skirmish between Taliban and U.S. Marines.

I pick up the receiver, put the Kid on speakerphone, and her tiny voice cuts through the air. *"Hi, Mommy!"*

"Hi, baby!"

"What are you doing?" she asks.

"Working. What are you doing?"

"Watching TV...why's that man crying?" In my haste to drown the wailer out, I realize I'd made it so she could hear him. Val, nicking tea for the ICU, takes her stash and closes the door behind

her. *Even if the man weren't wailing, Val would've still filed out eventually. All my mates did; they couldn't process such a sweet little voice smashed up against the cold reality of Bastion. They'd walled-off their loved ones, as I'd learned to do from them. Gemma told me after one of my* Kid Stories, *"You're a good mum, Kari. There are people here with four or five little ones back home, and you'd never know it." Whenever I talked about my Kid, though, they'd eventually open up. They'd given me permission to be weird and I, in turn, gave them permission to feel. The rub was I'd been simultaneously shutting down* (for good maybe) *and ratcheting up* (hello Phantom). *And Sangin? Sangin could destroy this sweet little voice if given half a chance. Just ask the father with the gored nine-year-old in Bay Three.*

I hang up the phone and eat some Otis Spunkmeyers because there's not a damned thing coming in. Val returns and sits next to me. She hands me a book, The Shepherd Boy.

"I wanted to give you a gift," said Val, "but I thought this would be better."

She inscribed the first page: Love your Mummy and have a happy life.

"Cute," I say.

"Pertinent subject matter in there, my dear," she tells me, then speeds off.

I set the book beside the Meerkat mug, the one with its play on words slogan from a popular ad campaign: Saving lives...simples.

Our regular shift ends without another CAT A, but we're still on call for another twelve hours. I head over to Camp Leatherneck before the vigil to grab a gorilla box: I have one already packed to send home--British uniforms and memorabilia. Benny said it best when he gave me his 16 patch, "This 'us' will never happen again." It won't. There will only be one Herrick 13.

I cross over the boundary to Leatherneck and see a Marine in a gun turret, regaled in battle-rattle. He's a young black kid smiling *ear-to-ear. He's getting into the shit.*

"Be careful!" I yell.

"Haha...okay, ma'am!"

I complete the errand and book it back because today's vigil begins in twenty minutes. Emma has somehow cajoled Mitch into coming with us. He's the strong silent type who doesn't like to leave himself open (and vigils are the pits).

Benny rushes up. "Rodney, the bastard, I tried to collect him but he's in the exercise tent having a wank with Smitty."

"Crossfit again?" I ask.

"Weights," he says, pumping his biceps, "OP MAXIMIZE!"

"Come on!" says Trevor, trotting past. "I won't have the Role Three looking like a bunch of arse wipes, AND REMEMBER TO FORM UP IN THE BACK!" All hospital staff line up in the back in case the Queen Mother calls us. Nightingale's quiet at the moment, and I see no little flies buzzing in the distance, so I hoof it over with Emma and Benny and the rest to the vigil.

An Irish kid died. I didn't know the details; the dead went to the morgue, and I never went in there. Not for all the alcohol and pills in the world. "He was a good lad," said his friend, addressing the formation. Just before the bagpipes kick off, the Queen Mother echoes:

STANDBY FOR BROADCAST...

ED STANDBY TEAM...TO ED...IMMEDIATELY...

I SAY AGAIN....

Just before the second incantation, I feel a beat, and on that beat I take one step forward. I look left, then right, and see my team peppered in a long line looking forward. And, just like that, we're away--scurrying boots in gravel, but otherwise dead silent.

I'm running behind Mitch.

BOOM! The first canon resounds, and I'm about shit myself.

"Come on, Rhyan!" says Mitch. "Seven months in the desert and you're still soft!"

There's nothing landing on Nightingale. It's too dark to see the mountains, so I keep my pace and tell Mitch to save "Sex Bomb" for me--I'm superstitious and, much like Bay One, that lead gown was my favorite.

BOOM! *goes the second. I stop to catch my breath.*

"Almost there," says Jeff, running up from behind, still with plantar fasciitis, still smiling, and still kicking my ass.

By the time I get there, Tully tells us it's a false alarm.

◆ ◆ ◆

Daily goals begins.

"Hi, I'm Kari."

"Hi, Kari," everyone says.

"My goal today was to finish my Combat Timeline, and I didn't do it."

"There's always tomorrow," says the group (*baluts*, every last one).

Chapter 13

"Ready to read your letter?"

"Sure," I say, "but it's not very good."

Riza waits.

"Okay," I tell her. "Enjoy."

Dear Teddy,

I hope this letter finds you not well. There's no pardon for trying to enter an eight-year-old girl. Not from me.

Go to hell.

"That it?!" asks Riza.

"It's a letter, right? Just like you wanted."

"That's not the point," Riza replies. "Go back to the notebook and try again." It's Day 36. I have to read my Combat Timeline, autobiography, *and* this piece-of-shit-letter before I discharge in six days. I'm to read the autobiography this afternoon, actually, and I'm scared shitless. None of the old crew will be there besides Tommy; a new batch of patients arrived last week, and they're bleeding (literally) into our circle. "Talking to strangers can be easier than talking to those we know, or even love," Riza had said on Day One.

Hokey bullshit.

Stefano discharged this morning, as did Noah. I'll miss them but I've met them before: Noah, initially like Rodney, was more of a Blake by the time he discharged; he'd been the one to call out Maddick in the Philippines for, well...being a dick, as did Noah when he comically rebuked the atrocious behavior of his fellow inmates. And Stefano, with all his natural talents, was like the golf caddie Blake and I'd hired from a Mom and Pop Nine-Hole just outside of our camp in the Philippines. (Stefano is more than an athlete or thug, of course, but the problem is Stefano really likes being an American thug--much in the way Zeke likes being an American bigot.)

But the Filipino caddie? He was just a very impressive golfer.

"I hate golf," I told Blake after hitting my last ball into Giardia

Pond, a contaminated water hazard on Hole Eight.

"Come on," he said. "What else we gonna do in this dump?"

The caddie gave us a *balut* to try, then pulled a club out of Blake's rented set. I passed on the morsel, but Blake ate it. "It's gross," he said, gagging. "I don't get it." After he spat it out, the caddie hit a 300-yard tee-shot with a 2-iron. With the round completed, the caddie walked over to a tree and fished out a black cobra (now that's gangster), and showed us a tuft of grass which shrank away from human touch. While flirting with the grass, I mused over the caddie: "He could be the best," I said to Blake in earnest. "He should really consider joining the circuit."

"Rhyan?" Blake said.

"Huh?"

"Don't be so fucking stupid." (Noah said the same thing when I wagered "Maybe Julien will get better.")

There are things we cannot change, the Canary reminds me. *Not with all the hope in the world.* I suppose she's right: A caddie ripping balls and a kid shining shoes in a third-world slum are just two of them.

That's not what I mean, the Canary says.

Julien, I think.

Yes, the Canary replies.

I can't change Rodney either.

No one SANE expects you to change them.

Yeah, but everyone is expecting me to validate them in some way. Rodney called again and, this time, he told me he nearly cold-cocked a fellow patient--a Vietnam Vet--yesterday for saying Operation Iraqi Freedom was "different from Vietnam." Rodney interpreted that to mean his own deployment, the one prior to Bastion and the one with the most collateral damage, was somehow inferior. Rodney had to be talked down by a magenta or an azure or whatever color the molls wear over there.

Crazy *Balut* Bullshit. *Viva Crank Vet!* And forget about civilians.

Rodney eats them for breakfast, scolding cashiers, shoppers, and cops all over Texas. He's got connection issues. Per *Trauma and Recovery: (The combat veteran) imagines that no civilian, certainly no woman or child, can comprehend his confrontation with evil and death. He views the civilian with a mixture of idealization and contempt: (civilians) are at once innocent and ignorant. He views himself, by contrast, as at once superior and defiled.*

True, but I don't go around and get in people's faces. Not that much.

Your PTSD isn't combat-related! the Phantom reminds me.

Well, then, call it the byproduct of combat, or call it nearly being busted by a Reptile: Tomato, tomato. I feel more humiliated than hostile, quite frankly. I'm a coward, you see. It's in my blood. I've been a host to pathogenic people since forever, and I've been trying to pick the tics out of my eyes ever since. So, I usually don't get all high and mighty. I just agree with everyone so I can maintain connections, albeit shitty ones like the kind I have with Rodney. There is, after all, something worse than being alive and feeling dead, and that's being alive and feeling alone. Sheryl has milked that shit for a while. *I'm sorry, Mommy. Don't leave me.* Rodney, in turn, is holding onto my family like a drunk holds onto a bottle of vodka in a deserted desert chapel. I can't double as Rodney's friends in Fallujah. Nor can I double as Sheryl's father. I'm just trying to do for me. I want to be with my Spouse and Kid now. It hurts to say it. I feel guilty because I kept Sheryl and Rodney around in the first place. Shane may be Shandy's "cross to bear," but Sheryl and Rodney are mine.

They aren't handicapped, says the Canary. *Not like Shane.*

So you think Shane is a cross to bear?! asks the Phantom.

"Never ever," I say to myself.

Tommy emerges from a session with his therapist.

"You have my list yet?" he asks, waiting for his next batch of words.

"Got'em right here...*banted, dross, and morass.*"

"Thank you," he says, copying them in his notebook.

I cruise over to the Kinkade, pen in one hand, a thumb in the other, and finish my autobiography.

◆ ◆ ◆

I'm the first and only presenter in the *Balut* Room. I completed my autobiography only five minutes ago. I'm not too sure how I'm going to find my flow: this isn't a morning snapshot, or a list of casualties written in my margins. It moves and breathes. It might tear me apart, until I remind myself that it's just Tommy and I and twelve breaths per minute.

I roll through my formative years, locking eyes with Tommy and Riza every now and then, but feel like I'm in a trance. I sink, and then bob to the surface. When I surface, I imagine standing at a podium. The last speech I'd given, about six months ago, was at a retirement ceremony for a Navy Nurse Corps captain. He'd asked me last minute if I could make a few remarks for his old buddy who'd gotten called away to Afghanistan. There I was, trying to give a sense of his twenty-four year career, and instead I blubbered about all the help he'd given *me* as *I* was coming undone from Bastion. My Commanding Officer, the same one who hasn't called, said it was the best speech he'd heard in ages. The Worm, who wants me to come back to work as if nothing happened, said zilch and slunk off. The Concubine, who thinks I'm spreading my gay and thinks me lazy, said I should write speeches for admirals. And the Troll? He sat in the audience and stared at me with red, watery eyes. Sheryl wasn't there. And, soon, neither was the good captain because he retired and went away, and I didn't feel like I could talk to anyone else until my Spouse came along, and that was that.

After the fallout from the "molestation revelation" died down, I settled into a routine of silence and sustained self-loathing. Though the cat was out of the bag with Teddy, and the family was good enough to keep him away for a while, Rich still found ways to humiliate me. He visited Sheryl's and my apartment one day, riding his Harley, decorated with two yellow cylinders.

"What's the yellow for?" I asked.

"That's Fat Man and Little Boy!" said Rich. "The bombs we dropped on the nips! Don't they teach you anything in that shit school?!" He scooped me up from behind and banged on my chest. "Kari's gettin' titties! Kari's gettin' titties!" They were mosquito bites at best, but when he hit them it felt like fire.

School wasn't much better. My promise to stay away from other kids was in full bloom. I tried to reach out to a group of kids who wanted someone to write a skit for our school variety show, but one of them told me I wasn't popular enough for such fun. Fuck 'em. I kept to myself, all the while feeling like I was going to explode any minute.

My only solace was Shane.

And there I stop.

I can't do this, I tell myself.

Yes, you can, says the Canary.

It's too much.

You're not a monster, Kari.

Shane had been in the bed every time Teddy molested me. "We're all alone," Teddy would say, but we never were. Shane and I slept together at The Fletcher Family Ranch. We'd been sleeping together since we were a few months old, actually, taking naps. So, it made sense that Shane would be there when the molestation started, and progressed. Teddy just nudged him over before starting in on me, as if Shane were Raggedy Andy. (Shane and I had even dressed up like Raggedy Ann and Andy that year for Halloween. Sheryl and Shandy were tickled. "You guys are so fuckin' cute!")

We sure were. Little muppets.

About a year into the abuse, I tried to touch Shane's penis while we were playing with Tigger. At first, Shane would push my hand away and say, "No more, Kari." Then, a few months later, I grew bolder and tried to unzip his pants. "No more, Kari! No! No!" he said, his tongue too big and his eyes half blind. I tried one more time after *that, when I was ten and just before I told Sheryl about Teddy. I went for Shane's zipper and he grabbed my hand and squeezed it so hard tears were coming out of my eyes; his nails, long and dirty, dug into my skin until the back of my hand started bleeding.*

"NO MORE, KARI! NO MORE!" he yelled, while tearing into his own thumb with yellow teeth.

He clamped down harder until I screamed.

"NO MORE, KARI!" He finally let go of my hand, then his own. "No more, Kari," he said softly. Then softer still, "No more."

Shane was the reason Teddy didn't penetrate me. He wailed whenever I started crying. What was Teddy going to do with two crying children?

"Motherfucker," I say, breaking from the script.

"True," says one of the new *baluts*. "He's a motherfucker."

My mother blames Teddy for my being gay. I'd heard her on the phone with Shandy after I came out. "Teddy made her that way! How else can you explain it? One minute she likes dick and the next she doesn't. I don't get it."

"I'm gay," I tell the *baluts*. "I was born a gay, quiet girl to a disgusting family with no scruples. I denied my true nature because that's what Sheryl and the Navy expected of me."

True-True, my cheerleader, is Foating. She's a senior enlisted Army soldier, and was a Pentagon first responder on 9/11. True-True, who's sole trigger is "ignorant people," is sitting next to Our Jolly Good Fellow. Zeke, late to the session, is Foating and wearing sunglasses. I look at Tommy and come clean.

"I'm tired of feeling ashamed."

I look at Riza, who's smiling at me as I do at my Kid when she practices her piano. A lifetime goes by, then she asks me "Anything to add?" she asks.

"Yes," I say and look around the room. "Never lose hope."

The *baluts* give a quiet, swelling round of applause, not unlike the response to the speech I'd given at the retirement ceremony. *No more shame.* I can't un-experience the abuse. I can't un-experience Bastion.

No more anger. (I'm still hoping that'll get better.)

◆ ◆ ◆

I go to the art therapy room afterwards to process my thoughts, or whatever. As with the unit gym no one uses, the Art Therapy Room is empty. I sit in my usual spot in the U, and Tommy, my Ginger *Balut,* comes in and sits next to me.

"I'm in a state of morass," he says.

"What for?" I ask.

"Did you ever forgive that boy?" he blurts.

"What boy?"

"Teddy," says Tommy.

"No, I can't forgive him. Not ever," I say.

Tommy starts crying.

"What's wrong?"

"Are you SURE you can't forgive him?!" he cries.

"Tommy?" (I wouldn't be any kind of *balut* if I didn't ask.) "*What* did you do?"

"I think I might've hurt this girl?"

"How old was she?"

"Eight," he says.

NO! Not this kid. Not the kid I've coddled. Not the kid who bounces his knees, runs from Julien, and calls his sister every day.

"How old were you?" A voice crack on the "you" and telegraph for the sucker punch that's surely coming because, if he doesn't give me the right answer, the Phantom is going to stomp his knees. Twelve breaths per minute--no more, no less. *Please God.* If Tommy's a child molester, then there is no hope because I can't tell a good guy from a bad guy.

It continues, says the Canary. It does. I just received a reply from the message I sent my younger cousin. Being that I had to write a letter to Teddy, I was morbidly curious about him. My barely-teenaged cousin told me he doesn't visit Shandy's anymore, not after Teddy appraised the backside of his twelve-year-old girlfriend. "Baby got back!" Teddy told her.

SMASH HIM! says the Phantom.

He's innocent and vulnerable, says the Canary.

SO?! Make your choice, the Phantom warns, *when Tommy tells you he was A MAN!*

"Same age. Eight," Tommy says. "She was my best friend," he says. "After the older kid...you know...I did the same thing to her."

"Did you keep in touch?" I ask.

"We talk sometimes."

"Talk to your therapist," I tell him.

"Are you mad at me?" he asks.

"No, Tommy. There's a world of difference between an eight year old and an adult. It doesn't make it okay, but there's a logical reason for why you did it."

"I don't know what I did!" he says.

"I understand," I tell him. "But listen to me. We were kids. Do you think *I'm* a monster?" Another voice crack, proof-positive that I think I'm a monster.

Tommy is looking at the ground. I crouch slightly so he can see my face. "You're not Teddy," I say. "Now go talk to your therapist. The nurses are watching us." Inmates are discouraged from hugging one another. Most are grappling, some are groping, and all want validation. It'd be just like me to stop my forward progress and focus on Tommy. That'd be the easiest thing to do.

Tommy gives me a nod and walks off to find his therapist, and I ask Miss Dorothea where Riza is.

"She's in the quiet room with an admission. She'll be out in a bit. Need anything?"

"Xanax," I say.

Miss Dorothea knows I'm joking. Miss Dorothea knows a lot of things, so I ask her, "Do you think I'm a monster?"

"That's enough crazy talk for one day," she says. "Here comes Riza. And, no, of course I don't think you're a monster."

Riza strides up next to me at the nurses' station counter. She has a huge smile on her face. "You did well," she says. "Much better than the letter this morning."

"Am I *Borderline*?" I ask.

"What?"

"Do I have a *Borderline Personality*?"

"Traits, yes. But your having asked the question in the first place tells me you aren't."

"Sheryl fits the *Borderline Queen* persona," I remind Riza. I bought a book online, *Understanding the Borderline Mother* by Christine Ann Lawson. We've been discussing it in our scab-picking sessions. *Borderline* mothers, or those who wax and wane between psychosis and neurosis, are typically described by their traumatized children as *Make-Believe Mothers,* all of whom fall into one of four categories. More often than not, though, a *Borderline Mother* assumes any one of the four categories based on their needs: *the Witch, the Queen, the Waif, and the Hermit.* The darkness within the Queen Mother is emptiness, within the Witch Mother is annihilating rage, within the Waif Mother is helplessness, and within the Hermit Mother--my favorite--is fear. The text goes on to explain that repeated childhood trauma shrinks the hippocampus, a part of the brain responsible for memory and emotional regulation. All that's fine and good but, granted even all that, I can't rise above the murderous rage I feel toward Sheryl. I guess I can't help it either. "You need to get your mother out of the house as soon as possible, and by any means necessary," Riza warned. According to Lawson, *Children must separate to survive, but separation threatens the mother's survival.* I hate my mother, but I love her. That's the sad, awful truth. And now Sheryl's probably got a raisin of a hippocampus.

"Considering her constant void, Sheryl's certainly a *Queen*," says Riza. "But the violent *Witch* within her cannot be denied. She's here.

It's only a matter of time before she takes everything."

Spouse and Kid are everything.

"Then I must be a *Hermit Mother*," I say. "I fit the bill. I'm scared shitless all the time." The military loves this type: able-bodied followers who are suspicious of everything and unable to think for themselves. Hermits want to matter, but need to affix themselves to somebody else's cause.

"*Hermit* and *Witch* traits don't make you *Borderline*," Riza says.

"I never said I was a *Witch*," I tell her.

"Witches, Phantoms, Wolves...it's all the same," Riza says. "But you're *not Borderline*. You know why?"

"Why?"

"You don't give me the Heeby-Jeebies," she says. "Working in mental health as long as I have, I can usually spot a *Borderline* from a mile away." Considering there's six-million and counting in the U.S. alone, I assume Riza gets the Heeby-Jeebies a lot.

"So," Riza continues, "if you *are* a *Borderline*, then you're the most dangerous one I've ever met."

"Right..."

"It's a good thing you're just narcissistic, anxious, and depressed!" she says.

"You're an asshole."

Riza laughs. "I'm staying a little late tonight. Have some work to catch up on. I'll meet you in the quiet room after."

"We're not done?"

"You're going to re-write the Letter to Teddy," she says. "And you're going to read it before I leave tonight. Before you start, though, I want you to read the first chapter of this."

"Another book? But I'm bleary-eyed."

Riza ignores me, and crosses the hallway to retrieve a book from our library. She hands me *The Drama of the Gifted Child*.

"I don't think I'm gifted," I tell her.

"That's what I like about you," she tells me before she leaves.

I read the first chapter, quickly gathering the book operates under the assumption that all children are gifted, or precious little sponges who accommodate their parents' every whim if that's what it takes to feel loved. We're born flexible, in body and mind, to survive. The author, Alice Miller, describes the role that children play for their damaged parents: *The most efficacious objects for substitute gratification are a parent's* own children.

The Skipper, my empty *Queen Mother*, is going to summon the *Witch*. She's going to take it all unless I stop her. Can a *Hermit* stop a *Queen Witch*? I don't know, but there's a five-year-old *balut* back home waiting to hatch.

◆ ◆ ◆

My letter to Teddy -- the second edition, the evening edition, the I'm-going-to-puke-my-guts-out-before-all-this-is-over- edition, is complete. Riza is waiting in the quiet room at the end of her shift, just like she said she would. I walk through her door and sit on the sixty-grit couch, only this one is blue, then realize Riza and Johnnie are not like Dr. Sutton, the shrink who was more interested in covering his own ass than reporting a pedophile and saving a bunch of future victims. Nor are they the shrinks who came to blows in the hospital hallways I used to manage. I'm not some "PTSD'er" on some "game preserve," nor are they trying to shoo me away. Riza and Johnnie are just trying to help.

"Are you ready, Kari?"

"Yeah. Let's get it over with."

Teddy,

How's life been treating you? I hope it's socked you square in the nuts. I hope the pain is excruciating because you are a monster and a coward, and I fucking hate you.

I hate your mouth-I hate your cravings-I hate your tongue-I hate your hands-I hate your smell-I hate your pocked skin-I hate your voice-I hate your arms-I hate your taste-I hate your leering eyes-I hate your dick-I hate its hardness-I hate your guidance...I hate your praise...I hate your weakness-I hate your power-I hate your ignorance.

I never want your pain to end.

I stop reading.

I can't breathe! I can't breathe!

Breathe, says the Canary.

"Breathe," says Riza.

I reset myself so I can say the last line, still gasping for air with each syllable. I don't need to read it because it's only three words, my silent scream finally surfacing, and True-True said it's no lie.

"YOU...ROTTEN...MOTHERFUCKER!"

Riza hugs me, retrains me more like, and pulls my head into her huge bosom.

"Shhh," she whispers. "It's okay to cry."

I cry and cry and cry until the upwelling darkens the tops of Riza's shirt and bra.

"Well," says Riza. "Only one more to go."

Chapter 14

Bastion.

Jesus, Mary, and Joseph. It's Day 40 and, though I have two days left on my six-week stint, my time is up. *The War Room* only holds court twice a week, and I've fallen a day shy of stalling the proceedings. Nevertheless, it's time to dust off, or come clean. My Spouse and Kid deserve a loving wife and mother because that's what I am (minus the loving part). Miss Dorothea says I'm lucky to have a family to come home to, and that's true. But Miss Dorothea doesn't understand that I haven't had a real family (sister notwithstanding) until recently. And the only passable family I had, up until that point, were the Brits. Although in The Stew, I never felt like a *balut,* just as Brian didn't with his fellow Marines. I'm pretty sure he'd have rather been the one injured, just like I'm okay assuming ownership of this...whatever *this* is.

"It's time to live," says my Spouse. "You've had such a hard life, Kari, and I'm so sorry." Me, too: I don't know how to love, never mind live. I've resided inside my head for almost forty years. If I *really* stop and think about it, I've always been one hallucination away from The Eff U all my life.

Come what may with Sheryl, it's time to kill or be killed according to the *Breitling* I stopped wearing (and the *Ray Bans* I'll smash when I get home). I can't replace Sheryl's love with rank and rubbish to escape my trashy roots. Nor can I bubble-wrap the world for Sheryl and pretend she's a nurturing figure. I love her, but I'm not her father, the perpetual subject of her unresolved issues. And what are Sheryl's issues? She's never told me.

The Canary tells me *it's time.*

I haul ass to Starbucky, resurrected by True-True, the Pantagon *Balut,* and I put the finishing touches on my Combat Timeline. This is the last piece, the last snapshot, the last file for the cabinet.

Miss Dorothea taps me on the shoulder thirty minutes later. "It's time," she says. Zeke, Tommy, and True-True file in behind and sit in front of me. *The War Room's* configuration is much like that of the Art Therapy room, except with a dot in the center and, today, that dot is me. I'm surrounded. But I got Zeke, Tommy, and True-True right there in the bend, so I think I'm okay. Riza isn't monitoring The War Room today; she's with the *baluts* on Thursdays. A young woman, barely older than Riza's student, is monitoring the group.

I'm gonna blow, I think.

No, you're not, the Canary says.

They're gonna think you're a pussy, the Phantom insists.

No, they aren't, says the Canary.

They're gonna think you're weak, the Phantom replies.

No, they aren't.

Coward!

Stop.

CRYBABY!

I may have had a tough past, but Bastion makes me scared for the future.

"You ready, Kari?...Kari?"

"Yes."

"Okay," the therapist says, turning to address the group. "Remember, 'What's said in The War Room, stays in the The War Room.' If you have to leave for any reason, please do, but I need a thumbs-up before walking out. Any questions?"

No questions. I look at the three in front of me. Zeke has his arms folded. I can't see his knuckles from this angle, but I need to believe they look better than they've looked all month. Tommy is leaning forward. His knees don't move an inch. He doesn't look relaxed, but he doesn't look scared, either. *Very good, Tommy.* True-True is rocking back and forth, hugging herself, and bouncing her knees to the palsied rhythms of her own troubled mind. *It'll get better, True-True.*

I read my Combat Timeline, coasting through my first two

deployments. *Filler*, I think, but I'm hopeful it'll provide the momentum I need to get through The Stew. I think I've got the hang of it until I get to my first day at Bastion--the one with the Quad Amp and his Buddy and the screaming and the locket and the blood. I put my hand over my mouth and try to hold in my wailing, but I can't. An Army sergeant in the corner stands up to leave.

"Angelo?"

Angelo stops after grabbing the doorknob.

"I need a thumbs up," the therapist says.

Angelo gives the therapist a thumbs-up without turning around and quietly leaves the room. Thank God, because the pause gives me just enough time to get a grip on my emotions, and it's not like I could look Angelo in the eye anyway. *I'm a pussy.* I glance at the three before me. Tommy gives me a tight-lipped smile. Zeke nods and spits. True-True keeps rocking.

I come to the seven year old with the burn and the bones and the glove. I feel like I'm in a trance. *I'm Foating,* I think. I didn't know it was possible to Foat and read, but then I stop and consider my last year has been one long tunnel.

I read about the insurgent in CT and the dead Dane and the doubles and triples and snips. I read about the Brits, my dear friends, who are helping me float to the surface at this moment. And it's all going well again until I get to the last entry on the last day. I stop reading and start planning a hasty exit. I look at the door.

"You ok, Kari?"

I give a thumbs up.

After the vigil and false alarm, I walk out to the ambulance bay, where I see Val arguing with Benny and a few Paras over which holiday destination is better.

"Marbella!" says Val.

"Ibiza!" says Benny.

"Bleh!" Val replies. "I wouldn't visit that slag-ridden cesspool for all the tea in China. Coming to the NAAFI tonight, Kari?"

"I'm not sure," I tell her.

"Awww come on, Kari-oke," Val says, knowing I'd never pass on a chance to make an ass out of myself, especially if it meant I could become someone else for three to four minutes a pop.

"Twist my arm," I say, and we gather-in for a picture at a Para's request.

We're bumped as we say 'cheese.' "Hey!" I say without turning around. "You ruined the shot!"

"Oh, well PARDON me!" says an Air Force nurse. She's transferring a Marine double amputee into an ambulance. (He's to fly to Landstuhl, Germany--the mid-point between Sangin and home.) The Air Force nurse grazed us with the gurney in her haste, but I thought it was one of our friends messing around. Her diamond studded earrings glint as she gives me a look of disgust.

It's okay, I think to myself. I deserved it. I'll absorb Diamond Girl's snub. *She gets to leave Bastion.* We had to stay. I was insensitive, which is to say, I was no longer human by that point. She, like everyone who made brief stops in Bastion, left aghast. I can only imagine what she'd think of us if she knew my friends and I amputated gingerbread cookies in the OR. We used red icing. We smeared it on our faces. We took pictures. We laughed and laughed like vampires.

"You all right, Kari?" the therapist asks.

"Yes," I tell her and resume.

After the picture and Diamond Girl, I go to my tent to nap. I dream about my second deployment--specifically my roommate who was an intensive care doctor. I asked her if what we were doing was right. "Well," she said, "I have to assume that the people in D.C. know what they're doing." I told her historians think we're wrong. She said those people don't have a clue. "That's why they're professors."

"Kari?" a voice whispers through the partition of sheets surrounding my cot. I wake to see Gemma in a devil mask. It scares the hell out of me. *"Ready to go to the NAAFI?" she asks.*

"Only if you take that off," I say.

She laughs and complies. "I thought you were going to shit your pants!"

"Wouldn't be a first."

Gemma and I walk out of the tent to find the whole gang waiting. Even Rodney and Smitty are there. Rodney's in the middle of one of his stories. "The club was bangin'! Then I saw this girl staring at me from across the room. So I figure I'm gonna go in and make my move. She starts shaking her body to the beat as I get closer and I'm thinking, 'Oh, shit! This bitch wants to battle!' So, I move in and start pop-lockin'. She needs to BRING it," Rodney insists, "if she wants to battle me! You know what I'm sayin'?"

"Oh, sure," says Tully, rolling his eyes. "Muppet."

"Then she seized!" Rodney says. "Right in front of me. I had to give her first aid until the ambulance got there."

The War Room starts laughing. I start laughing. Good old Rodney. He even made Smitty crack up. I want *that* Rodney back-- the one who tells stories and cracks people up. The one who rimmed Slime Ball's coffee mug. But I haven't seen *that* guy in a long time. After the joke, Rodney told me while walking to the NAAFI: "You know you're my sister, right?" *He must be my brother then,* I'd thought. He'd take a bullet for me. He put the group ahead of himself, period. He risked his life in prior deployments, time and again. But now, with me, he requires too much. *Pump him up, Kari. Make him feel wanted,* I'd tell myself. I'm good at that, right? Not anymore.

He wants to be somebody, the Canary tells me. *You want to be somebody.*

I do, but all eyes are on me in *The War Room,* and this isn't a Somebody I want to be. And none of us have enough ironic distance to get the dust off us. Worm told me he doesn't give a shit about Honor, Courage, or Commitment. "I take my uniform off and I switch gears," said Worm. "It's just a job." But Worm has never been to Iraq or Afghanistan. Worm still sees himself as somebody. If this is what it takes to be somebody, then I'm okay with fading away. It's all a lie and it's all gone.

"Kari?" the therapist says, breaking my train of thought, or my naysaying, never-believer, self-loathing self-talk.

"I'm okay," I tell her and pick up where I left off.

We arrive at the NAAFI, and cricket is on the television. Yay. "I don't get it," I tell Emma.

"That's okay. Neither do I," she tells me.

I think about what song to sing, while Gemma has hers all figured out. "I'm chuffed! 'Don't Stop Believin' is in the queue!"

"Again?!" asks Emma. Gemma belted Journey in pubs all over the motherland. I'd heard a similar rendition of "Believin'" in the Philippines when Blake, our General Surgeon, sang it in the lobby of a massage parlor. I was getting a back rub at the time, by an old woman with no teeth, on top of a table covered in plastic wrap. His falsetto distracted me from the thoughts of all the happy endings that must've come before, so I figure this could distract me from the amps I saw earlier.

I fill out a song slip to get in the queue. I have to make it quick. There's no telling when The Queen Mother will need us. It's Team Two's last night on call and anything can happen. I'm the first one on, and it's standing room only in the NAAFI, as fifty or so British have filed in, along with a smattering of Marines (fresh from Sangin). Their buddies are in the hospital, so they're here. It's time for some stress relief.

I chose "Dirty Deeds" by AC/DC.

I sing the song, which is to say I butcher it, but get a respectable applause and slink away. I like attention, but I don't like attention.

"Spot on!" says Tully.

After the "Deeds" and the "Believin'," came The Hammer.

A geeky white British kid starts singing "You Can't Touch This." The audience groans, but it turns out the geeky white kid is pretty good. So good, one of the Marines gets up and does The Worm. *His Worm kicks four feet high. Then a tall, pretty Irish girl with dark curly hair steps up to the Marine.*

"Oh, shit!" *says Rodney.* "She's gonna seize!"

"No mate," *Benny tells him.* "Watch her."

She doesn't seize. She battles. She pop-locks. She dances like Rerun from What's Happening!! *She couldn't have been twenty, or grown up further from Watts, but she danced better than LeShawn's friends all those years ago.*

Then, the blare:

"STANDBY FOR BROADCAST...

ED STANDBY TEAM...TO ED...IMMEDIATELY...

I SAY AGAIN..."

(Translation: Come on, Kari. This your Big One.*)*

"Damn," *says Tully.*

"Off you go," *Emma tells us.*

"Turah," *says Benny, and Team Two quickly exits.* (Benny left the QARANC after Bastion and lives at the top of Scotland with his bride. I'm sure he still wears a Tam O' Shanter fun. If not, he should.)

I hear the music resume a few strides out the door because Nightingale, for the time being, is quiet. We get to the ED and prepare for eighteen casualties--most of them kids. There's rumor of an amp. Unfortunately, I'm not assigned to Bay One. I have the overflow ward designated for less-injured children; Herrick 14 did a deal with Trevor, and 14 would be running the show in the Bays. (I don't know what Trevor is doing these days. He's not one to Facebook, but I *can* speculate with confidence that, wherever he is, he's not mincing his words--in his journals or otherwise.)

I lock eyes with Abi, now on a rapid transfuser in her lead gown and Green Butcher Smock, and I try not to appear as if I'm worried for her, but fail miserably. She looks away and starts wringing her hands.

I book back to the overflow ward and hear the helos.

"*Call for Terps!*" *Mary tells Rodney, both in the overflow ward. Rodney runs down the hall and is back before:*

"*INTERPRETER TO WARD 5...INTERPRETER TO WARD 5....*" *says the hospital loud-voice, or J-Chat, or Tully's punching bag. The new J-Chat has a heavy Scottish accent, or Glaswegian on account of it's peculiarity, and she doesn't take shit from anyone.* "*Aye can only go wae the info they gee me, ya cunt!*"

The kids arrive: some via gurney, some walk, and some are carried. The kids are in party dress with bells around their ankles and wear eyeliner. Brown eyes. Long lashes. The babies are plump and the kids are skinny. None of them cry. A head bonk here, a bit of exposed bowel there, but all will be fine. These are minor injuries. I book to the ED for extra supplies and pass J-Chat and Tully in the hallway still arguing.

The ED, however, is silent, or so I think given the blade noise that's now upon us. No one moves, except for the Padre, who's praying with his replacement.

A young corpsman, the runner, is at the foot of my Bay with his sheers in a diagonal slit made in his Green Butcher Smock. An ambulance pulls up and the brakes screech. I forget about Ward 5, the overflow ward. I'm standing behind the Blue Line with the Blue Scrubs. This is where I belong. A MERT doc waits in front of Bay One and reports, but I can't hear through the blade noise. A litter is carried in.

I can't tell if it's a kid or an adult, Afghani or coalition, alive or dead. They logroll the body onto our gurney. The MERT doc backs away to give Herrick 14 room, and I hear whispers. When the whispers make their way to me, I hear "little girl."

"*Little girl,*" *I say to no one in particular.*

"*No,*" *says the MERT doc, Foating behind me.* "*It's a woman.*" This made sense, I think, because Afghani women are usually small in stature. We'd always underestimate age, though the human being on the gurney left everything to question.

"Kari!" Tully shouts. "I want you to stay close. Observe the new lot--especially the Yanks. Field questions, but give them space. It's their show now."

"I'm jumping in if they balk."

"Well, you was a no-nothing muppet, and you did fine!" he says smiling, and darts off. (Tully is still in the QARANC Territorial Army, or reserves. Later, I'd ask him how he tolerated me all those months. He wrote: Your face was sad yet alive, and I warmed to it. I so wanted to befriend a preppy American man with blue jeans or chinos for an illicit, clandestine affair, but got you instead. Tully travels to New York regularly, and I hope to bump into him one day without coming apart.)

Everything inside me wants to hop on a transfuser or start a line, but that wouldn't help. There's no swooping in. There's no saving the day. I continue to stand behind the Blue Line and take note. When a man lost his arms and legs there was still some bulk. Not so much here, yet she's alive. A goodbye kiss, Sangin style. And this girl, sixteen, according to MERT (and a woman, according to culture), is dying. She has long hair and breasts. I look down at her womb, swollen.

"Is she pregnant?!" asks Pam.

"No, no, no," says Jeff. "She was a tough intubation. Esophagus was intubated twice." The forced air from ventilation that would've gone to her lungs, filled her belly instead. "But we'll know for sure when the blood test comes back." She wasn't pregnant.

"Remember!" Jeff tells Herrick 14. "This is not reality."

Yeah, ok, Jeff. (Jeff isn't doing well according to a Bastion surgeon I bumped into during a Training Evolution in San Diego a couple months ago. I have no further information, but I can probably wager, and I wager he'll be fine.)

"Fast Scan Positive!" says Smitty.

Ya don't say? (Smitty is still in the Navy and will probably make captain. He's got his robot down and his rooms darkened, hunting frags forever and ever.)

"Get her in the OR now!" says Pam.

Yes, ma'am.

I trail behind the gurney, giving the new team a wide berth, as instructed. Mitch is already in the OR with another amp and addresses a flock of 14 who spilled into the OR behind me to get a look. "IF YOU'RE NOT IN THE TRAUMA," Mitch says, "THEN GET THE FUCK OUT!" (Mitch retired eleven months after returning from Bastion. Twenty-eight years on the books. Between fifteen as a salvage diver and half a year in Bastion, I guess he'd had enough.)

I watch the runners deliver shock packs of blood. I watch Abi work the transfuser. They got this, I think. And they do. Abi stares at the girl in sixty-second-lags (the time it takes to administer a unit) while her partner, a Mitch of sorts, charts.

Abi says to no one, "Well, I guess I'm in the fucking Navy now."

"Do you need some water or a break?" I ask both.

"Nah," says Abi's partner, charting and Foating.

Abi says she doesn't need a break or a drink. "But I don't know how to process this," she tells me as the surgeons slice and preserve--a million little decisions that MUST add up to something.

"I can't tell you how to process this," I tell Abi. "You just do." Or don't.

Pam, standing behind us and observing our transaction says, "Listen," she tells Abi and partner, "I know you're both new, but you have to find a place in your brain that your heart can't reach and lock all the shit in there." (Step on your stool and clamp the bleed!) A few minutes later, Pam whispers into her replacement's ear, and I know what she's saying:

"Let her go."

Afghanistan can't handle wounds like these. And she's right. How would this girl survive, assuming she healed? (Pam's still in the Navy, still deploying, and still tormenting surgical residents. I'm sure they loathe her. I'm sure they love her.)

Abi will pump and pump and pump until the surgeons tell her to stop. (Abi would eventually be shipped out to a Forward Operating Base. A month later, she'd be the one wearing flight gear, reporting on patients over the blade noise after the ambulance screeched. All eyes on her. Mouths shut for the reports. She's married now, having two kids with a Marine she'd met at the FOB. They are The Abernathys of this new generation. They will be the ones who'll warn against war. She told me years later that she considered getting a tattoo: DULCE BELLUM INEXPERTIS, or *War is Sweet to Those Who Have Never Seen It.* "I decided not to get it," she'd tell me. "I lock it in a place I can't feel, and let it out slowly when I'm ready...or all at once when I'm not." She resigned her commission, as did her husband, after returning. There were no Skippers or Bearcats keeping them in. They just left. And that's the way it should be.)

I approach Tully's replacement. "They're doing good," I tell him.

"Thank you," he says. His eyes are like Mary's. "Would you mind cleaning up Bay One?" he asks.

"Love to," I tell him.

I return to Bay One. Gemma is already cleaning.

"I'm gagging for a fag," she says.

"But the Bay is a mess," I tell her.

"J-Chat is quiet," Gemma replies. "Come on. It'll keep."

I follow Gemma out to smoke. Mary has gathered up her gear in the break room for her eventual flight home tomorrow, and as we pass hands each of us a cup of tea.

Gemma and I sit opposite each other on a picnic table and don't say a word. Rodney's replacement, a new corpsman fresh from FMF School, sits next to us and lights up. He'd been one of the runners, and also needed a break. After a couple minutes, Gemma interrupts the silence. "It shouldn't feel different, but it does." I get it; doubles, triples, and even quads were a dime a dozen, but a girl cut down in such a way was just too much.

"That was the worst thing I've ever seen," says the corpsman.

That makes three of us.

I go back to the Bay, and see a Muslim elder doting over one of his sons. A minor injury, his son's forearm had been fragged by the blast that got his daughter-in-law (the quad in the OR). With the elder are a host of other men surrounding the son. They are talking and smiling. It's no surprise; most women didn't make it on the helos, the men preferring the women die at home than be touched by us.

They don't care about her, I say to myself.

I finish cleaning and walk past the Afghani men. With the exception of the nurse caring for the quad's husband, the ED is a ghost town. Everyone is either in the overflow ward or the OR. I walk out of the ED for the last time and see Emma in the ambulance bay.

"I need to talk to you," *I tell her.* "Alone."

"How many times do I have to tell you," *Emma says,* "I'm betrothed."

"Oh, for fuck's sake!" *I tell her.* "Get over yourself."

"All right then," *Emma says and escorts me behind the huge tanks for the hospital water supply.* "What's occurin'?"

The Big One, finally on top of me, breaks through my Foat and I collapse in the sand, and I scream. "EVERY KID DESERVES A MOTHER! EVERY KID DESERVES TO BE LOVED! IT'S NOT FAIR! IT'S NOT FAIR! NO ONE CARES! THEY DIDN'T CARE!"

"Go on," *Emma says.* "Get it out."

"I CAN'T BREATHE!"

"You're fine."

"I'M NOT! I'M NOT FINE! SHE'S NOT FINE! I DON'T UNDERSTAND! I DON'T UNDERSTAND ANY OF THIS! IT'S BURNING!"

"What's burning?"

"MY CHEST! IT HURTS-SO-BAD! SHE COULDN'T FIGHT! SHE COULDN'T RUN! SHE COULDN'T SCREAM! SHE DOES WHAT'S

BEST FOR THE GROUP! WE ALL DO WHAT'S BEST FOR THE GROUP!"

"LISTEN TO ME!" Emma says. "This place is SHIT, Kari. That's all it is. It's shit. You will go home and love your little girl and all of this will become a memory. Do you understand?" I tell her yes, but I didn't understand: How could any of this become nothing more than a memory?

I always tried to make light of Bastion, telling the cookie story to some unsuspecting soul who'd invariably ask me, "So, what was Afghanistan like?"

"We amputated cookies," I'd tell them, "and then we ate them."

Rodney would tell me he danced on top of trucks in Iraq to the song, "Too Legit to Quit," during Muslim call to prayer--the very same song Noah blasted when he was there. Except Rodney would tell me this story and laugh. I, of all people, should've thought it was funny. I eat legs and arms, after all, but it wasn't. None of it was funny. I imagined what would happen if Afghani soldiers came over here, blasting houses and killing, and dancing in front of our churches on Sunday. D.C. should be ashamed of itself. Not me. Not Rodney.

He's dusted, says The Canary, leave him. The truth is still too painful. He's yet to accept his own cruelty. It's all he knows. And it's all you knew until now. Rodney is in trouble, Kari, and there isn't a thing you can do to make it better. He has to see it on his own, and in his own time.

"Kari?" the therapist asks, rousing me from the trance. "Thumbs up?"

I give her a thumbs up and finish it.

Mary rounds the water tower and stops short, appraising the wake left by my Big One: me on the ground (again) trying not to throw up (again), but so, so tired. Mary says, "We've seen what no one should EVER see. It's changed your soul, Kari," then she crouches to meet my eyes, "and no one will ever understand how *much except us. But THIS family," Mary says, motioning to the three of us and, no doubt, the whole of 13, "is what will stay with you for life. You'll see."* (Mary is serving in KABOOM, or Kabul, presently. I miss my civilian punk mother and I hope she doesn't bite the dust. Even our tent cat, Cat A, only had one life. One and done.)

Mary looks at Emma, and Emma looks at me. "Come on, Kari...let's get you a nice cuppa of tea." (To this day, Emma acknowledges how heavy Herrick 13's casualty stats were, but that's the extent of it. She never talks of Bastion. We talk about our kids instead. She and Colin have two sons.)

"Sounds good," I say.

Mary and Emma smile.

"Brilliant!" adds Val, standing just behind the tower.

We go to the NAAFI. Benny is already in the queue for a black coffee. "How's the girl?" he asks me.

Emma answers for me. "Let's not discuss it."

I stop reading because that's the end, and I can't read the tally, or snapshot, in the margin because there's too many kids and the girl is at the bottom with the husband who didn't care, and I'm barely hanging on.

"Very good, Kari," the therapist says. "Okay, everyone. Let's hear some feedback.

"I don't know how you did that shit every day," says Zeke.

Usually the group takes fifteen minutes to give positive feedback, but I give them two seconds. I stand and give a thumbs-up, but, instead of taking a seat with the others, I run out of the room with my hand over my mouth. It's not a wail. It's a scream. I no sooner make it to my room when Zeke, Tommy, and True-True surround me. Miss Dorothea is in there, too. This time she stands back.

"It's okay, Kari," says Tommy.

"You're gonna be fine," says Zeke.

"It's okay to cry," says True-True.

They scoop me up in a group hug, and I scream:

"FUUUUUUUUUUUUCK!"

We hold each other tighter as we try to pray to God. When I feel my knees give out, Zeke eases me down on the bed and sits next to me.

"Thank you," I tell him.

Zeke has his chew in the front of his bottom lip and tells me, again, that I'm going to be fine. I have to believe he's going to be fine, too.

Miss Dorothea asks everyone to leave and pulls back my covers. "You sleep for a while," she says, and tucks me in.

I think about the chapel in Bastion as I drift off to sleep. Gemma, during our last meeting, gave me an old compass with a Robert Frost poem etched into the base. The poem was about paths, and Gemma hoped that I'd find the right one.

"There's something about you, Kari."

"I know," I tell her, "you said that before."

"It's true. And I hope one day you get what you want."

"And what do I want?" I ask her.

"Love and acceptance," Gemma tells me. "They're what we *all* want."

The next morning, I said goodbye to Herrick 13. The Americans piled into a bus bound for the flight line, and the C-130 that would wing us west. To Qatar, then D.C., then home. The Brits formed a line leading up to the bus. I was last one on. I turned around one more time, bumping against handrails, weighted in bulky battle-rattle.

"I love my Brits," I told them.

"And they love you!" yells Gemma.

(After going on holiday for a year, Gemma returned to Bastion for one last Herrick. A news crew captured Gemma in Bay Two, mid-resuscitation on a patient, her asking if the Royal Marine was wearing blast pants. The blurb, on YouTube, is her sole claim to fame. "Figures I'd be on telly asking about a bloke's knickers.") I waved goodbye to my old crew, and moved to the back of the bus, past Pam and Mitch, past Rodney and Smitty, and sat in the last available seat.

I heard a helo as we pulled away. I looked behind me and through the dust that'd caked the rear window. "Nightingale's kicking off," I whispered to myself, closing my eyes, wondering how Abi and Jeff would fare in the Bays. There was nothing left to say and, likewise, no one uttered a word during the ten-minute ride to the airfield.

Except Smitty. He and Pam got into it big time when she wouldn't let him return for his camera and clinical photos he mistakenly left behind. Doing so would have broken a rule or six, being that we were officially "in transit."

"I'M GOING BACK, PAMELA! YOU CAN'T STOP ME!"

"Easy Smitty," said Pam, who pulled him to the side after we stepped off the bus. Smitty could've given a shit about the camera; he needed *the photos* (I had mine on CD in my right cargo pocket). Pam knew this. "You be back in ten minutes or it's YOUR ass."

An hour later, as the whole of us loaded onto the C-130, I took my iPod, pressed play, and kissed Bastion goodbye, listening to "Comforting Sounds"--the Viking tune I played every night before bedding down with so much blade noise:

If someone else comes
I'll just sit here listening to the drums...
Blunted and exhausted like anyone

Chapter 15

Day forty-two. Six weeks over, and I'm homeward bound. I said my goodbyes to Zeke, Tommy, and True-True this morning. I declined the certificate ceremony in which Riza was to give me a paper for a job well done just prior to discharge, but I'm done with pomp and circumstance. Instead, we patients exchange emails with the promise of contact. The new unit President, a malingering Army captain who spends way too much time calculating his disability retirement on the unit's sole community computer, cut into my goodbyes anyway and dismissed the group before I could get a word in. I could've dressed him down. But why? He's still going to be an asshole long after I leave this place. *Fucking bearcat disguised as a balut, that's what he is.*

Nothing's for sure, the Canary corrects.

And that was it for The Willows: six-weeks of close contact evaporated. No one needed a transfusion. No one pumped. No one sliced. No one expired. Well, almost. Tommy, with his admission of kid-on-kid rape sliced away any remaining distortions I had about him being a pure soul. Pure souls, I'm convinced, don't inhabit the body of anyone over the age of three, and, as natural as the need was to save Tommy, it was egotistical of me to assume the role of savior. And so when Tommy and I said our goodbyes, it was with a healthy distance: a hug with a little less squeeze, a smile with a little less tooth, but he knew I cared. I don't have to save him to convince him of that. I just have to respect him as he goes about the process of saving himself. Yep, there's just me, now, walking out of The Willows with the same baggage I brought in--minus a bottle of bennies.

We start off in herds, the human race, be it as sheep or *baluts* or whatever. Rousseau said it best (my Spouse began reading Rousseau after finishing a story about Christopher McCandless, the disillusioned hiker who slipped away from the human race and into the wilderness where he'd never come out), "...the human species is divided into so many herds of cattle, each with its ruler, who keeps guard over them for the purpose of devouring them."

The only herdsman I'll ever listen to again stands forevermore in a yellow square in the sluice across from the Bay I loved so dearly within a hospital that no longer exists. Bastion opened my eyes, then closed them, then opened them again. *Thank you, Padre.* Why did Herrick 13 bother to save so many if people keep killing each other? Because it was worth it.

Goddammit.

"And what will you do?" Riza asks me. I don't know if she's talking about the Navy or the unspoken contract I'd made with Sheryl--the one where I agreed to save her forever.

"I'm going to live," I tell her.

Riza gives me a poem about fancy china and how it's better to be a paper cup. "It's not worth it," she tells me. *I get it.* I traded my humble beginnings for fancy rank and sparkle and got the same results: I'm still not sure who I am and, after doing a fair amount of research, realize there's no "app" to assist. I have to put in the work.

"Go with confidence," says Riza. "You have all you need."

Miss Dorothea escorts me to the van that'll drive me to the airport. On the walk, I pass the same lady with the same baby on the same bench. The baby's blowhole is gaping and her magenta must surely know the fire hazard it has become. I look at the lady and am thankful for my hallucinations that never materialized, and my deterioration that has, for the sake of all appearances, slowed. I stop looking at the blowhole, and try to make eye contact as I pass. When I do, the lady smiles and says something unintelligible, like Millie. Garbled, like Shane.

"Poor soul," Miss Dorothea says to herself. Or, at least that's what I think she says; my hearing aids arrived in the mail last night per my Spouse.

I step in the van as Miss Dorothea wishes me well. Before I close the door, she says one more thing, "You know what you have to do."

I give her a nod, and she gives me a card. As the van pulls away, I look out the rear window. Miss Dorothea has already started her walk back to the unit. I open the card. It has a flower on the front, and some Hallmark prose inside.

Sweet lady.

It's a thirty-minute drive to the airport--plenty of time to consider the last six weeks, but I don't think about The Willows. I think about the flower on the front of Miss Dorothea's card. It's deep orange, the same color as the flower I'd been given on my second day in Africa, just prior to my first deployment, while climbing Kilimanjaro. We started off the climb weaving our way through a couple of villages at the mountain's base. I passed an African kid standing in front of his family's shack while his mother tended to laundry. He could not have been more than four or five. He had rags for clothes, the same shade as the red soil covering the mountain trail. Though the kid's clothes were tattered, he was chubby. I motioned to his mother, asking if I could take her son's picture. She said yes, and corrected me, saying "he" was a she. The mother said something in *Swahili,* and her daughter posed like she must've for so many travelers on this well-worn route. I thanked her and proceeded on. The kid ran up a minute later with the flower and handed it to me with the sweetest smile I'd see in five years. I took the memento and pressed it into a book. I'd been taking Navy War College classes at the time, mistakenly figuring there was an intellectual side to war, and placed the flower in the only book I'd bring with me--Carl Von Clausewitz's *On War.*

I got this, I think, as the van pulls up to Departures. If I can climb a mountain, I can get well.

But you had sherpas that time, the Phantom says.

"I know," I say to myself.

"You know *what*?" asks the magenta driver, pulling my suitcase from the back of the van.

"Nothing," I reply.

I can't wait to see my Spouse and Kid.

◆ ◆ ◆

Two hours later, I'm in my window seat with my Domino, Sixties longboard surfing legend Robert August plastered to it this time. It's good morale *and* it's keeping me from picking my thumbs. Robert is lacquered to the bone, nose-riding on a three-foot wave, and he couldn't be happier. He ain't gonna drown, no sir, and neither am I as I watch all these sheep put their too large *scary-ons* in the overhead compartments.

I'm having trouble breathing. We're packed in like sardines. (Trigger.) The guy in front of me is drunk. (Trigger.) There are children screaming fore and aft. (Trigger, trigger.) The intercom, with it's deafening treble, is directly above me. (Trigger.) It tells us we're going to be on the tarmac for another twenty to forty minutes. (Trigger...*goddammit.*)

I grab my phone and get online. One thumb on Robert, and the other swiping through the news of the day. I read a *Time* magazine article about Miley Cyrus. Camille Paglia, the author, says America has an artistically bankrupt music culture as evidenced by Cyrus's tongue wagging, twerking, and clumsy stage persona at some awards show. I YouTube the spectacle: it reminds me of the Cyrus video we pantomimed to promote our hospital's executive farce--that we were caring, current, and approachable.

I had been controlled by a governing body of Zany Bearcats and Whimsical Skippers. Now, I have to get my mother out of the house. And, as for the Navy, I only have eighteen months left on this twenty-year stint. I can breeze my way through the last year and a half. I hope.

Sheryl has no money and can't breathe. *I'll pay for her medical insurance and give her a monthly stipend.* Yes, this sounds good, I think. *She'll agree to that,* I tell myself, though I know she won't. Sheryl will feel abandoned instead.

I'll clean it up, I think.

No, the Canary says. *Not anymore.*

My mind is racing. I put down my phone and Domino and have a go at my thumbs. I glance around, searching for something to ground myself. The plane is still inert (and getting hotter) in this sickening Florida heat.

I drift off to a moment just before my hospitalization. I was carrying groceries into my kitchen when a bag opened from below. A gallon of milk fell to the floor. The milk oozed out through a tear in the plastic, and my vision flashed red. My Kid came up to the milk. "We need to get more milk, Mommy."

"I KNOW THAT! DON'T YOU THINK I FUCKING KNOW THAT?!" I screamed. The Kid ran off crying and I yelled after her, "DON'T DO THIS TO ME!" I'm a fucking monster. *My Kid is drowning.*

I stare straight ahead at the drunk guy in front of me. I concentrate on the sweat ring around his shit brown Bass Pro Shop ball cap, but grounding isn't working.

I stand up. A flight attendant comes over and says I have to get back in my seat.

"I'm going to throw up," I tell her.

She allows me to lie down in the back as she confers with her fellow attendants on what to do. I lie just outside the lavatory on the sticky black rubber floor in front of two buckled attendants as they trade suggestions. They keep asking me if I'm all right, but they sound like they're underwater. I tell them I'm okay, though I'm breaking out in a cold sweat. I want to die.

This is what the last two years have felt like--a constant oscillation between wanting to die and wanting to unload. Because *I Am,* for lack of a better description, *a loose cannon.* I think about the hell I've put my Spouse through: having tantrums in traffic jams, pounding on the passenger window so violently as to break it and screaming; having a shit-fit at Haystacks in Oregon when parking was an issue, "I'M NOT FUCKING LEAVING THE CAR!"; and then there's the milk, and the New York, and the bracelet that'd torqued our dog down so hard. Anything...and I'd instantly transport to a fragged child screaming in pain. ALL those times I'd been one beat away from hurting someone. This annihilating rage, a rage that only leaves me whenever I entertain giving up, is going to be my undoing.

One minute feels like an eternity as, thankfully, I suddenly feel well enough to return to my seat. The flight attendants confer some more, gauging whether or not I can handle the flight. I stand up and turn on what little charm I have left, talking some medical mumbo-jumbo, and reassuring them I'm fine. Of course the attendants believe me: if I could convince my Commanding Officer I was well enough to assume control of a mental health directorate while in the grips of PTSD, I can charm the pants off of anyone. I'm *that* good, and I'm leaving Florida if it kills me.

"Can I have some tea?" I ask a flight attendant.

"Yes," she says, "as soon as we're in the air."

I sit behind Bass Pro Shop and stare at his sweat line, but look away. I'm sure he has a story. We all do. I reach under the seat for my backpack, pull out my *Trauma and Recovery* book, and pick up where I left off. *Rape and combat might thus be considered complementary social rites of initiation in the coercive violence at the foundation of adult society.*

Well, I think, *THAT's fucking depressing* (and isn't helping). So, I set the book in my lap and pass out, waking only when the wheels touch down in South Carolina, or Mars, or wherever.

◆ ◆ ◆

"So what's that do for you?" Sheryl asks as I unpack my suitcase. I'd put all my Art Therapy pieces on my dresser, unsure of what to do with them. Sheryl was pointing at the amputated boot I sculpted. It's in full *living* color, painted a couple days before I left The Willows. It sticks out like a sore thumb, or toe (so to speak).

"I don't know," I tell her and continue to unpack. "I suppose it helps me file the image away."

"Hmph," she says and returns to the living room to watch television.

My Spouse and Kid are at the grocery store, getting ingredients for a Welcome Home Feast so, after unpacking, I wait for them in the kitchen. A Rubbermaid bin sits next to the dining room table, the one I used to clear out my corner office six weeks ago. I open the top and see Bastion's cruise book on top. Navy cruise books, similar to yearbooks, commemorate deployments or tours. I put one together for Bastion. I open the cruise book and, indeed, it looks like a scrubbed high school chronicle: very congenial and totally sterilized.

My heart starts pounding, beating against the lie. The book is nothing more than the normalization of war, right down to the two-page spread in the middle where all the celebrity visits are documented. Hello Prime Minister. Hello Duke of York. Hello Mark Wahlberg. Leafing through, I see Emma, Val, Gemma, and me on page seventy, sitting behind an M240 in the rear of the Chinook fuselage. *All smiles.* I see Jeff, Pam, and Smitty in a doctor-only photo with the caption, "They've saved more lives than you can shake a stick at." My propaganda. There's a photo of Mitch with Benny behind him making muscles with the caption, "I'm gonna nurse the shit out of you!"

That's funny, I think, *but it's not enough.*

I tell Sheryl I'm leaving for a couple minutes and take the cruise book with me. I drive with it to a causeway that connects Parris Island to the mainland and, with a flick of a wrist, send the book over the bridge and into the murky water. A minute later, a fresh group of Marine recruits run past me. It's high tide and high time. The book will bury itself in the mud by sundown like a scavenger.

I get back into the car. My phone shows a text. It's Rodney. He's discharging next week and gives me his flight information.

◆ ◆ ◆

It's bedtime for the kid, and I've just the thing to read. *The Shepherd Boy.* It's one of the Kid's favorites. I lie next to her under the covers because I'll stay with her until she falls asleep like she's accustomed to. One day, she will be able to fall asleep on her own.

One day, so will I.

I read Val's inscription because that's become part of the story. "Dear Little One...love your Mummy and have a happy life." (Val is still in the QARANC, cranking out directives as a Lieutenant Colonel, or a Principal Matron, or a Bearcat--the good kind--who keeps wolves and Glory Seeking Cunts contained, or tries to. She'd written to me a while back saying the best part of Bastion was taking care of everyone, regardless of race, religion, or uniform. "I had to travel to Afghanistan to realize every ounce of training I'd been given. The place, for all its blood, connected us because we treated everyone the same.")

After the inscription, I begin, "James' father was a shepherd. Every day he got up very early, took his crook and his collie, and went off to see his sheep. James longed to be a shepherd too...." I knew a James of sorts. I met him after I came back from Bastion. He was eating lunch in our hospital galley, and having a hard time at it being a triple amputee. I sat down next to him and my vision flashed red. I asked him how he was coping, to which he told me he was glad it was him that got hit and not one of his buddies. "I can handle this better than they could."

"I want a collie, too," says the Kid, snapping me back.

"We already have a dog," I say, motioning to Arnold.

"But Arnold is so old and boring."

I glance at Arnold, our red "Blanche-Point" Schnoodle, or *Golden Girl* Dog--all ginger with thin gray roots sprouting from the top of his head. Already dreaming, Arnold kicks his legs and whimpers a little. I pat his backside until he settles down and starts snoring again. I look at my lamb, cuddled in close, with her big blue eyes and big blue optimism. *She's better than me,* I think. They're better than all of us.

After I close the book, the Kid takes her index fingers, sticks them into the corners of my mouth, and literally turns my frown upside down. "I'm making a V," she tells me.

Chapter 16

"You don't talk to me anymore," Sheryl says. My mother, freshly released from a night in the county jail after her DUI, sits on the couch to plead her case. Though we moved to a peaceful mountain town-- one with the longest running Peace Vigil in U.S. history--we, which is to say my mother and I, are very much at war. I haven't said anything to Sheryl in days, not even after she slurred, "I love you," before walking out the door yesterday. I assumed she was taking a walk. A couple hours later I'd noticed the car was gone, then we got the call from the jail this morning.

"You expect too much from me," I tell Sheryl, then look down at the Persian rug and take note: *You need a wash.* It's been a year since I medically retired from the Navy, and a year since the hasty government move that soiled this rug. I think I expect too much from Sheryl, too. She can't live in peace. I still try: My new job, since medically retiring, is to walk my Kid back and forth to school, and log volunteer hours at her kindergarten class in between. One of my Kid's classmates approached me on one such morning.

"My mommy says God is going to come down from heaven and kill us all." Cydney also says my eyes look like gumballs.

I told the kindergarten teacher, Mrs. Pierson, and she threw her head back and laughed like a dame. "Well, let's hope *that* doesn't happen!" she said, handing me a box of wooden nubs. "Now go sharpen these pencils."

I also went to the Kid's Veteran's Day celebration at school and, with considerable prodding, donated a picture of my flak and Kevlar'ed self for the all-school assembly. The slideshow of parent-veterans played as the kids sat Indian-style on the gym floor. When my smiling face flashed across the projector, the kids "Oooh'ed" and "Aaahh'ed" like they'd done with the rest. After the assembly, I gave my Kid a quick kiss, and hauled ass down the path to our house, stopping only once to throw up in a blackberry bush.

So it's no wonder that Johnnie Walker threw down the gauntlet not long after I'd returned from The Willows. "May as well face the music," she said. "You won't last a year. We gotta get you out of this environment, and we have to do it *now.*" By *environment,* she meant the military environment. By now, she meant yesterday, or two years ago, or after my Big One. She was right. It's possible I wouldn't have lasted a month.

Yet a year, one year, was all I needed to get to twenty years of service, when I could've retired with a few extra hundred dollars a month--crucial when considering I couldn't work. Still, twenty years is twenty years. I can't do anything about that. I'm worth *less* (a total of twenty-five percent less to be exact). I'm in the red, according to the matrix.

"So apply for Combat-Related Special Compensation," said Troll. I did, knowing it was a shot in the dark. The reply from The Secretary of the Navy Council of Review Boards: *There must be a definite causal relationship between the armed conflict and the resulting disability. Witnessing of life-threatening events such as* actual combat *qualifies. Your PTSD from caring for victims of horrific combat related injuries occurring in a combat zone as a result armed conflict was not a result of armed conflict but from witnessing carnage. Congress intended to require a specific combat related nexus. In the opinion of the Board, it was not Congress' intent to include any and all hazardous duty. Using that rationale, every service member in a combat zone who suffers from PTSD would otherwise qualify for combat-related special compensation pay.*

Translation: "You, Commander Rhyan, are not entitled to the extra scratch. You never made it to twenty. You never made it to combat." My herders had spoken: our rulers devoured me just as Rousseau said they would. I get it; it would cost the government a lot of money if they paid for those affected by combat's *ripples.* Establishing such a precedent would also open up the opportunity to *malingerers,* which, let's face it, is what they think I am. Still, I could care less about the measly pay; it's always been about the perception. The gravity of my wounds cannot be seen with the naked eye. Therefore, they doubt, and have the carte blanche right to categorize our injuries. Actual combat? It's the actual disconnection that has always hurt more.

I don't say this lightly. I'd never compare my pain to that of someone's physical and mental torment of having to cope after being torn apart by an IED. But arguing with the Navy and Sheryl, clinging to the escarpment between what they think I deserve and what I know I deserve, is grinding me down. (That, and Rodney is on my heels: He closed on a house last week only five miles down the road. He's still looking for his older sister and battle buddies. I wonder what'll happen when he finds out they aren't here either.) Having to reduce my Bastion casualties to currency, as I'm doing now to bolster my own purse, seems beyond perverse even to me. I never put my life on the line. No, sir! But is life defined by heartbeat or spirit? I need to know because my spirit is gone. My heart beats, but I am no longer living.

Carl von Clausewitz wrote *War is the realm of physical exertion and suffering. These will destroy us unless we can make ourselves indifferent to them....* I must've reread that passage a hundred times, more for the fact that the flower I'd been given, the orange one from Africa, had long since stained the page.

I've pled MY case (thank you very much, Sheryl), begging the Navy *and* my mother to open their eyes. They haven't. They won't. My pain, culturally wrapped around the axels of *MASH* and *China Beach,* has somehow become...*jejeune.* And I don't know what I'll do, or so the song goes.

So, I smoke weed. I'm in a perpetual fog. My vision still flashes red. Red on the Persian rug. Red as my mother tells me "You're going to fuckin' HELL!"

"Get out," I say.

"You'll have to call the fuckin' cops! They'll have to drag me screamin' out the fuckin' door!" she says, then tells me again, "You're going to FUCKIN' HELL! YOU SHIT FACE!"

My Kid starts laughing because she always laughs when her grandmother, the witch, gets whimsical.

"Oh, come on!" says my Spouse. "She's not going to hell. And stop with the name-calling!"

"Yes, she IS! And YOU mind your OWN FUCKIN' BUSINESS!"

I flash red to the last time I saw Rich. He's in front of his mother's television watching a boxing match with other hog outlaws. Marvelous Marvin Hagler had just won a by knock out. "The only reason Marvin Hagler is so marvelous," says Rich, "is because a nigger's skin is like leather!"

Mine has worn thin.

I pick up my phone and call the cops. Riza told me to kick her out, and it's taken too long. I tell my Spouse to take the Kid and seek refuge next door while I sit in the front yard waiting for the police as I did all those years ago in front of the kerosene heater. I hate my mother--not because she drove drunk or is presently embarrassing me in front of my new neighbors. I hate her because, chances are, Sheryl gets to leave this God-forsaken world earlier than me. I want to be dead, though I'll never admit it to my Spouse. I want my mother to love me, though I know she never will. I need the Navy to acknowledge my PTSD is combat-related, but their response is absurd. I was born into this world, like everyone else, incapable of protest. I did the good non-combat service of cleaning up messes others hadn't the guts to see, and now I want to leave this place. I want to leave it all. I'm dying as I sit on this lawn. I'm dying as the cops pull up to the corner. I'm dying as an officer says after talking to Sheryl, "There's nothing we can do, ma'am."

"Give her an eviction notice," the other cop tells me. "She'll have thirty days to vacate." *But what if I kill her tonight?* I chose not to admit my emotional state to the police. I'm doomed to these circles and cycles. The Phantom burns within. She's around so much now I can't tell the difference between us. And the Canary? I can't find her most days. Lord knows I've been looking high and low.

The police tell me one more thing before pulling away, "She says she's an old woman and doesn't know what she's doing half the time, but she promises to behave now." *Well, that's fucking great!* I go into the house and notice Sheryl has locked herself in her room.

I JOURNAL. I paint the house gray and deep purple. I keep my hands busy--anything to keep me occupied. Sheryl is a week out from leaving; I served her the eviction notice as the police instructed me to.

Rodney comes over twice a day now. He walks my Kid to and from school. Rodney and I smoke together and discuss our marijuana dreams and caviar revenge and talk about how the world owes us. I love to smoke, though Riza has warned us all about the dangers of marijuana. "Here's a review on a strain," she said on my last day, picking up a print-out from an online review: "'It has a sweet, lemony taste.' This one was written by Piff Cakes 420."

I laughed my ass off, as usual, to which Riza commented, "You must be Piff Cakes 419."

True-True, next to me, asked, "Why in the hell would someone wanna smoke some shit that tastes like lemon?!"

Because it takes the pain away, like it did for Stefano, and like Opana did for Zeke. I don't care if there isn't a proper medical review. It makes me feel better. Rodney, by contrast, is like a news pundit, stoned or not, who thinks the only charitable contributions he need make to the world are all the fucked-up opinions he bestows upon anyone who'll listen. He's a real Charlie Krauthammer. I'm Charlie Bucket at best: Marijuana is my Fizzy Lifting Drink. I just want to fly far away. Rodney is my "brother," sure, but it comes with a trade. I'm exchanging a Circus Bear for a Crank Vet.

Still, I use words like "was" and "had been" when I journal to try and put the past where it belongs. But the Phantom looms. Those times when I'm not smoking or cranking, I'm ignoring the two people who matter most. "I hugged the Kid three times today," I told my Spouse. "That's enough, right?" She looked sad and sorry that I even had to ask the question. After a few moments, she asked:

"Do you know how precious we are?"

"Yes," I told her, though she had no arms at the time.

My curiosity for this world is nowhere to be found. My sister doesn't sugarcoat it. "You've changed, Kari. I don't know you." That makes two of us. And my memory, compounded by my drug use, is shit. I can't remember anything, not so unlike my dad, Andy, who couldn't remember his siblings when he died of dementia. I can't hear squat, much like Millie couldn't on our last visit together. And I can't see what's precious, though it's standing right here in front of me with no arms.

◆ ◆ ◆

I "emerge" from the TV room, a cave I use to hide from the world, and walk downstairs. It's Sheryl's last day in the house, and I'm careful to stay away. No sense in interacting this late in the game.

"You know what?!" Sheryl says out of the blue, standing outside her door. "SHANDY AND I DIDN'T MOLEST YOU!" I found out Sheryl is to live with Shandy, and no doubt Teddy, through phone records, and thus told Sheryl I was reneging on my promise to give her a monthly stipend. She was a little ticked off about the whole thing. Tough shit. I'd been a catcher of abuse for decades, but supporting the woman who, not only protected, but is to live with the man who tried to fuck me for two years is a no-go.

"I'm done talking to you!" I tell Sheryl. "PERIOD!"

"Mommy?" my Kid asks, watching from the dining room table. "What's 'period' mean?"

"End of story," I say.

I go up to my room. On the way, I pass the baseball cards I'd once collected to buy Sheryl the house she always wanted. I move toward my nightstand. Bon Scott is crooning behind my eyes, "Freedom, I am chasing..." Make no mistake; *this* is a Jailbreak.

"OP VAMPIRE, OP VAMPIRE, OP VAMPIRE..."

I open the bio safe with my prints and pull out the revolver. *One cavity ripper in the slot.* A good home defense.

I'm a Monster. I ignore the people who matter most.

I'm a Vampire. I'm sucking off amputees to line my pockets.

I'm a Killer. Of who? I don't know yet.

It's time to dust off.

BOOK IV

HOT WASH

Chapter 17

If I die before my time
Bury me upside down
- Cat Power

There are pillows of spider eggs in the outside corners of my kitchen window. The eight-legged traffic patterns have left white residue in the dark purple paint I recently slapped up. Some spiders have already hatched, their wispy webs fluttering just outside the glass. It annoys me a little until I stop and consider even spiders need a place for first steps. It may as well be here. I don't brush the pillows away. Nor can I chop down the 80-year-old pear tree littering the lawn with rotten Bartletts every August and, later, with bees that torment the dog during Indian summer--this being Arnold's last (people know these things). But, spiders and bees aside, I've become a recluse.

The gun did go off, unfortunately, but no one died. I couldn't pick a 'cide. My bed bit the dust a month after my mother left, surprisingly, without much ado. Sheryl returned only once to give the Kid an advent calendar full of chocolates. I watched her leave the gift on the porch and drive away, knowing it would be the last time I'd ever see her again.

As for the gun, I was performing a monthly safety check. Anyone considering suicide should let a round loose in a mattress first: The ringing silence snapped me back. In that moment I pictured my end. In that end, I decided to stay. The hollow point got as far as the comforter where it expanded upon impact as was intended. The casing landed on my pillow--the same tattered, drool-covered cushion I used in Bastion. After the pop and shock, my vision flashed white. White, not red: The room rained goose feathers. Thankfully, my Spouse and Kid were off on errands.

I wanted to get rid of the comforter, naturally; a negligent discharge is a cardinal sin in the military (and doesn't feel much better as a civilian), but my Spouse told me to keep it for the reminder. So, I stitched up the tear, and the seam still holds after a dozen washes. Not so for the gun.

I hocked my revolver at a pawnshop, and bought an ounce of *Gorilla Glue* at a pot dispensary next door. I don't blame anyone for my drug use, not even the Navy. Marijuana may be erasing my memory little by little, but it also lengthens my reaction time between a trigger and (what would've been) annihilating rage. I'll keep using *The Glue*, a lemony strain with crystals and orange hairs.

Simply stated, marijuana helps me feel everything without bleeding out. Thankfully, it's legal where I live. I *live*. My new norm, this trickling without hemorrhaging, is how I get by. My Vietnam Vet buddy Chuck says, "Hey, man, at least you're not on Benzos!" Chuck, who barely survived his own childhood, went on to tell me I was a victim of my own compassion. "What's common sense to us isn't so common in our old circles. But we can't fault our families for being so mean and ugly when they were just scrounging to get by. They don't know any better."

Chuck gave me a bumper sticker last week: *Vietnam Veterans of America: NEVER AGAIN Will One Generation of Veterans Abandon Another.* "You're not perfect either, Kari. You aren't supposed to be perfect. But you made me believe in the *good* again. I'm glad I'm the one who gets to help you through it." Chuck, also a recluse with a supportive family, tells me how to live, "Keep your circle small. Stay inside it, go out when you have to, smoke weed whenever you want, and never EVER watch the news."

The only gun left in our house is the one in my Spouse's painting, "Walking Doll." There's a woman's face in the upper corner, and breasts in the lower. The gun takes center stage, representative of the collision between sex, violence, and control. Such will never be a rite of passage for the Kid, nor will she ever feel compelled to own a weapon to feel safe. We teach her about the differences between boundaries and borders. I tell her the only way a person can notice their own boundaries being crossed is to cease crossing others' first. So, *be the change*, or the ball, or whatever.

"Pfft!" the Kid replied. "I don't understand any of that stuff. How are the England people?"

◆ ◆ ◆

I pick up my Greyhound diary from the desk in our study. Its lock is in a permanently picked position, evidence of a boundary crossed thirty years ago. *Why lock it?* I hold the diary to my chest and pray for the lonely; I usurped Rodney last month, reassuming the duty of walking my Kid to and from elementary school. I wear no Eisenhower. I post-up, instead, with my headphones, sunglasses, and pocketknife (one can't be too careful these days). I try not to talk to anyone. There's nothing to say right now. I have too much work to do, and the frivolity of the weather and the PTA are things I can't entertain. But I hope to some day.

Along with Rodney, I've cut ties with most of my military friends. That's a life I can no longer identify with. I'm eking out a new existence--something Rodney never understood, even when I gave him his walking papers.

"WHAT ABOUT ME?!" he said.

"You're killing me," I told him. "And now you have to go." I also added expletives, threats, and gibberish. I wish I could have simply told him:

Dear Rodney,

I sent you away because I didn't want to become you.

Before he left town, he emailed my Spouse about how awful I was. Sheryl had done the same thing. I asked my Spouse if she thought they were right.

"They've never wanted you to be happy, Kari," she replied. "Love doesn't act like that."

◆ ◆ ◆

We take hikes around our mountain town. I still have to work up the motivation: trailblazing takes practice, especially in the Cascades, where there's too much space to think. We're making our way to Blue Lake today, so I concentrate on sights and sounds.

"I see a red-breasted robin," I whisper--a grounding technique Riza taught us to stay present.

"I hear a waterfall." Other veterans have also moved here. They're going off the grid. The men have long beards and leather boots.

"I see a bushtit." The tit is a local bird as common as pigeons in New York.

Just then, my Kid interrupts, "I saved five ants, Mommy." She rescued them from a puddle of gathering rain. I kick the puddle. The British military boots I wear are brilliant on slick rock. (Gemma nicked them for me from a stash in a back room of the hospital--the very same brand Jeff wore to relieve his plantar fasciitis.)

We resume our trek, and I pick my thumbs, littering the trail with little red poppies.

"I see fawns," I continue, then think of Shane and dig deeper.

A canopy of cedars and firs keep all of us dry, not so unlike the oak trees in South Carolina that provided cover from the frequent thunderstorms. The Carolina oak, according to locals, takes one hundred years to grow, one hundred years to live, and one hundred years to die.

I don't have that kind of time.

We reach Blue Lake in an hour, thanks to my slow stride. My Spouse and Kid skinny dip while I watch over them on a huge tree root that juts out from the top of a twenty-foot drop. I pull my Bastion Journal from my backpack, debating whether or not I should toss it in the lake, but decide to hold onto it after noting the last entry-- penned the first month I reported to South Carolina, just after returning from Afghanistan.

There's a cadence on Parris Island. Only one road, The General Edwin Pollock Causeway, links the recruit Depot to the mainland. Though the bridge is a mere quarter-of-a-mile long, there's a perceptible change in the rhythm of things: Palm trees march out in perfect two-by-twos; sudden gusts of wind stall scads of island herons and egrets; and wetland cord grass leans out from the salt marshes, giving hints of bottom-dwellers and razor-sharp barnacles.

Each drive over the causeway yields a different impression. High tide comes just shy of the grass tips, capturing the southern sky in its glassy surface. Four hours later, low tide washes the effect away, stripping the marshes to their muddy bones. Motoring on, the meter isn't yet audible until the causeway ends at a roundabout and bifurcates to parade grounds or barracks.

I spot the first group of marching recruits. A block further reveals another group, and then another. The cadence is always there. Their one hundred-year old song resounds through the base, back up the bridge, and falls like clockwork onto The Lowcountry, the geographic stretch from Savannah, Georgia to Charleston, South Carolina. Parris Island is my new home. Seventeen thousand recruits are my new neighbors.

The oak trees the recruits navigate between are massive. South Carolina's most popular oak grows only eighty yards away from my new office. Slaves gathered around the tree one hundred and fifty years ago on what is now Naval Hospital Beaufort's military compound. There, The Emancipation Proclamation was read for the first time on January 1, 1863. The area, considered hallowed ground, is honored each year on the first Friday morning of the year after our nation's colors are raised.

I stand with the hospital formation and render a half right face toward The Oak's general direction while The Proclamation is read. This year's ceremony was ushered in by a bursting orange sky that lit up the Spanish Moss, and their clinging red chiggers, like tinder.

It looked like fire. It felt like deliverance.

The End

CPSIA information can be obtained
at www.ICGtesting.com
Printed in the USA
BVHW080103210722
642678BV00001B/28

9 780692 901458